WELCOMING CHILDREN

For Barbara Jean Mercer,
with whom I share a childhood

WELCOMING CHILDREN

A Practical Theology of Childhood

JOYCE ANN MERCER

FOREWORD BY
Bonnie J. Miller-McLemore

CHALICE PRESS
ST. LOUIS, MISSOURI

Bible quotations, unless otherwise noted, are from the *New Revised Standard Version Bible,* copyright 1989, Division of Christian Education of the National Council of the Churches of Christ in the United States of America. Used by permission. All rights reserved.

Bible quotations marked AT are the author's translation.
Bible quotations marked KJV are from the *King James Version Bible.*

An earlier version of chapter 3 appeared as "The Child as Consumer: A North American Problem of Ambivalence Concerning the Spirituality of Childhood in Late Capitalist Consumer Culture" in the *Sewanee Theological Review* 48: 1 (Christmas 2004), 65–84. The author gratefully acknowledges STR's permission to reprint portions of this original article in the chapter.

Cover art: © W. P. Wittman Limited
Cover design: Elizabeth Wright
Interior design: Hui-Chu Wang

ChalicePress.com

Library of Congress Cataloging-in-Publication Data

Mercer, Joyce.
Welcoming children : a practical theology of childhood / Joyce Ann Mercer.
    p. cm.
ISBN 978-0-827242-51-7
    (pbk. : alk. paper)
1. Christian education of children. 2. Church work with children. I. Title.
    BV1475.3.M47 2005
    268'.432—dc22

2005013223

Printed in the United States of America

CONTENTS

FOREWORD

Last weekend the United States celebrated one of its high holy days—the Super Bowl. Although the football match-up is the presumed focus, the game itself is often unspectacular. Instead, what millions of viewers—including children across a wide age spectrum—eagerly await are the multimillion-dollar advertisements. Long before the commercial breaks had ended this past Sunday, the youth choir director at my church had already sent an e-mail to all the kids ranking her favorites. This, in a paradigmatic nutshell, is the world that houses North American Christianity and captivates the hearts and minds of children. It is the "imperial regime" practical theologian Joyce Ann Mercer is eager to overthrow for the sake of today's children.

What exactly is the problem with this market empire? It commodifies children and turns them into consumers, rendering them of little or no value unless they benefit adults and advance the purposes of the market. But it is not just these global aspects that Mercer decries. Consumption creeps into daily patterns and practices, shaping a way of living completely at odds with the Christian life. A pervasive consumerist lifestyle betrays what Mercer has learned about children's intrinsic value from her immersion in congregations, sojourns into contexts outside the U.S. where responsibility for children is widely and gladly shared, and travel through classic texts of the Christian tradition itself that prize children.

Welcoming Children is uncompromising in its advocacy for children and for embracing them more wholly within the Christian faith. Moving deftly across scripture, prime theological texts, sociological research, and faith practices, Mercer invites us into a vivid exposition of the invaluable place of children in Christianity and within our daily lives. Christianity has the capacity to foster a "counter-narrative" that values children not as consumers but as amazingly wonderful creations of God. Welcoming children means recognizing them as fully human, whole-yet-broken gifts and participants in God's realm. To welcome children requires challenging the social and political forces that diminish them, celebrating the turmoil and gladness they bring, and enfolding them in all aspects of Christian life. Children have the capacity to make God known and to embody a rich nonmaterial divine abundance.

Mercer brings immense resources to this task. She has worked closely with children as a church pastor, social worker, and teacher. She is raising three elementary school children of her own. She has extensive knowledge of the methods and contributions of feminist practical theology, with special interest and expertise in education and Christian ministry. She is extremely widely read. Her orientation as a practical theologian compels her to "start small," looking at the nitty-gritty details of life with children in families, congregations, restaurants, stores, schools, and so forth. But Mercer does not shy away from big questions, showing how such small matters impact how we think about the nature of God and life as a whole, and how we act toward our neighbor. Her book raises probing questions in three important areas: theological meaning, faith practice, and child advocacy. What is the meaning of children? What practices of faith best nurture them? How can we advocate for children plagued by oppressive social circumstances?

Answers emerge from a deep well of resources–experience, congregational life, local stories, strategies and tactics of ministry–as well as from conventional sites, such as the gospel of Mark and the scholarship of Reformed theologian Karl Barth and Catholic theologian Karl Rahner. These texts and figures are chosen in part because they offer the kind of counter-narrative that Mercer seeks. In Mark's incriminating exposure of the social and political powers of his time, for example, children usher in God's reign precisely because they most embody the least and the lowliest in social rank and class. Both Barth and Rahner, in quite distinct ways and for different purposes and communities, also echo countercultural Christian claims about God as supreme authority, children's inherent worth, and the Christian obligation to cherish and sustain lively engagement with their developing faith.

Here and throughout the book, Mercer builds upon, yet nicely extends, recent publications in theology on children. She locates the formation of children's Christian identity as a communal, rather than individual, enterprise. She includes two excellent chapters on particular ecclesial practices of education and liturgy. With a solid command of the current state of children's Sunday school on both scholarly and local levels, she proposes an alternative vision of learning as a "communally situated activity" in which children are involved more directly in mission and congregational life, faith, and relationships in general. Regular worship, at the heart of church life, not only needs to find ways to involve children on equal footing with adults, but will be enriched by what is learned from children by doing so.

Mercer makes the most of her orientation as a practical theologian. In fact, in addition to her penetrating portrait of the challenges faced by children and religious communities, one of her contributions is her exposition of good practical theology. The book circles from engaged struggle, to understanding, to action, and back around again and again. In moving through this hermeneutical circle Mercer hopes to create "useable theology." The goal is not just to help readers think differently or critically about children. Our whole "habitus"–the "multidirectional" influence of practices upon beliefs, beliefs upon practices, and systemic, cultural forces on beliefs, practices, actions, and decisions–needs consideration and transformation. This commitment to shaping an entire ethos evolves partly out of penetrating feminist sensibilities. In particular, one cannot improve the lives of children without significantly improving the lives of those who care for them and the complex network of ideologies and social structures that oppress both children and their caregivers, often women.

Many congregations do attempt to welcome children and many do an excellent job. Yet Mercer makes clear that vigilance, reflection, and action are needed. Complaints about the impact of consumer culture upon children are common, but few people really press the deeper question of genuine change. A market-driven consumer culture forms North American Christian life, not Christian discipleship. This has particularly insidious consequences for children. Even seemingly overt affirmations, such as five-minute children's sermons, innovative educational programming, or the sequestering of children's ministry in the education wing, can become yet another reflection of children's token status, marginalization from "real" worship, and exploitation as a means to promote church growth. Although the destination of a genuinely hospitable church and world often eludes us and dreams are sometimes our only guide, *Welcoming Children* takes the reader on a fabulous excursion that does not disappoint in its suggestive vision of the road leading toward a more "child-affirming theology and church."

Bonnie J. Miller-McLemore

PREFACE

Finding a Welcome for Children

It is Sunday morning. My husband and I are about to make an extremely countercultural choice for residents in the place we live: we are about to go to church with our children. Many of the families around us make a different choice. They go to the zoo or to soccer practice or just stay home together. People make the choice not to be part of a congregation's work and life for many reasons. One reason particularly concerns me. Sometimes families choose not to participate in the church because the church fails to welcome their children.

This book is my search for a child-affirming theology and for a church that genuinely welcomes children, cares about their well-being, and advocates for them in situations in which they are marginalized or harmed. I became interested in issues of justice and the well-being of children long before I became a scholar of Christian theology, even long before I become a parent.

As a pastor in the 1980s and 1990s I worked in a hospital with chemically dependent teenagers, and later with people of all ages in an urban congregation. I heard stories every day from youth and adults about enduring various forms of emotional, physical, and sexual abuse in their childhoods. In both locations I also heard stories of family love and care, of right relationships lived out among family members. As a social worker in children's hospitals and a community-based clinic for youth, I encountered the extreme vulnerability of children oppressed by the violence of poverty and by the interlocking oppressions of gender, race, and class exploitation. I met children exploited for their cheap labor, children treated as objects for all kinds of gratification of adult desires, and children who were simply alone, with no family and no home. Before my own children were born, these children taught me about the power of the human need for just relationships between children as vulnerable people and the communities of care and support on which they depend. Now that I am the mother of three elementary-aged children, the stake I have in such issues expands considerably.

I care about the faith lives of my own and other people's children because I view Christian faith as an identity into which persons are formed. Such Christian identity has the power to oppose the destructive identities consumer culture offers today. Our family had the privilege of living and working in the Philippines from 1997 to 2000. We experienced that culture's remarkable affirmation of children, along with the many wonderful ways Filipino culture gives a different shape to childhood. There I also learned firsthand about the impact North American consumer practices have on children's lives even in very remote communities of the world. I witnessed globalization's long reach into the lives of children.

Such experiences only intensified questions about how church leaders can support families in their efforts to nurture children in Christian faith, which stands in such contrast to the consumer culture swirling around us all. Along the way I began to ask questions and search for theological resources related to children: what is the theological meaning of childhood? How can the church best affirm and celebrate God's gift of children amidst all the complexities and difficulties they bring? What practices of our faith communities will support and nurture children to grow in Christian faith that liberates rather than oppresses? And how can we advocate for the well-being of children oppressed by violence, poverty, and the absence of caring adults in their lives?

The search for a child-affirming theology and church began for me as a search grounded in the realities of children's struggles and, in some cases, their oppression. It began also in my deeply held theological conviction that God in Jesus Christ is at work transforming the whole of creation, including and especially the situations of struggling children. So I began to look for theological resources that could fund our practices and ministries with children in the church, both with children who are hurting and with those who are not. This book represents a portion of that search.

ACKNOWLEDGMENTS

Writing, like the Christian life, involves one in ever more active and deepening forms of gratitude to others. I am grateful to the many children whose stories populate these pages and my memory. Special thanks go to the congregations participating in the Children in Congregations Project, and to the Louisville Institute for generously supporting that research. Although this book is not a report on the project, my experiences with its congregations, pastors, teachers, and children inform these pages in countless ways. Nancy Ammerman and Bill McKinney provided skillful consultation, and Nancy's mentoring friendship helped me over numerous hurdles. Deborah L. Matthews, Shelly Holle, Chandler Stokes, Gail Doering, Di Pagel, Sarah Reyes, and Mary Wright Gillespie are inspiring minister- and educator-conversation partners who care deeply about children and the church. Thanks also to Lynn and Steve Bicknell and their daughter Jenny—we could never do this parenting thing alone.

Karen-Marie Yust, my long-distance colleague and "conference companion" read the manuscript in its entirety when she really did not have time, for which I am in her debt. Herman C. Waetjen read and commented carefully on chapter 2. His generous help along with that of other readers surely saved me from my own excesses and blind spots numerous times, though any errors that remain are my responsibility alone. Charles Foster, mentor and friend, offered encouragement and assistance through several key conversations on practice and education that were crucial in my formulation of chapter 5. James Fowler similarly has provided substantive feedback and sustained conversation about faith and children over the years. Friends and colleagues from Union Theological Seminary in the Philippines, especially Mariano Apilado and Elizabeth Tapia, remain treasured and inspiring partners from whom I continue to learn much about life, postcolonial realities, and the transformative love of God. I am grateful for supportive colleagues at San Francisco Theological Seminary and among the practical theology and education faculty of the Graduate Theological Union. Trent Butler at Chalice Press offered helpful editorial guidance along the way. Members of Old First Presbyterian Church in San Francisco give our family a congregational home with many adults committed to children.

My dad remembered to ask, "how's the book?" at regular and supportive intervals. My brother Walt and sister Barbara got me through several periods of near despair with moral support and reminders of my roots, however tangled. I dedicate this book to my sister Barbara, who is one of the most accomplished, kind, and generous people on the planet.

I have the good fortune to be with a partner in marriage, Larry Golemon, who truly shares parenting. Although he never read a word of this manuscript, many moments of informed theological conversation and parenting talk, along with countless extra hours of everything from carpooling and cooking to supervising children's teeth brushing and play dates, provided tangible forms of love and support that facilitated the completion of the book. Larry, you are everywhere in this book. Thanks again and again.

Last, I am grateful beyond words to our three children, Andrew, Micah, and Sarah, who give me the gift of who they are every day, in addition to the gift of being their mom, an identity I treasure. Other writers on childhood comment on the irony that such work inevitably requires long periods of absence from one's own children, a reality in my case as well. To my children: I am thankful to each of you for your patience and your many ways of blessing this work and me. And yes, I can play with you now.

Joyce Ann Mercer,
San Anselmo, California
July 26, 2005

CHAPTER ONE

Starting Small

A Way of Doing Theology of Childhood

A Scene from a Restaurant

A few years ago, in a family-oriented pizza restaurant in California, my then two-year-old daughter Sarah began to fuss and cry in a high-pitched voice. It was late in the day, and I knew that her crying probably came from hunger. So I immediately went to the salad bar to try to find something that would quiet her until our meal arrived. I reached for a few crackers while she kicked and screamed in my arms. A man stood up at a nearby table, walked over to us, and remarked loudly as his finger pointed only inches from Sarah's face, "For Christ's sake, can't you shut that kid up? Why don't you take her out of here? I don't pay to eat out only to have to listen to that screaming."

I was shocked! The shock came not so much by what he said. I am in complete agreement that it is far nicer to dine in a restaurant without the sounds of a screaming child punctuating the air. I was shocked by the aggression in his voice and his gestures. Perhaps even more astounding was the fact that no one else in the restaurant appeared to see anything inappropriate in this man's words or actions. For me the irony of a supposedly "family-oriented" establishment in which no one blinked an eye at overt hostility toward a child and her parent was surpassed only by this man's choice of epithets: "For Christ's sake!"

"For Christ's sake, shut that child up"? The very idea of associating Christ with the silencing of children appears preposterous to anyone even vaguely familiar with New Testament stories about Jesus' interactions with children. Of course, the man in the restaurant was hardly engaging in theological reflection with his use of religious language! But this experience caused me to think about the way in which children constantly receive ambivalent messages from the society and from the church about their worth and their welcome. The family-oriented appearance of the restaurant seemed to say to children, "you are welcome here." But the aggressive behavior of the man toward a crying child, and the passive acceptance of bystanders witnessing his actions, communicated something very different.

The Church's Ambivalence to Children

In a similar way the church often manifests its ambivalence toward children in a set of "double messages" that seem to welcome them, but only if they do not act like the children that they are. For example, congregations generally view themselves as "child-friendly" places. Most church members speak of the desirability of having plenty of children in the church. At the same time, however, many congregations demonstrate that they in fact do not want children to be present in worship, the central gathering of the church's life. They express this ban of children through their "adults-only" styles of worship and through the disapproving words and glances they give to noisy or disruptive children. In the church, no one stands up and shouts, "For Christ's sake, shut that child up!" like the man did in the restaurant. But for all practical purposes, the message to children is, "For Christ's sake, or at least for the sake of we adults who consider ourselves followers of Christ, either be quiet or leave!"

Of course, for anyone who has ever been seated with or near a young child during worship, the situation appears more complex. When children are present in worship, particularly younger children, their needs for attention often clash with adult needs. Adults seek quiet, reflective space to meditate on faith that engages adult critical thinking capacities. These also are legitimate needs, and if the adults accompanying children in worship (most often but not always women) are constantly called upon to sacrifice their needs to attend to children, then having children physically present in worship hardly becomes a liberatory act for anyone. That is, in part, the reason adults in local congregations continue to struggle with questions about how to live well and hospitably with the children in their midst.

The Search for a Theology of and a Church for Children

This book is part of my search for a child-affirming Christian theology and for a church that genuinely welcomes children amid a culture and church tradition that at best embraces them ambivalently. I use the notion of a search metaphorically here, for it is not as though I expect to find a fully formed, adequate theology of childhood waiting under a rock somewhere out there. The image that comes to mind is more like that of a child's three-dimensional wooden puzzle that is missing some parts. Putting it together involves sorting through the available pieces to see what sort of figure might emerge as they are put together in some meaningful way. But it also involves imaginative envisioning of what the finished figure might look like even in the absence of certain readily available parts. With such a vision in mind, one can then construct some new pieces (sometimes out of surprising materials!) to complete the puzzle. As I speak of a search for a theology and for a church that welcomes children, then, I envision a constructive, imaginative theological activity that takes place in critical relationship to available resources and perspectives that can contribute to the construction of emancipatory practices with children in church and society. Such a view sees theology as a highly imaginative activity out of which real emancipatory practices can come, at the same time that these practices themselves fund the imagination that generates theological insight. It is a "both/and" process.

A central question within my search for a welcoming theology of childhood concerns practices of education with children. Such practices should invite and welcome children's participation together with adults in communities shaped around the stories, symbols, and practices of Christian faith. Such practices must be observed amidst a culture bent on shaping persons and communities around the stories, symbols, and practices of consumption. How can communities of faith invite and educate children into a Christian alternative way of life to the dominant consumerist life into which the wider culture continually schools them? The search for a theology and church that welcomes children is a search set within a contemporary North American social context in which the very nature and meaning of childhood are undergoing rapid transformation in relation to the forces of globalized consumer culture.

As children and childhood take on new shapes, social practices with children, including religious ones (such as practices of worship and liturgy, education and care with children), also undergo transformation. The search for a child-affirming theology and a church in which children are genuinely welcome necessarily concerns itself with children as they are formed within contemporary culture and also with those cultural and social forces at work to reshape childhood in our time.

No Return to Nostalgia

Such an understanding of the task at hand for theological work differs considerably from that of scholars who see their task in terms of the recovery of a supposedly more natural and authentic childhood identified with its dominant construction in an earlier time. Amidst the changes wrought by postmodern cultural forms and a national social fabric tenuously held together by fickle market forces, it becomes tempting to revert to nostalgia for some bygone era when life seemed simpler and childhood appeared less problematic. Indeed many voices, most of them situated within a conservative theological and political perspective, take precisely that tact in contemporary conversations about childhood. They critique the current contexts in which childhood takes form by yearning for an earlier time in which various elements within the culture appeared to "match" the view of children and childhood of that era. Many of these critiques speak of the need for a "return to innocence," or of the "disappearance" or "fall" of childhood.[1] These writers can sound like magicians of nostalgia with the solutions they pose, longing to magically revert to earlier constructions of childhood and critiquing whatever in the current social context does not match those constructions. They tend to assume innocence as a natural and given characterization of childhood and fail to recognize the historicity of this view of children.

In my search for a child-affirming theology and church that genuinely welcomes children, I, too, critique the contemporary social context in which children are situated. But my agenda is not to turn back the clock to an earlier age of supposedly natural innocence characterizing childhood. This is our time and not some other. We cannot go back, even if doing so were desirable. (We should recall that the past of nostalgic memory was not equally good for all groups of people within the larger society.) Instead, I come to such a critique from the perspective that every society, culture, and historical period constructs and embodies its own peculiar understanding of childhood. Amidst competing perspectives of what a child is, certain understandings rise up when they find support from dominant social, political, economic, and religious trends that reinforce them. These dominant constructions of childhood, while not to be confused with the lives of children themselves, have formative, shaping power on children's real lives as they set forth what a particular society means by the idea of childhood. They come to appear natural, taken as normative of childhood for all times and places rather than valued in a relative sense for the historically situated constructions that they are. But not all of these dominant constructions support the thriving of children, as they may reflect other interests and agendas bearing certain antipathies to children's well-being.

Current North American constructions of childhood need to be critiqued, then. Such critique does not seek to get back to some supposedly more originary and natural view of children. Rather, such critique seeks to name and resist the points at which the regnant constructions of childhood serve the needs and agendas of other interests and power arrangements at the expense of children's flourishing. While I share in common with the "nostalgicians" the view that contemporary culture contains much that is hostile to and fundamentally unwelcoming of children, I disagree with their proposed solution of recreating an earlier vision of childhood formed from nostalgic imaginings of a bygone era. Contemporary constructions of childhood need to be understood and critiqued with a view to put forward a more adequate vision of childhood for this time in which we live and to enable resistance to those aspects of contemporary constructions of childhood that thwart the thriving of children.

An Alternative to Children as Consumers

In a consumerist society, the wider culture lifts up a dominant vision of children, namely, children as consumers. Christian theology can offer an alternative vision of the meaning of childhood. This vision will provide alternative practices that compose a way of life for children and for the adults who accompany them. Together they must seek to walk in the way of Jesus, a way opposed to the hostile and inhospitable visions so prevalent in North America today.

Christian theology also can be co-opted and engaged to endorse and affirm the vision of human life held out and blessed by globalized late capitalist society. In this case no tension exists between the market's vision of childhood and that found in the church. I contend that such uses of Christian theology lack legitimacy when held up to norms within scripture and tradition. These norms identify the good news in Jesus Christ in terms of human flourishing and freedom from oppression, as freedom for captives and sight for the blind (Lk. 4:18). These norms consistently uphold as an ethical mandate the need to "care for orphans and widows" (Jas. 1:27; see also Isa. 9:17, 10:2; Acts 6:1).

In this book, I offer one particular lens on Christian theology's alternative vision of childhood. This lens comes from the vantage point of feminist practical theology and takes as its critical principle the liberation, thriving, and well-being of all children. This critical principle includes their liberation from oppressive manipulations of the market. In what follows, I will describe what I mean with this language as I also frame a way to proceed with constructing a theology that genuinely welcomes children for this time (the beginning of the twenty-first century) and in this place (North America and in particular the United States).

While I intend to focus on issues concerning children and childhood, the issues impacting children may well have broader implications. Perhaps children in a given society operate like the proverbial canaries in the coal mines in relation to wider cultural critique. What places childhood and children at risk, fails to welcome them, and cannot support their thriving may also be what threatens the rest of humanity as well, if only we heed the warnings. At the same time, perhaps the thriving and well-being of children also can signal what is most hopeful, most generous, and most gracious about the society they inhabit, pointing the way to transformation for us all.

Starting Small: An Approach to Doing a Theology of Childhood

Most Christian theologies start big. That is, they begin with the largest of matters, such as the nature of God as the creator of the universe, and work their way down an invisible hierarchy to smaller concerns such as men, women, and only much later children and other creatures. They create vast, multi-voluminous systems of theological thought in which one of the primary concerns is coherence between one part of the system, say, the doctrine of salvation, and another part, such as the doctrine of the nature of God. Problematically, children often get "lost in the system" of systematic theologies, as a relatively small area of concern within the entire and vast universe of theological thought.

I am not writing a systematic theology of childhood. Nor am I engaging in the kind of theological reflection that places children at the center and then attempts to relate every facet of theological thought to the lives of children (although that would be an interesting project). Instead, in my construction of a feminist practical theology of childhood I will start small. I will focus on a particular situation and problem, the welcome and flourishing of children in North American mainline[2] congregations, who simultaneously participate in the church's education in Christian practices and in the culture's education in consumer practices. Concentrating on this situation and set of questions means I will not consider every theological doctrine in relation to children. I will pay particular attention to theological ideas–such as the call of Jesus to welcome children–that have some potential to contribute to the construction of emancipatory theology and practices with children. This work, then, represents an admittedly partial perspective, a specific topic and voice within the whole conversation, and not the whole of Christian theology itself.

"Starting small" also means starting with the lives and stories of some of the particular children who inform my thinking and action and with whom this theology is ultimately concerned. How does one gain access to the lives and stories of particular children? As a mother, of course, the lives and stories of my own children comprise an important source of children's experience informing this theology. Another key context from which I have access to the lives and stories of children comes from participation and research in local congregations. Between 2001 and 2003, I directed a research project to study practices with children in congregations. This research is known as the Children in Congregations Project. Its ethnographic studies in congregations allowed me to come to know and interact with many children in the context of their faith communities. While this book is not a report on that research, the Children in Congregations Project constitutes another important source of connection with the lives and stories of particular children. I will refer to this study and offer some of the stories of its children from time to time.

Yet another point of access and connection with children's lives informing this theology comes through my local Christian education resource center. In addition to offering a library for church curricula and educational materials used by churches, the center hosts a periodic gathering for a small group of pastors and educators. We share ideas and resources, engage in problem solving together, and offer mutual support for our work with children in various church-related contexts. Through this sharing I "meet" a number of children in the churches.

From time to time, in my role as a professor of practical theology and Christian education in a seminary, I visit these congregational and other church-related contexts in which children participate. Thus I have opportunities to get to know some of the children more directly. It is a wonderful way to gain knowledge about the experiences of children and of the adults concerned with educating them in the Christian faith tradition. It also provides a window on educational practices with children among a cross section of mainline congregations, and on the problems those called to ministries of education in the church face.

The Children Who Inform Our Study

In this group at the resource center, we often hear about Elliot, a lively and joyful three-year-old Korean child. An Anglo couple adopted Elliot when he was almost nine months old. Elliot bangs loudly on the church sanctuary's wooden pews during silent prayer and "talks back" to the preacher during his sermons. Elliot usually brings a bag full of small action figures to play with in church. He especially likes those with special shooting weapons. Our educational ministries group talks often about the relationship between church teachings about conflict, peace, and war and children's toys. We explore how we can educate children such as Elliot and support their families to nurture them in faith.

We also talk about Dana and Devon, five-year-old twins from an upper-middle-class, European American congregation. The twins fight with each other constantly as they vie for the attention of their exhausted parents and anyone else who will offer some. At their church, they often sit with Jean, an older widowed woman who has become their unofficial grandmother on Sunday mornings. Their own grandparents live far away, and the twins are glad to have this relationship with "Grandma Jean." Jean holds the hymnal between the two of them during worship, helping them to follow along with their beginning reading skills, before they run up to the chancel steps for the children's sermon. Their parents sit in the pew behind this little trio, grateful for an hour of respite and a chance to worship together in relative peace.

Dana loves Sunday school, where she and her peers rotate between four different "workshops," involving different media and approaches to the same biblical story over four weeks. Her favorite rotation is the video station, where films and video clips become the curriculum for the morning. Devon, on the other hand, fights with his parents every Sunday about whether he has to go to Sunday school, saying that church is boring. The Christian educator at Devon's church notices in Devon many of the same behavioral features of older boys diagnosed with attention deficit disorder. Our educational ministries group holds many lively and controversial discussions about the media, medication, behavior, and attention problems in Sunday school. We want to know how to educate the children like Devon in our congregations.

Carol pastors a struggling urban congregation. Each month Carol updates the group about Jo-Jo, a young boy from a mixed-race family (African American and Mexican) who began attending his church's after-school computer lab for youth. Jo-Jo is ten years old and has a learning disability that makes it difficult for him to keep up with his peers' computer skills in the classroom. He likes the church computer lab because it is a pressure-free environment where he can go online and surf the Internet. Jo-Jo is more interested in the Internet than participating in the rest of the life of the church. As he told me when I visited Carol's church and met him for the first time, "sometimes I go on Sundays because Pastor Carol asks me to come and help with something, and the people here are nice." Last winter, Jo-Jo spent several days in the hospital with asthma. His family does not have health insurance. Since they are not members of the church, they were surprised when several church members helped them out with rides and childcare for Jo-Jo's younger siblings while he was hospitalized. Jo-Jo's parents come to worship with him a few times a year and have told the pastor how glad they are that Jo-Jo can come there to "get some good values."

Katie, a six-year-old European American girl, is the oldest of three children in her family parented by a single mom who works as a teacher's aid. Every year Katie's mom is laid off from her job in the county school system due to budgetary problems, only to be rehired again as an "emergency hire" a few weeks into the school year. The family has moved many times over Katie's life, each time connecting with a neighborhood church that has "good programs for kids." Katie's pastor works hard to make sure her church has those "good programs for kids," but the congregation's budget problems meant that last year they had to cut the position of the part-time Christian educator who worked with children. The pastor is concerned that her congregation does not prioritize children's ministries, but realizes they must also deal with the realities of the budget and competing priorities in an aging congregation. Still, it concerns her to sense the congregation's lessening tolerance for the restlessness and noise children make during worship and its diminishing commitment to support those ministries of the church most directly related to children.

To "start small" as a way of doing theology means to begin with the lives and situations of my own children, and children such as Katie, Jo-Jo, Elliot, Devon, and Dana. It means to continue with other children not personally known to me. These unknown children are part of the web of connection in which all children's lives are situated. This web of connection makes the faith commitments and choices of U.S. children relevant to the suffering and well-being of children elsewhere in the globe. Starting small means engaging the conditions of their lives–the toys with which they play, the instabilities of their parents' employment, the hostilities they encounter in public spaces, the congregations in which they worship–as part of the "raw material" of theological work. Starting small as a way of doing a theology of childhood means listening to the stories of these littlest ones in relation to the story of Jesus.

A Small, Personalized Perspective

Starting small also refers to the particular writing perspective from which this feminist practical theology of childhood emerges. In some traditional theologies the identity of the theologian remains hidden, deemed insignificant in relation to a theology written for the purpose of addressing universal questions for all people. In contrast, I offer this theology from a much smaller or more specifically located perspective. This is not a "God's eye" view of all children as seen from no place in particular. It is *my* view of the lives and situations of children in mainline congregations in North America, as shaped through the lens of the particular social location out of which I write and engage in practical theological work. The fact that I am a European American woman formed within the progressive side of the Reformed Christian faith tradition affects the particular theological questions I pursue in relation to children. It affects the ecclesiology out of which I write and the way I interpret biblical and theological texts in my search for a grace-filled theology that welcomes children.

I am a woman raised in a lower-middle-class family in a conservative southern town in the United States. My socioeconomic, racial, and gendered context was highly problematic for me from an early age. This personal background and identity places certain issues, such as critiquing socioeconomic class issues and the maintenance of status distinctions between groups, in the foreground of my work.

I am a woman whose consciousness has been raised by my formal education and work as a pastor, social worker, and teacher and scholar of practical theology. The informal pedagogy of direct experiences with diverse communities in the United States and beyond it has also affected my values. Thus the kinds of theoretical resources I engage for analysis of children's situations take a different shape than they might in another person's work. I am interested in engaging interdisciplinary resources that can contribute to more multifaceted perspectives of children's situations both globally and locally. I seek resources that lead toward children's liberation and flourishing. And finally, but not unimportantly, I am a mother caring for three children together with my partner in marriage. This impacts the stake I have in theological questions concerning children. So does the perspective I hold that my faith commits me to work within a community of persons engaged in parental and other forms of care and commitment not only for my own but also for "other people's children"[3] as a key practice of faith.

A feminist practical theology of childhood involves persons and communities in actions on behalf of children, based on the conviction that in Christ, God already is at work on behalf of children to bring about transformation toward the reign of God. In that sense, a practical theology of childhood concerns the church's participation with God in what God is doing on behalf of the emancipation of children. Starting with the smallest human creatures, this theology of childhood thus "starts small" as it considers and aligns itself with how God is at work in children's lives, choosing children as partners, and effecting transformation for and with children. In this case, though, small does not mean unimportant or less valuable. Small is a good place to begin.

A Theology Informed by Practical Knowing

A joke has circulated about a person flying in a plane. Suddenly he had to parachute down to land for safety. After drifting through the sky over unknown terrain, he found himself tangled in a tree, safe but totally uncertain about his location. After this pilot had hung from the tree for several hours, unable to free himself, another person came walking along on the ground below. The parachutist called out, "Hello, can you tell me where I am?"

"Yes," came the reply. "You are in a tree."

"You must be a theologian," said the parachutist in response.

"I am. But how did you know that?" asked the person from the ground in surprise.

The parachutist replied without pause, "I could tell immediately that you are a theologian, because what you told me is true but absolutely useless."

From the perspective of this humorous story, some people might suggest that to use the term *practical* as a modifier for *theology* creates an oxymoron. Practical theology, as both a discipline within theology and as a method for going about theological work, describes a theology intending to be both true and useful. Practical theology is concerned with truth, insofar as it seeks to offer a valid and adequate account of the praxis of Christian faith in a particular context in which human beings strive to live lives in relation to God's reign. To be a credible account, such theological work must be recognizable both in terms of the adequacy of its description of a particular context or situation of human experience, and in terms of its description of God and God's activity.

For instance, some descriptions of children's lives tend toward a flowery, fairylike notion of innocence. This kind of description belies the truth of the everyday struggles of children and their families—at least, those in our family and others I know. In our experience children appear quite the contrary of innocence. Indeed, they scheme up new ways to best their parents or siblings, shout angry epithets or even spit in the face of someone who loves them, or commit acts of real harm (sometimes with intention, other times not) to friends. Accounts of children as theological or moral innocents lack credibility when measured against the actual experiences with children I encounter. The same is the case with similarly positioned, *in*-credible accounts (i.e., those without credibility) of children as special embodiments of depravity. When descriptions of children posit them as essentially oriented toward rebellion and wrong-doing, such accounts lack credibility in relation to experiences with other types of children. These other children exhibit deep empathy and care toward others or display great courage and determination in the face of some obstacle such as an illness, loss, or disability. To be seriously imaginable accounts of human experience, practical theological descriptions of human situations, including those of children, must be recognizable in relation to actual encounters with people, communities, contexts, and practices.

In a similar vein, an account lacks theological credibility when it features a claim about God, God's action, or humanity in relation to God that violates what Christian faith affirms about God. Such accounts suggest that God acts toward humanity in some way that is contrary to God's own being. Some descriptions of God's relationship to children, for instance, pose a "trickle down hierarchy." On this basis they name nuclear families as the one religiously sanctioned family form. They make this claim by asserting a parallel between a patriarchal father God and patriarchal human fathers. Such perspectives claim that because God is father to humanity, human fathers necessarily act as stand-in figures for God in relation to their children.

Such a theological perspective embodies an important Christian truth, namely that of God's parentlike care for God's creatures and of the power of human relationships to make concrete the love of God. At the same time this perspective violates several important norms within Christian tradition. These include the claim that God's very nature is love and justice. Identifying the Divine with particular structures for human relationships that oppress some persons (e.g., women and children) cannot be adequate or credible in relation to the justice of God. Similarly, assertions that identify or sanction any single, fixed form of human governance or family life as divine violate the theological claim that God is free to work in and through whatever structures and institutions God wills.[4]

Practical Theology as Useful Theology

Practical theology, then, seeks to offer accounts of human experience and of the character and activity of God that are true in the sense of being "seriously imaginable" credible accounts of both. What about practical theology as useful theology? A central feature of practical theology as a discipline and as a method for doing theological work is *praxis* or the mutual engagement of theory and practice for the sake of emancipatory action in the world. That is, practical theology as a praxis-centered theology intends to be put to work in the lives, communities, and situations of people. It is not a theology centered on abstract questions asked as some form of academic exercise with no engagement in the real lives of people. Practical theology involves strategies and tactics of transformation.[5] Practical theology creatively and constructively develops alternative visions and practices for human activity that work toward justice and the reign of God in particular situations of struggle. For example, practical theologians are not content with abstract proclamations that God cares for all persons as God's children. Practical theologians ask about the meaning of God's parentlike care for children in contexts in which particular children experience pain and suffering. They work out visions of such children experiencing and manifesting that care in their everyday realities. They combine such visions with action strategies effecting transformation.

Some persons easily mistake the assertion of practical theology as a "useful" theology to mean that it entails the mere application of some biblical or theological proposition to a problem posed in human experience to generate a supposed theological solution to the problem. Such a distorted perspective on the practical aspect within practical theology confuses usefulness with simplicity. Paradoxically, this distortion originates in the idea that certain foundational ideas exist that come prior to actions and practices. Actions and practices in this view serve as the ideas' (secondary) application, after which the theory may be dispensed with as irrelevant to everyday life.

These notions of usefulness, in the name of being practical, reduce complex realities to straightforward matters with easy solutions in the form of "how to" manuals for religious life. As a discipline within theology and as a theological method, practical theology is a way of engaging in theological action and reflection in connection with life practices of persons and communities. But practical theology is neither untheoretical nor anti-intellectual. Practical theology is not hostile to theoretical complexity. Rather, it is a way of doing theology that takes seriously local contexts and practices and the everyday lives of persons in those contexts as they seek to walk in the way of Jesus. Its practitioners must therefore be, in the words of Robert Franklin, "skilled cultural exegetes."[6] They must be grounded in practical knowing in which a wide range of theoretical perspectives come into engagement with particular contexts, persons, and situations. They must have such knowledge to advance toward analysis and interpretation that can generate creative, constructive actions.

Practical Theology's Goals

The goals of practical theology are not about creating new abstract principles or theological doctrines for their own sakes. Practical theology takes as its *telos*–the intention toward which it is oriented–transformative practices of Christian faith in the world. As such, it intends to be a usable theology, one that offers resources to persons engaged in a praxis of Christian faith. In the case of a practical theology of childhood, then, such a theology should be able to fund emancipatory practices with children.

Currently, "practice" is something of a buzzword in theological circles spurred on by recent developments in the field of practical theology as well as by some scholarly border-crossings into sociology, philosophy, and ritual theory. Craig Dykstra, Dorothy Bass, and others influenced by the philosophy of Alasdair C. MacIntyre[7] have put forward a new perspective. They claim that practices are "those shared activities that address fundamental human needs and that, woven together, form a way of life...Christian practices are things Christian people do together over time in response to and in the light of God's active presence for the life of the world."[8] They assert that persons become Christian primarily in and through their engagement in Christian practices.

In other instances of its increasingly popular use, the term practice simply functions as a synonym for human activity–a practice is merely "what people do." I use the term practice in two ways throughout this book. Practice refers to the productive, person-forming power of practices as socially shaped and shared forms of action. It refers also to the strategic and tactical ways in which persons engage in actions in a particular context. In this usage, I therefore am following Rebecca Chopp's notion of practice as containing both subjective and objective dimensions, individual instantiations of socially constituted realities.

At the same time, differences within any given practice, like encounters with alternative practices, express the dynamic and transformational potential of practices. These differences call into question attempts to render a singular, fixed meaning to a practice. Thus, in addition to being bearers of tradition, practices are also sites for resistance, transformation, and change.[9] This critical dimension often finds expression in that aspect of a practice that refuses to mean what, at face value, it appears to mean. In emphasizing the critical and transformative aspect of practice, as opposed to merely focusing on its transmissive capacities, I am also engaging the perspectives emphasized by sociologist Pierre Bourdieu and ritual theorist Catherine Bell. Each of these defines practice as a form of activity that is situational, strategic, embedded in a misrecognition of what it is doing, and which both structures and resists power/status relations between groups.[10]

In a later chapter I will explore at length a good example related to children. The example may be seen in the practice of offering children's sermons during worship, a modern liturgical innovation now fairly widespread among mainline Protestant churches. Congregations often identify their explicit intention in this practice as offering something special just for children. Such children's sermons seek to render the substance of the day's message understandable at a child's developmental level. At the same time, though, the practice of offering a separate children's sermon may also operate implicitly to further marginalize or exclude children by segregating them from the worshiping community as a whole and by trivializing their ways of knowing through moralisms.[11] The marginalizing action of a children's sermon generally is misrecognized in the face of the more recognizable and explicitly owned meanings attributed to the practice of children's sermons.

Social Enactment and Transformational Possibilities

My choice of the term *practice* will become clearer through its specific usage in what follows. Still, I will simply highlight the importance of two key ideas to my understanding of practice—social enactment and transformational possibilities contained in practice. A practice is not merely an individually chosen action. It also involves the enactment of socially constructed meanings through actions or behaviors that are also socially mediated. Practices include an element of misrecognition. They can "mean things" beyond or even different from what they appear to mean at face value. Practices can even mean something different from what their practitioners may articulate as their meanings. This misrecognition is a key to the transformational potential of a practice because it indicates the ability of a given practice to bear alternative meanings within its purview. Many theorists of practice rely heavily upon MacIntyre's more individualistic understanding of the term *practice*. In so doing they have often obscured these two features of social enactment and transformational possibility. In any event, an important aspect of practical theological work is its attention to the faith practices of persons and communities. In the case of this practical theology, I focus on practices in relation to children situated within those "communities of practice"[12] we call congregations.

To call my work a practical theology locates it within an unfolding conversation among scholars today about the very nature of theology. Practical theologians claim, as Don Browning puts it, "that Christian theology should be seen as practical through and through and at its very heart."[13] As a practical theology, this work is a way of thinking about God and human experience in which actual, present-tense human experience and practices matter. Such theological reflection is always intimately bound up with action. What does this mean for a theology of childhood? This theology cannot exist simply at the level of ideas. Practical theology must be a practice, and a practical theology of childhood must represent a way of being in God's world in which the well-being of children is of prime importance. From that viewpoint, a practical theology of childhood in effect becomes a way of "doing theological anthropology." It names and enacts the meaning of human life in connection with God from the perspective of a theological understanding of childhood and calls forth actions toward the well-being of children. In this way of doing theology, actions and reflections, meaning-making and practices in relation to childhood are deeply interrelated.

Practical Theology's Sources of Knowledge

Practical theology is, in the words of Pam Couture, a theology "informed by practical knowing...a more formalized version of the thinking process through which an average person attempts to bring social science, cultural traditions, and religious convictions into dialogue with one another."[14]

Several kinds of practical knowing inform my theology of childhood. This practical knowledge comes from many sources. First among these is a lifelong engagement with Christian texts, stories, and communities in my efforts to walk in the way of Jesus. Other fountains of knowledge include my own and others' experiences with children along with the collective experience and reflections of various faith communities in which I have been privileged to participate or study. The practical knowing from which I draw also includes several disciplines of study grounded in practice-based knowledge (social work, education, cultural theory, pastoral care, ethnography), and various kinds of biblical, theological, and sociopolitical analysis.

Accordingly, this work in practical theology of childhood is highly interdisciplinary. Traditional studies have often built hierarchies of knowledge in which some forms are viewed as "higher forms of knowledge" and therefore more credible than others. In such cases philosophy and logic, empirical sciences, and the Bible have occupied the higher places, while education, early childhood development, pastoral care, and any knowledge from personal experience were assigned to lower realms. In this practical theology of childhood I enthusiastically mix various disciplines and forms of knowing toward the goal of creating a credible and playful–yet "seriously imaginable"– theological perspective on children and childhood.

Readers will find within these chapters a mixture of the kind of intimate, personal knowing that comes from hours spent breastfeeding babies, coaching a child who struggles to learn how to read, and teaching third grade Sunday school classes. Such knowing includes the personal-political knowing of standing in line during a time of unemployment anxiously waiting for WIC vouchers to help feed growing infants, of writing letters to legislators in an effort to impact policy in favor of children's access to health care, and of assisting a mother and her five children to find shelter space for the night. These pages also involve the academic technical knowing of how to perform exegesis of biblical texts in search of clues for God's purposes for children, and of exploring economic theory in an effort to better grasp the character of contemporary social injustice toward children in different parts of the world. All these forms of practical knowing and more make their own partial contribution to a feminist practical theology of childhood.

A Theology Informed by Norms of Justice for Women and Children

This theology of childhood is distinctive. It is a feminist theology of childhood. What makes this practical theology of childhood feminist? Not every practical theology concerned about matters of justice is feminist theology, nor is a theology feminist solely by virtue of being written by a woman. Feminist theology is theology that takes as a central concern the liberation of women, together with others, from various forms of injustice. Different varieties of feminist theologies feature different emphases, but all have in common some analysis of women's oppression and give central place to thinking and action that support women's freedom and flourishing.

As I suggested above with my example of how children's physical presence in worship may pose certain problems for their predominantly female care providers, a theology of childhood that portends to be liberatory for children must also take into account those who care for them. In present-day U.S. society those who care for children overwhelmingly continue to be women. A theology that welcomes children while contributing to the further oppression of women cannot ultimately embody justice as a practice of faith. Feminist theology employs various theoretical perspectives in the self-conscious analysis of gender and gendered power relations within church and society. Therefore, in this practical theology of childhood I attend to the effects of gender distinctions and gendered power relations coming out of discourses about childhood, as well as to the pragmatic implications for women of particular ways of understanding and living with children.[15]

As a specifically feminist practical theology of childhood, then, this work foregrounds the concerns, interests, and struggles of women. It highlights issues of justice for women as it explores the relationship between children's lives and childhood and the emancipatory reign of God proclaimed by Jesus. By calling this a feminist theology of childhood, I claim that an emancipatory theology of childhood necessarily engages one in the struggles of justice for women. Of course, one could write about children from other than feminist perspectives. In placing the concerns of women together with those of children, I am not suggesting that these are necessary links that cannot be uncoupled (such that women rather than men must necessarily be the ones to take responsibility for the care and well-being of children). This relationship needs to be strongly critiqued and not merely accepted at face value.

What I mean to do by placing them together is to address the reality of the contemporary situation in which women's interests and women's work tend to be closely tied to the interests and needs of children. Justly or unjustly, the concerns of women remain solidly linked to those of children in ways that are simultaneously relational, personal, and political. This close linkage means that advocacy for the full humanity of women cannot happen apart from advocacy for children. In a similar vein, though, I would argue that any true advocacy for children must take into account the needs and situations of women. Consequently, a part of this feminist practical theology of childhood seeks to address the issue of the theological meanings of childhood in a way that also takes account of women's lives and liberation, rather than adding to their burdens.

Speaking of Children

Issues about the politics of language constitute an important part of feminist theological discourse and so have a bearing on my use of language about children and childhood. Voices from Asian, mujerista, womanist, and other groups of theologians writing emancipatory theologies out of a particular context justly critique the use of masculine terms and hierarchically generated language to express human understandings of God. Many of these same theologians appropriately critique the use of the term *woman* as a universal signifier that enfolds all women into a single, homogenous unity. Such stereotypical language ignores the contexts of particularity such as race, class, sexual orientation, or social status. These contexts make for important differences between women.

Similarly, the terms *child, childhood,* and *children* must be problematized. Is there a group of persons defined by age and transcending boundaries between cultures that can be referred to as "children" without qualification? Is there such an identity as "the child," existing across all times and places as a natural and essential status of humanity? My response to both questions is a qualified no. I say no because it is clear to me that childhood and children take shape in relation to particular cultural, historical, and social contexts. To speak of children in general risks imposing an uninterrogated norm of childhood drawn from one social location onto all children. Similarly, to speak of "the child" is to employ an "essentialized," homogenized view of childhood as a generic age-defined human status occurring in some natural and pre-social form separable from the effects of its construction in a given historical and social context.

Such uses of language can meld diverse children into a false unity and abstract them from cultural specificity. In this view, if we could strip away all the features of social, cultural, and historical particularity like layers of an onion, we would end up with some common core called "the child." Speaking of children in this way denies the role and power of social forces (such as those that reproduce status distinctions coded by race or gender) to construct childhood in ways that have very concrete, material effects in the lives of actual children.

However, banning all common or general uses of these terms does not solve all of the problems. One must still determine how to write or speak meaningfully about children without falsely "essentializing" them. The qualification I place on "saying no" to all uses of universalizing terms to name children or childhood comes from both a simple pragmatic issue and from the Christian theological norm of justice. To involve "children" as subjects in theological discourse, we need some meaningful ways to speak about them in all of their sameness and particularity. Likewise, we must have linguistic terms to advocate with and for these children in the church and in the world.

Any concern I have over the "disappearance of childhood," thus, is not so much about Neil Postman's notion that some essential view of the nature of "the child" is disappearing under the influences of culture.[16]

Rather, my concern is that children and childhood will disappear from being subjects of theology by virtue of the difficulties inherent in talking about them as a group, right at the moment in history that children finally begin to show up as subjects of theological discourse.

I cannot purport to solve this problem in its totality here. For purposes of this writing, when I talk about children and childhood, I will adopt a solution described by feminist theologian Serene Jones and others known as "strategic essentialism."[17] In brief, essentialism is the approach within feminist theory that emphasizes a given or "essential" gender difference. Theorists working out of this perspective on gender posit a notion of fundamental or essential womanhood or woman's nature that underlies cultural overlays and constructions. These thinkers want to emphasize a natural or given basis for difference. They see this as a positive element in women's gender identity and feminist theory, unlike others who claim such a difference as the basis for discrimination against women, as has been done at various times in history. An alternative perspective, that of gender constructivists, posits the gender identity of women and men alike to be a creation of societal influences and historically constituted norms that are malleable and changeable rather than being a given state of nature. Constructivist thinkers emphasize the power dynamics embedded in how differences of various types are constructed and maintained.

Similar essentialist and constructivist ideologies are at play in discourse on children. I do not wish to take a hard-line essentialist approach that asserts an originary notion of "the child." On the other hand, I cannot commit myself to an equally hard-line, radical constructivist view leading to the logically necessary but silly affirmation that there is "no such thing" as childhood or children since these represent mere social constructions. A strategically essentialist approach to language about childhood asks whether, in a given situation, it is pragmatically helpful or useful to put forward a particular view of "the child." This approach fits well with practical theology's emphasis on the practical effects of discourse, or the notion that our ideas and practices exist in deep co-integration such that the ways we think and talk about something can produce real and practical effects. Within the framework of a "strategic essentialism," decisions about the appropriate terminology concerning children must be made contextually. We must keep an eye toward the consequences of any particular usage and apply norms that concern whether a given use of terminology about children works toward their flourishing, or in support of their further oppression.

For example, in arguing for children's rights to health care, activists often find that it is pragmatic and helpful to make the claim that "a child is a child is a child." In so doing they imply–if they do not outright state–that all children, regardless of their cultural group, economic and social status, or geographical location, ought to have access to basic health care. On the other hand, these same activists also try to redress the imbalance in health care services available to racial-ethnic minority groups compared to those received by Anglo children. In this case they might find it more strategic to argue from the perspective that childhood is differently constructed in different cultural communities so that different "delivery systems" for health care become necessary to ensure an equal standard of care. Decisions about language thus take place as strategies in an overall emancipatory agenda.

I tend to lean in the direction of those thinkers who see gender with its norms and definitive practices as socially and historically constructed (and thus deeply implicated in the structuring of power in a given society). For purposes of this feminist practical theology of childhood, though, it makes sense to me to adopt a posture of "strategic essentialism" for talking about children. Sometimes it is helpful and important to speak of childhood or children in an open and general way without need to add multiple qualifications to the terms in the service of the flourishing of children. At other times, specifying more particularity best serves these interests. In general, I do not use the term "the child" except when referencing other thinkers who do, since, even within a practice of strategic essentialism, this term takes on such an archetypal and wooden quality that its use poses more problems than it solves.

A Theology Critically Situated within Christian Scripture and Tradition

Finally, I identify this theology of childhood not only in terms of its relationship to feminist perspectives but also to Christian tradition. Calling a practical theology "Christian" involves another rather specific claim. Such theology takes place within, and by persons in, Christian faith communities in a constructively critical relationship to the sources and traditions of Christian faith. I addressed one aspect of this earlier in my discussion of theological credibility. As a specifically Christian theology, my reflections on children and childhood critically engage practices, symbols, and stories from Christian scripture and tradition as both primary content and interpretive lenses. Of course, Christian communities and theologies across their history have functioned as sites for the oppression and exclusion of women and children as well as for their empowerment and liberation. Therefore, I highlight the importance of critical interrogation and appropriation of Christian scripture and historical theology for use as resources in constructing a child-welcoming theology and church. Unlike some feminist theologians and scholars for whom the patriarchal taint of biblical texts or theologies renders them null and unusable, I continue to find in both kinds of texts resources for life-giving thought and practices. Christian scriptures continue to be for me a liberating word of God when, enlivened by God's Spirit, they witness to the news of God's grace for women and children together with others.

My way of engaging biblical texts can be seen directly in chapter 2. But the place of Christian scripture as a source for my way of understanding children in light of the grace of God requires me to comment further here about the method I use for interpreting biblical texts. In the same way that I assert above that the use of language about children is a strategic practice, I believe that textual interpreters also operate with different strategies for how they engage biblical texts. These depend upon variables such as their own social context, the context for the particular act of interpretation, and what is at stake for them and their community. I might, for example, utilize a different strategy for hearing and interpreting a text in the context of a liturgy or devotional setting than I would use in exegetical work of a strictly academic interest.

In this work of searching for a theology and church that welcome children, I adopt a feminist sociopolitical strategy for interpreting biblical texts. That is, I read texts through the lenses of feminist critical concerns about the positioning of gender and power in texts, and I seek to see these texts and their meanings in terms of the social and political relations they involve. Such a reading takes seriously both the context of the interpreter and that of the text's "community of witness." This reading strategy then gives appropriate attention to the dynamics of its historical context. Let me describe this feminist sociopolitical reading strategy in relation to the primary text I use in this work, the gospel of Mark and its stories about children.

A Strategy for Reading Mark's Texts

I read Mark's story of the Jesus movement from a critical feminist sociopolitical perspective in particular solidarity with children. I thus see it as a counter-narrative to the dominant discourse of the imperial regime of the time. Accordingly, I am especially interested in how children and women appear in Mark's counter-narrative and in the kinds of social relations and social practices the story portrays. To make sense of the counter-narrative depictions of children and women, though, I will need to give some attention to how the children and women of the Markan communities are positioned in the dominant discourse of empire. Such a reading strategy puts context in the foreground. Thus I see the fact that Mark's version of the Jesus story was produced out of a particular social, political, economic, and religious context to be of paramount importance for interpreting it.

Reading Mark's gospel from a critical feminist sociopolitical perspective means attending to the whole more than to the parts. I am less interested in taking its pieces apart—that is, creating a "catalogue" of all the places the gospel mentions children and dissecting these as independent units of meaning that will allow us to draw conclusions about children in the Bible. My interest centers in hearing the story as a whole communication of a particular message in which children and women figure significantly. For reasons of space, I cannot treat the entire gospel of Mark in chapter 2, so I necessarily choose to focus on several specific passages from it that involve children. My aim, however, is to read these particular stories within the framework of Mark's story as a whole, with its overall narrative agenda as the guiding structure for making sense of these stories.

Texts such as Mark's gospel have rhetorical intent, that is, they constitute some kind of argument. They are told to communicate a particular perspective, ostensibly in an effort to persuade hearers and readers to that point of view. To read using critical feminist sociopolitical practice involves interrogating this story's communication. I must ask about its intended message of "good news" in its version of the Jesus story. Much more, I must inquire about what in the text constitutes good news for children and women. All the while I remain critical of the text's potential to submerge the interests of children and women by working out power relations. Mark's story, like other texts and forms of discourse, constitutes a site of struggle for power. Yes, even a text produced as counter-narrative to the forces of empire may also involve certain concessions and compromises to those forces that render its message confusing or even contradictory at points. Here, feminist methods of interpretation call for a *hermeneutic of suspicion*, interrogating the gaps and inconsistencies in Mark's gospel as they may relate to the subordination of women and children.

This same hermeneutic of suspicion must be applied to the history of interpretation of biblical stories in which children appear. The history of interpretation reflects a bias against interpreting these texts in relation to the children in them. A feminist sociopolitical strategy for reading these texts, then, is one of *compensatory privileging* of the place of children in the text to see what new perspectives may emerge. Such a strategy assumes that just because children may be relatively invisible and silent in a particular text does not mean they are irrelevant to the meanings made and communicated by that text. Reading texts with an originary intention of privileging the place of children results in what is admittedly a partial and biased reading, contributing to what Letty Russell terms the "unfinished dimension"[18] of theology. That is, this partial reading adds a generally overlooked part, the stories of children, to the existing interpretations that attend to other themes and agendas. It does not purport to be an unbiased reading. Indeed, no reading of texts can make such a claim, as all interpretation comes from the particular standpoint and location of the interpreter. My commitment in this interpretation is toward a bias in favor of and in solidarity with children.

An additional feature of my strategy for reading biblical texts concerns texts as multivocal and resistant to fixed meaning. This strategy makes it possible for multiple interpretations to operate side by side or even simultaneously. While not exclusive to feminist interpreters, this postmodern perspective on how meaning resides in language certainly finds a home among many of us. We resist the tendency to fixity and to notions that to be meaningful a text can carry only one dominant structuring principle.

Finally, treating Mark's gospel as scripture means similarly allowing the text to interrogate me and the communities of faith and struggle in which I participate. I must engage this story not simply as interesting literature but as a means through which God's spirit may work to transform the hearts, minds, lives, and actions of God's people today. With that in mind, in chapter 2 I will focus on several of Mark's stories about children. I will seek out their contribution to a reading of Mark's story as a narrative about God's reign meaning freedom from empire and leading to a reordering of all relations in terms of justice for the "littlest" ones.

Biblical Texts as Source and Norm

I have just described the approach to biblical texts and their interpretation that I use in this book. Underlying my description is the assertion that Christian scriptures, though not unproblematic, constitute both a source and a norm for me in constructing a feminist practical theology of childhood. As a source, biblical texts provide some of the "raw material" for building a theology by offering a variety of witnesses to God's nature and activity in relation to children. Other sources include human experience, the heritage of Christian tradition, and new sources of insight that can come from various analytical or theoretical perspectives such as educational or social theory.

As norms, biblical texts offer criteria for judging the adequacy of theological claims, in effect "disqualifying" certain theological claims as falling outside of the bounds of how communities of faithful persons across many different times and situations variously have understood God's interaction with the world. For example, a theological claim or belief that only adults may truly be members of the body of Christ would need to be tested against criteria for membership and discipleship presented in Christian scripture. Where biblical criteria conflict or show evidence of being co-opted to subordinate children and women, I utilize the critical principle named above, that of the liberation and thriving of children. This norm is drawn from the Bible's larger overall witness to a God whose very being entails freedom, love, and justice and whose actions in relation to humanity work toward the realization of liberation in the lives of all peoples, including children.

Christian Tradition as a Resource

In addition to resources from scripture, I will draw from theological resources within Christian tradition to construct this feminist practical theology of childhood. In my work I make particular use of two twentieth-century theologians who might be considered unlikely candidates to provide assistance in constructing a feminist theology, Karl Barth and Karl Rahner. Barth was a Swiss Reformed theologian identified as one of the most influential theologians on the Protestant church in North American, and a primary voice for neoorthodoxy in twentieth-century theology. Use of his work engenders the suspicions of many feminists because of his emphasis upon divine transcendence in contrast to most feminist theologies' corrective focus on the immanence of God.[19]

Barth places Jesus Christ and scripture in high roles as divine revelation and witnesses to that revelation that have authority in human experience. Such a move does not sit well with feminist theologians concerned with addressing and redressing the harm done to women by exalting a male Christ and by oppressive uses of scripture. For them human experience constitutes the starting point of theology.[20]

Finally, Barth betrays his own embeddedness in the sexism of his time and context, in an argument about relationships between men and women as those of complementarity within difference. In his now infamous "A and B" discussion, he compares men and women to the letters A and B, insisting that they are different and not interchangeable but that this does not bring B (the woman, of course) any disadvantage: "A preceded B, and B follows A. Order means succession. It means preceding and following. It means super- and sub-ordination. It does indeed reveal their inequality. But it does not do so without immediately confirming their equality."[21]

These critiques serve as an invitation to read Barth critically. But just because I, too, find much to criticize in his theology, I cannot discard his theological perspectives altogether, as do some feminists. Perhaps I continue to return to Barth and others for resources in thinking theologically because of my own social location as a feminist theologian in the Reformed faith heritage. Such location places on me commitments to engage theology as an ecclesial practice.

Similarly, Karl Rahner was a twentieth-century Roman Catholic theologian. He was a German Jesuit scholar best known for his work in relation to the second Vatican Council. The Council significantly reshaped Catholicism by bringing Catholic theology into engagement with modernity. Some feminist critics charge that his work, with its underlying philosophical framework in retrieving Thomas Aquinas for the church, is too philosophical and abstract. Furthermore, some might argue that Rahner, as a priest living in celibacy, has little to offer as a resource for a feminist theology of childhood. Rahner's writings are philosophically complex and abstract, and he did not have personal experience as a father of children. Nevertheless, Catholic educators like Maria Harris credit him with reshaping the whole experience of Catholic Christian education (including education for children) and with bringing a positive understanding of childhood to the church. Rahner's theological anthropology has been a key element in the work of Latin American liberation theologians' assertions of the "full humanity" of marginalized persons. He makes the same argument in relation to children. I find the latter to be especially helpful in a culture and world that often treat children as less than fully human and therefore less than fully entitled to human rights and just treatment. I appreciate Rahner's unsentimental affirmation of children, and therefore find that I continue to return to his theology.

In chapter 4, as I engage in an exploration of contemporary North American religious discourse on childhood, I will consider in more detail the contributions that Barth and Rahner make to critiquing that discussion and to my own constructive theological work.

The Relationship between Thinking and Action in Theology

To speak of the Bible, theology, and norms as I am doing is to suggest a connection between beliefs about God and the way people live their everyday lives such that it matters what people believe. But how do theological beliefs relate to life practices? Specifically, how do Christian beliefs relate to personal and social practices with children? In recent years a flurry of writing has emerged on the subject of children and childhood in theology that assumes a direct link between thoughts and actions in relation to children. Feminist theologians began much of this work. They critiqued traditional Christian doctrine's support or even encouragement of the abuse of children. Such support came as the tradition lifted up the violent and abusive death of the Son of God on the cross as a central symbol.[22] The reasoning guiding such critiques follows the logical paradigm that "if we believe (X) about God, Jesus, Humanity, and Children, then (Y) actions are the consequences." Such reasoning gives a rather high place to the power of beliefs or ideas to directly and unilaterally influence actions and practices. In this particular example, of course, positing such a powerful and singular connection between a belief and a practice constitutes a problem because it suggests that holding a certain religious belief necessarily leads to a certain action, namely child abuse.

In the wake of the critique implicating Christian beliefs in the maltreatment of children, practical theologians, historians, and others responded with their own initiatives to critically address the way Christian theology deals with children.[23] Many set out to retrieve or reclaim child-affirming elements from within Christian tradition to construct contemporary Christian expressions of a child-friendly theology. Their answer to the implicit logic formula posed above is to say, in effect, that "negative" beliefs or those involving violence are not the only beliefs in Christian tradition. The constructive efforts of these thinkers then involved selecting doctrines or ideas from within the tradition that promise to lead to different actions or practices with children.

Such interests in retrieving a usable past from Christian tradition regarding children lie close to my own, and I benefit greatly from the work of these thinkers. At the same time, however, the method behind this mode of constructing theology still involves an uninterrogated assumption about the relationship between thought and action, or theory and practice in theology. That assumption holds that if we can just get our thinking about children right, then right actions with children will necessarily follow. Therein lies the difficulty: can problems with social practices be resolved solely at the level of ideas? Stated differently, How can this account for all the times people act in ways contrary to their explicitly stated beliefs?

I want to believe that what people think influences how they act. I particularly want to believe that religious beliefs can affect people's everyday life practices. I do think it matters what we believe about children, about God, and about human personhood. The question is, *How* does it matter? How do religious beliefs (which are thoughts and ideas) matter to human actions and practices, religious and otherwise? These are huge questions to which I cannot devote the space of a full exploration in this work. But it is important for me to briefly clarify how I see the relationship between thought and action, as my perspective differs considerably from some others who write about theology and children.

Theologian Kathryn Tanner[24] helpfully demonstrates that there is no single, unidirectional, and fixed relationship between a particular belief in Christian theology and a particular practice. She notes the way in which, for example, the same Christian belief in God's sovereignty can be used to support radically divergent actions by Christian communities. One group of Christians may take the belief in divine sovereignty as the legitimization of a particular form of government that they deem to be mirroring divine rule. Another group may see in the same doctrine the relativizing and critique of all forms of human rule in relation to God, who alone is truly sovereign. One community finds in the doctrine of the fatherhood of God a rationale for patriarchal family relations, leading to authoritarian family styles. Another community sees there a call to repentance from all human fathers who lack the kind of compassionate and faithful care God demonstrates, leading to practices of parenting not centered around authoritarianism.

How does this relate to theological thinking about children? The absence of a straight line between a particular theological idea and a corollary practice calls us to do more than merely come up with a more adequate idea of childhood. Such an idea cannot guarantee either more just and loving practices with children or a "better childhood" in the day-to-day experience of any particular child. Put differently, the content of theology does not alone dictate its effects and meanings at the level of practices.

From this perspective, to return to an earlier example, the Christian belief in the crucifixion of Jesus as salvific does not, based on content alone, issue in practices of child abuse. And at the same time, discourse does effect the world beyond its intention. Thus a climate of normalizing violence or glorifying suffering can be created through certain renderings of this Christian idea about salvation. This climate could then create a relationship between Christian soteriological beliefs and child abuse in some instances. But as we think about the ways religious ideas relate to human actions, we need to find other ways beyond the content of an idea alone to account for its impacts on human actions, both positive and negative.

Accounting for the Relationship of Beliefs and Practices

Tanner identifies four such "other ways" of accounting for the relationship between beliefs and practices.[25]

1. Changes in the meaning of a term or belief (i.e., in a different historical time period or in a different cultural or social context) can alter actions associated with it. For example, the meaning of the term "faith" differs considerably in Protestant mainline contexts steeped in the legacy of Horace Bushnell's *Christian Nurture* from the mid-1800s and in evangelical contexts rooted in the revivalist Christianity against whom Bushnell wrote. These diverse interpretations lead to different practices with children and to different responsibilities for parents. Bushnell's followers emphasize gradual education, while evangelicals seek to bring children to the point of conversion.
2. The way beliefs are combined with each other forms a major factor influencing actions. For example, the Reformed emphasis on divine sovereignty and human sinfulness might easily issue in human lives oriented around actions to appease a despotic ruler-God. But beliefs about sovereignty must be held in tension with beliefs about God's nature as Love itself. Affirming that God's being and nature are love means that God's sovereignty takes different forms, such as that of providential care for all creatures and of God's saving grace and sanctification of humanity. Otherwise, we might all be in a constant state of groveling before God to appease God's wrath. Our other beliefs about who God is (theo)logically disallow such appeasement-oriented enactments from being deemed appropriate manifestations

of the Christian life. An example in a different direction combines Christian beliefs about God as ever loving and forgiving with those about the power of prayer and confession in the lives of believers. Such a combination might well issue in nonaction/passivity on the part of believers. The same understanding of God combined with emphasizing other beliefs about God's justice or God's preferential option for the poor might logically lead to a response active efforts to change the social structures perpetuating poverty. As I will show in a later chapter, particular Christian beliefs amplified and placed in combination with other beliefs issue in distinctive theologies of childhood.

3. Power differences between persons constitute a factor in how ideas relate to actions. The practical working out of a particular theological belief may be quite different depending upon the context and social location of believers. For example, some groups of Christians often use beliefs about divine sovereignty to justify hierarchical relationships in families. Their logic claims that human social relations between parents (particularly fathers) mirror God's relationship to the world.[26] Such an engagement of this Christian idea about God calls for quite different actions from children and adults. This doctrine seems to invite children to behaviors of obedience and subordination, but to call parents to various kinds of actions associated with a superior social positioning. The church has a long history of using Christian doctrine differentially to enforce relations of domination by some at the expense of others. Later in this book I will affirm in more detail Tanner's arguments against such use of Christian doctrine. Use of particular Christian beliefs to affirm hierarchically fixed social relations between groups is extremely problematic in light of other Christian beliefs that limit human relations from being structured around social inequalities.

4. The "scope of a belief's application" is a factor influencing actions. This asks whether a particular theological belief is applied to all people or only to some people in certain situations. For instance, in the above example, the parallel between God as ruler and human power to rule only applies to fathers. Those who hold this perspective limit its scope to the member of the family deemed closest to God in use of power. It is not applied across the board to all members of the family—for example, children are not positioned in the family in a parallel role to that of the sovereign God. Hence the kinds of actions that relate to the Christian belief in divine rule, when used as a model for human relationships, necessarily will differ depending on whether they are seen to apply to all persons or only to certain persons.

Tanner's identification of four factors influencing the relationship between a belief and various potential practices is not exhaustive. It does point out the insufficiency of treating this relationship between ideas and actions as one of simple correspondence. Tanner demonstrates that a particular use of Christian doctrine justifies certain social practices and orderings of social relations. However, norms within Christian beliefs "rule out" their use to foster oppression.

Evaluating the Habitus of Faith and Practice

I will use this method of internal critique in my feminist practical theological search for a child-affirming church and theology. With this method I will assert that certain uses of Christian beliefs to support certain practices with children are problematic both in terms of the simple and one-way correspondence they pose between belief and action, and also in terms of their consistency with other aspects of Christian theology. I will engage this internal critique not only on the side of how beliefs fund practices, but also with reference to how practices give rise to beliefs.

To do so will involve examining various factors, such as the four named above, at work in influencing the relationship between belief and practice with children. I am working in the more multidirectional view of the relationship between Christian beliefs and practices. In this view actions and ideas, beliefs and practices, are already deeply intertwined with one another. They are often shaped and influenced by larger social forces of which persons may not even be aware. The late French sociologist Pierre Bourdieu wrote of practices taking shape in relation to a larger social arena or "habitus" within which persons come to be apprenticed in a whole set of beliefs and actions.[27] Bourdieu's notion of habitus includes the various institutions, social and cultural forces, and underlying structures that may promote or constrain actions. It is not as though we choose independent, isolated beliefs or practices from some sort of menu, as individual actions to be selected apart from the wider habitus in which they co-occur with other beliefs and practices. In short, this method will lead me to examine the larger "habitus" in which belief and practice take shape—that wider social and cultural space within which people experience and learn a way of life. I will evaluate the adequacy of how this larger "habitus" renders any particular form of Christian life with children.

A certain coherence exists between some practices and ideas and others. This coherence is based on the habitus that forms persons who engage these ideas and practices, and that also produces and reproduces a particular form of culture and ordering of social relationships. Therefore, one might occasionally find a person who genuinely prefers paintings of Elvis on velvet and listening to classical music. However, the notion that our preferences, ideas, and actions take shape in relation to a wider habitus in which they come to make sense suggests this as a less likely scenario than some others. Accordingly, in such a perspective on how ideas and actions relate, transforming practices with children depends not only on having "right ideas" about children and childhood. It also depends upon the larger habitus that forms a system in which ideas interact with and shape practices.

Here is what I am suggesting, with the help of Tanner and Bourdieu:

1. Our ideas about children (theological and otherwise) and our practices with children (religious and otherwise) mutually influence each other. Both are formed socially and culturally within the various "communities of practice" we inhabit. Beliefs do influence actions, although there is no single, fixed formula for this influence. Actions also influence beliefs.

2. It is both unnecessary and impossible to posit either ideas or practices as "coming first" in the relationship between the two. We find it more helpful and more important to notice that both beliefs and practices with children occur within a wider system or habitus, within which particular aspects of both belief and practice become amplified, while others recede into the background or are nullified altogether. Some of our ideas and practices with children are quite explicit. Others take shape without our awareness, shaped and constituted within the particular social arenas in which we live.[28] That is, sometimes practices emerge apart from any particular supporting beliefs as an effect of the wider ethos or discourse of which they are a part. For example, some congregations engage in liturgical practices that exclude children's participation in worship. They do not link this practice to a belief that children should not participate. Rather their habitus involves a highly literary and word-oriented religious culture. Their overdependence on written words in liturgy leads to exclusionary practices with children who do not yet read. In such a situation no explicit doctrinal belief is at fault.

Considering the wider context in which beliefs and practices exist may also assist us to understand why it so often seems that beliefs actually fail to influence actions. Vincent Miller offers the compelling example of theological students who articulate strong agreement with various aspects of liberation theology's call to live and work with the poor, yet do not evidence any connection between these beliefs and how they live their lives.[29] Similarly, congregations frequently express beliefs that Jesus had a special concern for children and therefore they also should manifest particular care for children. Many congregations believe in a general and abstract way that children are important and valued in the church, but these beliefs do not seem to translate into practices in the lives of persons or congregations. They go on voting for legislation that denies health care, housing, and food for poor children. They continue to give disapproving looks to children in their sanctuaries during worship, as if the presence of children poses a problem and an obstacle to communion with God.

We must do more than interrogate the content of an individual belief or, conversely, to look to a particular practice as a direct (unmediated) expression of meaning. A practical theology of childhood has to consider beliefs and practices with children as part of a wider "habitus" or community of practice. This habitus, with or without intentionality, forms persons into a way of life. This practical theology of childhood will thus take seriously the power of transpersonal social forces to shape human ideas and actions.

To answer the question of how Christian beliefs and actions are related, I examine the ways both are situated in relation to a wider social and cultural environment. In that environment a variety of factors may influence what will be intensified and what will be diminished in a particular rendering of Christian life. For North American children, the habitus in which thoughts and practices take form is a society structured around consumption. Market forces often easily co-opt the intended coherence between what we think and what we do in relation to children. We structure patterns of social relationships around consumption and treat religious beliefs and symbols as disposable commodities. The effect is to disable beliefs about children in the church and society from any connection to practices with children. A person can believe, therefore, that Jesus loved and blessed children, and go on with life as usual.

3. The question of how thoughts and actions relate fundamentally concerns what other factors are present in the wider "habitus" in which both are formed. We must also consider the various forces at work that structure how persons live and make meaning of their lives. In a habitus of consumerism, market forces constitute a powerful shaping energy underlying practices, habits, relationships, and identities. Theological ideas and practices concerning children do not occur in a vacuum but take form in the context of this consumerist habitus. As Miller suggests in his helpful analysis of how consumerist culture impacts religious life, we need to "consider how underlying structures and practices of consumer culture transform the function of Christian symbols and practices."[30] While theologians might retrieve child-affirming elements from Christian theology and construct a more consistent and coherent connection between the visions expressed with these ideas and the related practices with children, the habitus of consumer capitalism can place real constraints on how these ideas are embodied.

In this work, I therefore address consumer capitalism and the North American social and cultural environments spawned by it as the habitus in which contemporary Christian beliefs and practices with children take shape. The problem, then, is not merely the cultural construction of a distorted idea of children as consumers, against which a better, Christian understanding of childhood can constitute a correction. The problem is that consumerism as a habitus forms persons into patterns of action, attitudes, dispositions, and habits of interpretation that inform how they engage the various elements of Christian faith, including beliefs and practices with children. Constructing a more adequate vision of childhood or retrieving a better theological view of children from within Christian tradition is not at all incidental to the work of transforming theology and church life to welcome children. Such a construction, however, cannot alone respond to the problem of finding/constructing a welcoming theology of childhood within this situation. We must also address the mechanisms by which consumerist societies operate as the wider ethos in which congregational and individual beliefs and practices with children take shape in Christian faith communities. It becomes critical to pay attention to the impact of living in a consumer culture on theological beliefs and practices with children. And so I will inquire about the effects of participation in globalized consumer culture on Christian beliefs and practices related to children individually and in congregational life.

Mainline Churches, Children, and the Habitus of Consumerism

What is the situation of mainline congregations in the United States, and of their children, at the start of a new century? Congregations in the United States have been understood as one among several important mediating institutions that foster the well-being of families by contributing to the families' ability to be a "haven in a heartless world" of the labor force, and an important source of "social capital" for families and children.[31] Prior to the 1970s, people expected "that religion and child-rearing were connected to each other, and that both were women's work. Congregations existed in part to help families do their jobs, and families were expected to support in their homes the work and worldview of the congregation."[32] But the entry of large numbers of more affluent women into the workforce in the 1970s shifted the balance between work, family, and religion in the United States. This changed the patterns of religious affiliation among different types of families, particularly in relation to the workforce participation of the women in these families. These women were no longer as available, or no longer had interest in, performing the domestic labor of congregational life in addition to that of their homes.[33]

Popular wisdom, backed up by denominational census reports, holds that nondenominational "megachurches," evangelical denominations and congregations, and Pentecostal churches are booming, while the mainline denominations continue to decline both in numbers and in influence. Analysts attribute this decline to various factors. Demographic studies show a population decline in those demographic groups typically drawn to mainline churches. Theological differences have brought a movement away from more liberal theologies to embrace conservative theologies with more clear-cut boundaries and expectations. Generational shifts have produced the so-called GenXer's and Generation Y adults, who seem less drawn to mainline congregations.

Some observers, looking back on the past fifty years of Christian education in churches, hastily proclaim mainline Christian education as the chief culprit in its decline. They claim a failure to adequately pass on the faith to a new generation has created the current gap between a loyal but aging cadre of members and a transient group of young adults returning–perhaps only temporarily–to church "for their children."[34] Others, such as sociologist Penny Marler, maintain that Protestant congregations remain nostalgic for a traditional family structure that no longer exists as the predominant family form. The decline of these congregations' populations is proportionate to the decline in the number of persons in so-called traditional family forms in the general population.[35]

Many congregations, anxious about their own survival, have quickly seized educational ministries with children as a way to bring adults into the church. Some use the situation as a moment of opportunity to strengthen their ministries and outreach to children. As a result many vital ministries of Christian education with children live on the mainline Protestant landscape.

Beyond this positive and creative impulse another dynamic is at work in situating Christian educational ministries in congregations. It has to do with the shaping power of consumer culture on religious life and practices in North America. Mainline churches have become anxious about their declining numbers, vitality, and public influence. They find themselves reshaped around an ecclesiology of the market economy, focused on what needs people have that the church might meet with programs and on what niche groups within the population to target for their church growth (advertising) campaigns. These anxious efforts are oriented around institutional survival, to keep people on the membership roles by providing them the services they want and need, but these efforts have the reciprocal effect of training mainline Christians to live out a view of their congregations as "service stations."

Traditionally, such congregations have seen themselves as a local community of practice, constituted around a corporate and companioned walk in the way of Jesus and centered around shared practices of hospitality, love, and justice. In short, these congregations want to be the body of Christ given and sent out for the life of the world. Instead, congregations formed by the discourse of consumerism have become service-providing institutions where persons find programs to meet their needs. Thus the habits and dispositions by which persons engage in commodity exchange in the market economy come to shape life in the church as well.

In such a regime of commodity exchange, it is hardly surprising that Christian education becomes yet another mechanism of this consumption-oriented process. The church alternates between treating children like commodities to be obtained in a competitive market ("How many kids did you have in your Sunday school this year?...Oh, that's too bad. Our numbers are up since we started using the rotation curriculum."), and treating them as "clients in need of church programming."[36] Some senior pastors in larger congregations who otherwise show little concern or interest in the lives of children speak of children as one of the best ways to get adults (their parents) into the church. This reflects a utilitarian view of the smallest humans that reduces them to being merely the means for achieving some more desirable end. Other church leaders speak and write about the need to attract families with young children so that their congregations will have vitality. The desire for vitality is not in itself wrongheaded. But the interest in children primarily for the purpose of getting adults onto the church rolls or of making the congregation appear to have life objectifies and commodifies children. This is simply more evidence of the church's captivity to market forces. The theological notion of welcoming children easily slips into advertising to adults through children.

I am not saying that all mainline congregations have devious intentions with children, or that none are engaged in strong and faithful educational ministries with children. Rather, I simply note that in the United States, institutions including congregational and family life operate within and are subject to the processes of consumer capitalism's domination of social and political life.

I offer this too-brief description of how contemporary ecclesiology is being reshaped under the forces of the market regime because that is part of the situation of children in the church today that needs description in the work of theology. One of the most significant effects on children is the ambivalence in which they are held by churches that do not wish to be in the position of "needing" children and yet cannot escape the fact that they do need children, if only to meet their own images of vitality.

A second crucial effect of the consumerist shaping of congregational life with children is the difficulty it creates for churches whose theological understandings move them to resist domination by market forces and the way of life posed by the market as "the good life." Efforts to educate children and adults in a different practice and understanding of faithful living come up against the pervasive and powerful pedagogy of the market empire's ability to absorb and co-opt various forms of resistance. Let me offer an example from my monthly Christian educational ministries group, whose gatherings at our local resource center for sharing and support I mentioned earlier.

The weeks leading up to the Advent season always present challenges for pastors and educators in this group as they work toward creating events to involve children and families in learning Advent faith practices and deepening their knowledge. In our November gathering this autumn, Larry, a Methodist pastor and father of two children, described the dilemma he faced in his church and family: "Last year our congregation decided to covenant together to simplify our Christmas holiday celebrations in our homes, to cut down on our emphasis on spending money on gift giving, and instead to put our focus on being together and on religious meaning. What actually happened, though, is that people felt so uncomfortable not participating in the usual kinds of gift exchanges that they ended up shopping and giving gifts any way–and then feeling guilty about not sticking to what we agreed to do as a church.

"My wife Jan and I also become aware that one of the ways our kids connect to their peer group is by the 'stuff' they all have in common, you know, the computer games. We want a less consumer-oriented holiday, but we don't want to deprive our children of their connections with friends. We are surprised at how much those connections happen through sharing things you buy."

Asked by other group members what they did in their family and in the church, Larry sighed heavily and acknowledged, "We just had to give in–the Goliath of Christmas traditions built around buying and giving gifts was too big, and the pressure was too much. We knew we would start losing children and families if they heard us saying, 'Don't do Christmas this year'–and 'doing Christmas' means buying stuff."

Annika, a minister of Christian education in a UCC congregation, nodded her head in an understanding way. "We talk about simplifying our holiday celebrations, recovering the religious meanings of Christmas, but it feels as if the 'real' shared meaning of the holiday is buying stuff. We add on religious stories and language in a feeble effort to make it more meaningful." Many in this group of concerned clergy and educators spoke about consumption-oriented holiday celebrations as the norm onto which religious significance becomes an extra, added-on feature.

Annika smiled wryly as she described the way her efforts to invite the congregation to a deeper kind of celebration beyond consumerism became converted into another, different kind of marketing campaign.

"As I started writing curriculum for the children, the congregational growth and outreach committee decided it was a good way to advertise our church—you know, 'Jesus is the reason for the season' and all that. So before I knew it, what began as an effort to invite people to an alternative to the shopping mentality at Christmas time became a marketing ploy for the church! We had slogans and banners along with a direct mail campaign to households in the neighborhood. Our children's choir was suddenly off on a 'reason for the season' tour of performances in local shopping malls!"

What descriptions such as these point out is the power of market forces to shape congregational life and practices, even to the point of co-opting resistance. With Vincent Miller, I see congregations in the United States today standing within a market regime that shapes people into an ecclesial way of life tied to practices of consumption. That is, under the pervasive influence of market forces, persons come to treat religious symbols, narratives, and practices, including those concerning children, as commodities—isolated, disposable elements that stand alone, apart from any mooring in a wider tradition. Miller argues that the habits of use and interpretation learned from living in a consumerist culture leak into religious life. Persons come to practice their faith as consumers and to hold their religious beliefs in such a (commodified) way that those beliefs have little impact on people's life practices. What might this mean for children in congregations? In a situation of high anxiety about their own institutional survival, mainline congregations inadvertently operate out of a consumer-driven ecclesiology in which children are used to uphold an image of vitality of programs or to bring adults into the church.

A Method for a Christian Feminist Practical Theology of Childhood

Above, I have been describing in some detail the senses in which I use the terms "practical theology," "feminist," and "Christian" as I embark on an endeavor to construct such a theology in relation to the welcome of children. Now it is time to identify in brief form what such a method of doing theological work looks like.

The basic framework of my practical theological method involves a movement between three primary activities:

1. engagement with and description of a particular context, community, or situation in which people struggle for justice and work to practice the reign of God announced by Jesus
2. engagement of multiple and interdisciplinary resources toward more adequate understandings, analyses, and interpretations of that particular situation of struggle or life context held under the norm of emancipatory justice

3. the construction and engagement of strategies and tactics of action and hope that can participate in God's transforming work of love and justice

These primary activities are far less a given order of discrete operations than they are a continuous and fluid movement among children's experiences and situations, biblical and theological resources, critical analysis, and constructive actions and responses. As I described earlier, by adding the modifier "feminist" to practical theology, in this method I give a primary place to the analysis of gender. This involves the gendered use of power and issues of justice for women and children together with men in light of God's grace, an emphasis that takes place across all three activities of theological work.

The context, community, and situation of engagement for this feminist practical theology of childhood consists in the community of children in mainline congregations in North America. In this chapter I have begun the first of the three activities in my theological method, namely, that of offering some description of contemporary North American children in the churches. I do this through sharing some stories of children and through describing the situations of congregations in which children come to be nurtured in faith.

That descriptive work will continue in the next two chapters, albeit in a different vein. In chapter 2, I describe the children with whom Jesus interacts in the gospel of Mark and offer a feminist sociopolitical reading of Markan stories concerning children. This chapter is at once both a descriptive activity–telling about children in a situation of imperial domination–and an interpretive-analytical move, as it initiates the bringing of biblical resources to contemporary understandings of childhood.[37]

I believe that the stories of Jesus with children constitute some of the "spiritual capital" with which children interact in congregations. These stories of Jesus' regard for children constitute an always present but often unarticulated backdrop to the meanings children hold in congregational life.

Chapter 3 continues the descriptive activity with a depiction of children's lives in relation to changes in the contemporary economic landscape and other shifting cultural forms in the United States that impact the shape of childhood. This chapter describes the situation of children in congregations in contemporary U.S. culture. Simultaneously they are educated into practices that form a Christian way of life and into practices constituting a way of life shaped around the marketing, acquisition, consumption, and display of commodities. The chapter shows the ways childhood itself becomes reconstructed in terms of the market. It uses the metaphor of empire to describe the way market forces dominate the lives of children.

Like the children in Mark's gospel, children in contemporary North American congregations also live in a situation of imperial domination in which their welcome and well-being is at stake. At the conclusion of chapter 3 I consider the similarities and gaps between the vision of childhood held out by Mark for those seeking to walk in the way of Jesus and the vision of children and their thriving embodied in consumerist culture today.

Chapter 4 continues this analytical and interpretive activity by exploring contemporary American religious conversations on childhood. This discourse reproduces the wider culture's ambivalence toward children and in so doing falls prey to a commodified process of engaging children and childhood in theology and church. At the same time, within this conversation may appear some helpful theological resources that can contribute to an alternative vision and practice of welcoming children. I will explore these as resources for the constructive work of the remaining chapters. There I explore theology of childhood as a practice of theology with children, which necessarily embraces the ambivalences and ambiguities inherent in the messiness of childhood. Chapters 5 and 6 constitute a preliminary attempt to explore what this theology looks like in action. They will bring theology to bear on two areas of practice involving children that remain highly contested: liturgy and education. The final chapter is my effort to summarize the feminist practical theology of childhood issuing from the descriptions, analyses, and strategic actions in this volume.

A Scene from a Different Restaurant: Creating a Welcome Table for Children

I began by describing an experience in a restaurant in which a man asserted his supposed right to be in a space free of the messiness, bother, and noise of children by virtue of his having paid to be there. While I am writing this book primarily in and for a North American Protestant church context, significant parts of it, particularly the vision of children's flourishing that it develops, came into view during the years our family lived and worked in the Philippines, where my daughter Sarah was born. I want to end this discussion of theological method at the starting point of my practical theological method, that is, beginning with the situations and experiences of children, by sharing another story from a restaurant in our little town of Dasmarinas, Cavite (in the Philippines).

One day, I took my infant daughter into town. After a jeepney ride in which several adults assisted us, Sarah and I went into a restaurant. We ordered some rice, *buko* (coconut) juice, and *lumpia*. While we waited for the food to be prepared, Sarah began to cry loudly. It was late in the day, so I knew that she was probably hungry. I began to rummage around in her diaper bag in search of something to quiet her screams.

Before I could find anything in my bag, though, the woman at the next table stood up, stretched out her hand toward us, and thrust a banana into my hand. "She is hungry. You give her this." As I thanked her, the proprietor of the restaurant stepped out of the kitchen with our rice wrapped in a banana leaf, saying, "Take this now for the baby. I will bring the lumpia soon." I sat down and fed my baby, and she stopped crying. The woman who gave us the banana held Sarah on her own lap for a few minutes when my lumpia came, allowing me to eat more easily. The proprietor came out from behind the counter and played a Filipino version of "peek-a-boo" with Sarah and another young child who was there.

In a country where material poverty pervades, in that moment the room was filled with riches: we were all connected. No one was hungry. There were no more tears. The children laughed and played and sensed the respectful care of everyone around them. I cannot be overly romantic about this vision. I long for the richness of that moment to become the material reality in the lives of all children in the Philippines and the rest of the world. Surely the call of Christian discipleship is a call to work for transformation of children's sufferings, especially in solidarity with peoples of the Two-Thirds World, where children's suffering is omnipresent.

As a beginning, that day in a Filipino restaurant we beheld a glimpse of God's transforming power, a foretaste of the divine realm that keeps alive my hope for finding a theology and a church that genuinely welcome children. Jesus said to his disciples as he held a child in his arms, "Whoever welcomes one such child in my name welcomes me, and whoever welcomes me welcomes not me but the one who sent me" (Mk. 9:37).

SOURCES CITED

Albrecht, Gloria H. *Hitting Home: Feminist Ethics, Women's Work, and the Betrayal of "Family Values."* New York: Continuum, 2002.

Ammerman, Nancy Tatom. "Golden Rule Christianity: Lived Religion in the American Mainstream." In *Lived Religion in America: Toward a History of Practice,* ed. David D. Hall, 196–216. Princeton, N. J.: Princeton University Press, 1997.

Ammerman, Nancy Tatom, and Wade Clark Roof, eds. *Work, Family and Religion in Contemporary Society.* New York: Routledge, 1995.

Barth, Karl. *Church Dogmatics.* Vol. 3, part 4, ed. G.W. Bromiley and T.F. Torrance. Edinburgh: T. & T. Clark, 1961.

Bass, Dorothy, ed. *Practicing Our Faith: A Way of Life for a Searching People.* San Francisco: Jossey-Bass, 1997.

Bell, Catherine. *Ritual Theory, Ritual Practice.* New York: Oxford, 1992.

Bendroth, Margaret Lamberts. *Growing up Protestant: Parents, Children, and Mainline Churches.* New Brunswick, N. J.: Rutgers University Press, 2002.

Benhabib, Seyla. "The Generalized and the Concrete Other: The Kohlberg-Gilligan Controversy and Feminist Theory." In *Feminism as Critique: On the Politics of Gender,* ed. Seyla Benhabib and Drucilla Cornell, 77–95. Minneapolis: University of Minnesota, 1987.

_____. *Situating the Self: Gender, Community, and Postmodernism in Contemporary Ethics.* New York: Routledge, 1992.

Bourdieu, Pierre. *Outline of a Theory of Practice.* Translated by Richard Nice. Cambridge: Cambridge University Press, 1977.

_____. *Distinction: A Social Critique of the Judgement of Taste.* Translated by Richard Nice. Cambridge, Mass.: Routledge, 1984.

Bourdieu, Pierre, and Jean-Claude Passeron. *Reproduction in Education, Society and Culture.* Trans. Richard Nice. London: Sage, 1990.

Browning, Don S. *A Fundamental Practical Theology: Descriptive and Strategic Proposals.* Minneapolis: Fortress Press, 1991.

Bunge, Marcia J., ed. *The Child in Christian Thought.* Grand Rapids, Mich.: Eerdmans, 2001.

Chopp, Rebecca S. *Saving Work: Feminist Practices of Theological Education.* Louisville: Westminster John Knox Press, 1995.

Cooey, Paula. *Religious Imagination and the Body: A Feminist Analysis.* New York: Oxford Press, 1994.

Cornell, Drucilla. *Transformations: Recollective Imagination and Sexual Difference.* New York: Routledge, 1993.

Couture, Pamela D. *Blessed Are the Poor? Women's Poverty, Family Policy, and Practical Theology.* Nashville: Abingdon Press, 1991.

_____. *Seeing Children, Seeing God: A Practical Theology of Children and Poverty.* Nashville: Abingdon Press, 2000.

de Certeau, Michel. *The Practice of Everyday Life.* Berkeley: University of California Press, 1984.

Delpit, Lisa. *Other People's Children: Cultural Conflict in the Classroom.* New York: New Press, 1985.

Dunne, Joseph. "Arguing for Teaching as a Practice: A Reply to Alasdair MacIntyre." *Journal of Philosophy of Education* 37, no. 2 (2003): 353–70.

Dykstra, Craig. *Growing in the Life of Faith: Education and Christian Practices.* Louisville: Geneva Press, 1999.

Fuss, Diana. *Essentially Speaking: Feminism, Nature and Difference.* New York: Routledge, 1989.

Greven, Philip. *Spare the Child: The Religious Roots of Punishment and the Psychological Impact of Physical Abuse.* New York: Alfred A. Knopf, 1991.

Harvey, David. *The Condition of Postmodernity: An Enquiry into the Origins of Cultural Change.* Cambridge, Mass.: Blackwell, 1990.

Held, Virginia. "Care and the Extension of Markets." *Hypatia* 17, no. 2 (2002): 19–24.

Jones, Serene. *Feminist Theory and Christian Theology: Cartographies of Grace Guides to Theological Inquiry,* ed. Kathryn Tanner and Paul Lakeland. Minneapolis: Fortress Press, 2000.

Keller, Catherine. *From a Broken Web: Separation, Sexism, and the Self.* Boston: Beacon, 1986.

Lasch, Christopher. *Haven in a Heartless World: The Family Besieged.* New York: Basic Books, 1977.

Lave, Jean, and Etienne Wenger. *Situated Learning: Legitimate Peripheral Participation.* Cambridge, Eng.: Cambridge University Press, 1991.

MacIntyre, Alasdair C. *After Virtue: A Study in Moral Theology.* Notre Dame, Ind.: University of Notre Dame Press, 1984.

_____. *Whose Justice? Which Rationality?* Notre Dame, Ind.: University of Notre Dame Press, 1988.

Marler, Penny Long. "Lost in the Fifties: The Changing Family and the Nostalgic Church." In *Work, Family and Religion in Contemporary Society,* ed. Nancy Tatom Ammerman and Wade Clark Roof, 23–60. New York: Routledge, 1995.

McFague, Sally. *The Body of God: An Ecological Theology.* Minneapolis: Fortress Press, 1993.

Mercer, Joyce Ann. "Gender, Violence, and Faith: Adolescent Girls and a Theological Anthropology of Difference, 1997." Unpublished Ph.D. dissertation. Emory University, Atlanta

_____. "Children and Religious Education in an Age of Globalization: Learning from David Ng." *Religious Education* 97, no. 3 (2002): 208–25.

Michel, Sonja. "Childcare and Welfare (in)Justice." *Feminist Studies* 24, no. 1 (1998): 44–55.

Miller, Vincent J. *Consuming Religion: Christian Faith and Practice in a Consumer Culture.* New York and London: Continuum, 2004.

Miller-McLemore, Bonnie J. *Let the Little Children Come: Reimagining Childhood from a Christian Perspective.* San Francisco: Jossey-Bass, 2003.

Ng, David, and Virginia Thomas. *Children in the Worshiping Community.* Atlanta: John Knox Press, 1981.

Noddings, Nel. "Is Teaching a Practice?" *Journal of Philosophy of Education* 37, no. 2 (2003): 241–52.

Postman, Neil. *The Disappearance of Childhood.* New York: Delacorte Press, 1982.

Pritchard, Gretchen Wolff. *Offering the Gospel to Children.* Boston: Cowley Publications, 1992.

Putnam, Robert D. *Bowling Alone: The Collapse and Revival of American Community.* New York: Simon and Schuster, 2000.

Roof, Wade Clark, and William McKinney. *American Mainline Religion: Its Shape and Future.* New Brunswick, N. J.: Rutgers University Press, 1987.

Sommerville, C. John. *The Rise and Fall of Childhood.* Vol. 140, Sage Library of Social Research. Beverly Hills, London, New Delhi: Sage Publications, 1982.

Sonderegger, Katherine. "Barth and Feminism." In *The Cambridge Companion to Karl Barth,* ed. John Webster, 258–73. Cambridge, Eng.: Cambridge University Press, 2000.

Tanner, Kathryn. *The Politics of God: Christian Theologies and Social Justice.* Minneapolis: Fortress Press, 1992.

_____. *Jesus, Humanity and the Trinity: A Brief Systematic Theology.* Minneapolis: Fortress Press, 2001.

Wenger, Etienne. *Communities of Practice: Learning, Meaning, and Identity.* Cambridge, Eng.: Cambridge University Press, 1998.

Wood, David J. "Rebuilding Community: Let's Meet." *The Christian Century* 121, no. 3 (2004): 24–29.

CHAPTER TWO

Whoever Welcomes One Such Child

Children in the Gospel of Mark

Elliot comes to church prepared. He brings a bag with a few snacks—a small box of raisins and some crackers. He brings his most beloved action figures and usually takes them out about mid-way through the sermon, when the long minutes of hearing one person's voice stop being interesting enough to hold his attention. And he brings his Bible, in this case a children's story bible with bright pictures and engaging renditions of various narratives from the Old and New Testaments. On a recent Sunday morning in Elliot's church, as members of the congregation settled into their pews to listen to the gospel reading for the day, Elliot already had his action figures out and moving on the pew beside him. As the pastor began to read the story from Mark 10 in which Jesus tells his disciples to let the children come to him, Elliot froze in his seat. Looking up at the pastor quickly, he grabbed his story bible and began frantically turning the pages, as he began to cry out loudly, "I know that! I have that story! Look. I know that. It's 'Yes-Jesus-Loves-Me.'" Elliot's parents, rosy-faced with embarrassment over the attention of this "disruption," worked to quiet him. Elliot would not be quieted, however, until he found the page in his story bible with the picture of Jesus gathering children around him.

Many Christians "have that story" of Jesus and the children engraved as an early template in our memories. The image of Jesus surrounded by and blessing children (Mk. 10:13–16; Mt. 19:13–15; Lk. 18:15–17) references one of the most well-known stories from the Bible. We may know the story in the form of children's songs like "Jesus Loves the Little Children," or in paintings ranging from Sunday school poster art to various museum pieces that take this story as their subject matter. In this chapter I want to explore the story of Jesus blessing the children, with its portrayal of children as gifts of God, as one among many richly textured narrative images of children in Christian scriptures. I will do so by focusing on the gospel of Mark and its depictions of children as central to how Mark tells the story of Jesus and, therefore, as central to the larger story of God's grace in Jesus Christ. In this reading, children are indeed gifts, but that gift status may mean something different than is readily apparent in popular depictions of children from the Bible.

Choosing Mark's Version

Why Mark's gospel? Mark's way of telling the story of Jesus has long appealed to me because of the active place it gives to women, its attention to reordering relationships and power arrangements, and its oddly interesting ending. I have a deep personal interest in Mark's take on the Jesus story for the way it clearly and directly addresses issues of social and economic class difference as central rather than peripheral concerns of faith. And this gospel's continual reiterations of the themes of the reign of God and the meaning of Christian discipleship draw me in and challenge me, as someone who wants both to understand and to live my faith in the world.

But in my more recent forays into scripture scholarship focused around children, Mark's gospel comes to the foreground primarily because of the place of children in the story. Children in Mark's narrative mirror the journey of Jesus. They embody the reign of God in human history. Through stories of Jesus' engagement with children who struggle with illness and spirit possession, Mark communicates what it means to be a part of the reign of God. As Mark's text portrays Jesus blessing children whose low social position places them in sharp contrast to the desired positions of honor and power sought by Jesus' adult male disciples, Mark offers his view of what it means to follow Jesus. Children in Mark have a primary role in moving the story along to its highly unusual and surprising ending. In short, children become a primary means for Mark to tell his version of the story of Jesus with its good news of God's grace. It seems likely that we might find clues in such a story for a liberatory theology of childhood.

From the standpoint of feminist theology, however, one of the most important reasons to look to Mark's version of the Jesus story in the search for a theology that welcomes children concerns its sociopolitical context, a context with certain parallels to our own time. Mark's gospel took shape in a context of expansive, oppressive imperialism that wreaked havoc and incredible suffering on many people for the benefit of an elite few. New Testament scholarship locates the communities in which Mark's story circulated as being in the village culture of Palestine. These communities in the Galilean region struggled under both the conditions of agrarian life and those of Roman imperial rule, conditions I will describe below in more detail. In addition, Mark's gospel took shape in a patriarchal context in which cultural patterns of honor and shame[1] amplified the oppression of women and children. That is, in the combination of factors at work to produce the contexts inhabited by the hearers of Mark's stories, women, children, and families experienced particular hardship. Mark's version of the Jesus story came into being as a *counter-narrative* to the discourses of empire.

Literature from Below and from Above

Mark's gospel was thus produced "from below" by a community experiencing imperial domination under the *Pax Romana*. Mark's story thus comes out of a sociopolitical context with marked similarities to our own time as the world experiences the imperial domination, expansion, and rule under the *Pax Americana*,[2] a situation that likewise has a significant impact on children.

One critical difference, of course, is that Mark's gospel emerged as a counter-narrative to the dominant narratives and discourses of empire, produced by people struggling to resist the totalizing grip of empire on their existences. In the contemporary imperial context of *Pax Americana*, North America stands positioned "from above," as the one *producing* the discourse of domination and as *perpetrators* of the extension of empire. Certain commonalities exist in the sociopolitical context of imperial domination between the *Pax Romana* of Mark's time and the *Pax Americana* of our time, but the positioning of contemporary North American readers and hearers and that of the Markan communities of the first century stand in antithesis to each other. Readers might misunderstand what I am doing here and see me as drawing a too quick parallel between Mark's context and the twenty-first–century, middle-class Anglo community of my social location. So let me be clear: I see myself as standing (however unwillingly) among those who produce and benefit from imperial discourse and practice, a factor that positions me among those "critiqued" by the way Mark tells the Jesus story.

Even from such a position, perhaps *especially* from such a position, Mark's counter-narrative is important. As counter-narrative, Mark's gospel can help to expose the dehumanizing effects of empire, not only upon those subjugated by it, but also upon the ones who appear to benefit most from it. Put differently, Mark's gospel can help in North American privileged contexts to unmask the way our roles in the *Pax Americana* harm us and our children. At the same time, Mark's gospel exposes the direct effects of such power on subjugated persons, especially children, who constitute the objects of imperial domination in our time.[3] In chapter three I will address that issue in greater detail, looking at North American children as consumers under contemporary market forces.

For now, I will simply note that, like many majority-culture women in North America, I live as one variously positioned in relation to issues of power and privilege, sometimes experiencing both privilege and marginality in the same context. With other women (and men) of faith who participate in movements for justice for children both locally and globally, I am committed to use experiences of marginality as resources for identifying in solidarity with those who have little power or privilege. I am also committed to use those positionings of relative power to which I have access as resources in solidarity with those who struggle for justice from far less advantaged situations. From such a position it becomes clear that the privilege and benefits of empire in early twenty-first–century North America are related to and implicated in destruction and suffering in the lives of children and women wrought by the globalization empire. As Christians aware of this situation, we must join together and attempt to construct a counter-narrative to the dominant narrative of imperial domination. Mark's story as counter-narrative to the destructive narrative of empire of its time may offer some clues about how to walk with children in the way of Jesus in our time.

The Sociopolitical Context of Mark's Gospel

The sociopolitical context for Mark's gospel was that of agrarian village life under the so-called *Pax Romana*, the "peace of Rome," a peace secured through military might along with political and economic subjugation of many peoples. Features of this imperial domination included occupation and rule by Rome (or its designees), often through the co-opting of a subject people's own political and religious institutions for the benefit of the empire. That is, Rome actively involved members of the occupied people's upper classes and ruling elite, allowing them to maintain a privileged position by acting as client-rulers on behalf of the emperor. This had the appearance of "local rule" and thus ostensibly lessened resistance. An important feature of the *Pax Romana* was its program of state-sponsored terrorism, with mass slaughter and enslavement as the common imperial responses to rebellion. Finally, the so-called peace involved severe economic oppression of subjugated peoples as the empire exacted huge taxes in coin and in kind to support its building programs and feed its armies.

For the Jewish agrarian village people in northern Palestine at the time of Jesus and of Mark's gospel, such a program of imperial domination brought particular hardship. Horsley describes the heightened impact of Roman conquest on Galilee:

> The Roman conquest of Palestine was particularly hard on the Galileans. Whenever the Roman armies conquered and reconquered the area, they started in Galilee, with devastating effects. For example, in Magdala–hometown of Mary Magdalene, one of the three women who witnessed Jesus' crucifixion and empty tomb (Mk. 15:40; 16:1–8)–the Romans enslaved thousands of people roughly fifty years before Jesus was born.[4]

Theological Support for Opposing Rome

Jews living in Palestine were undergirded by a theological tradition of assenting only to the rule of God and not to any human ruler. Thus they especially resisted both Roman imperial rule and coming under the authority of a priestly centered religious leadership based in the Jerusalem temple. So determined was their resistance that Palestinian Jews underwent not one but four experiences of conquest by Rome before finally being subdued. When Herod was appointed as "client king" of Judea in 40 B.C.E., he experienced sustained resistance, particularly in Galilee and the area around it. This resistance, close enough in time to the birth of Jesus, would undoubtedly have been a part of the corporate memory and consciousness shaping the lives of people at the time Mark's gospel took shape.[5]

In addition, "Temple Judaism" was centered in Jerusalem and vested power in high priests and kings. Agrarian groups of Jews had long resisted Temple Judaism. These northern farmers had separated and formed their own kingdom in the area of Samaria and Galilee rather than being subject to forced labor for temple construction under a king. At the time of Jesus, then, inhabitants of these areas stood in a tradition that rejected urban temple religion in favor of local assembly-based (synagogue) religious and political practice.[6] Around two hundred years before the time of Jesus, however, after the Maccabean revolt, Galilean Jews again became subject to the rule of Jerusalem. When Rome then subjugated Palestine in 63 B.C.E., these Jewish peasants found themselves under an imperial Roman domination that co-opted the temple-based religion as collaborators in its system of local client king-rule.

Roman Exploitation of Galilee

Thus the agrarian Jews of Galilee became subject to three levels of economic exploitation. First, they were obligated to pay tribute to the emperor. Horsley notes that at the time of Julius Caesar, Palestinian Jews paid roughly 12.5 percent of their annual harvest to the emperor. The tribute, as "a symbol of domination and subjection as well as the economic means by which the Romans supported their empire," was strongly enforced such that "Rome regarded nonpayment as tantamount to rebellion."[7] Second, Palestinian Jews also paid taxes to their local governors, client kings such as Herod. Last, the people were also now subject to the Jerusalem religious authorities and their system of temple taxes and "*korban*," the system by which the religious leadership siphoned off support that rightly needed to be available for support of families, instead requiring these payments in land or its produce as a substitution for temple service.[8]

For an agrarian peasant population whose existence was already barely at a subsistence level, such economic hardships created unbearable, inhuman conditions. Families had to sell off land, and some even had to sell off children or other household members into debt slavery.[9] Adult males who no longer possessed land to work necessarily left their families behind as they traveled in search of labor as well as to avoid forced conscription into the imperial army or enslavement. Such conditions often meant leaving children, women, and the frail elderly in extremely vulnerable positions, without any viable means of support. Women and children, whose wage earnings were never enough to sustain them anyway, could scarcely survive alone. The huge, destructive impact of such economic hardship on family life can scarcely be overestimated.[10]

Even when families and households remained together, imperial domination heightened the oppressive circumstances in the lives of women and children who already lived in a patriarchal family context in which they existed as virtual property of their husbands or fathers:

> In circumstances of imperial subjection such as prevailed at the time of Jesus, alien political-military rule and compounded economic exploitation intensified patriarchal domination. As lowest in status, women received the brunt of the pressures passed down along the chain of domination. Jewish men, who were experiencing humiliation and frustration under the effects of Roman rule, would have reacted by demeaning their own women. And the society would have sharpened and intensified their concern with the ordinances governing the proper behavior of their women.[11]

Women's exploitation under patriarchy and under the economic exploitation of the Roman Empire went hand in hand, with the resulting reality that

> in the first century—as today—the majority of the poor and starving were women, especially those women who had no male agencies that might have enabled them to share in the wealth of

the patriarchal system. In antiquity widows and orphans were the prime paradigms of the poor and exploited.[12]

Mark as Counter-narrative

In such a context, Mark's gospel emerged as a counter-narrative, a story against the dominant story of empire. In this counter-narrative, the conflict of power stands at the center. Jesus' proclamation and embodiment of divine rule, or the "kingdom of God,"[13] in opposition to the rule of empire takes center stage in the drama. And as a counter-narrative written a generation apart from the events it narrates, Mark's gospel constitutes a bitingly critical commentary on the conflict in his day. This conflict pitted the radical reconfiguration of power Jesus proclaimed in his ministry against the substitution of that vision with a "replacement hierarchy" by male leadership as the Jesus movement began to shift from being a populist movement to a more established form.[14]

Children's Roles

Where do children figure in this story of political power and economic exploitation? Ignoring the sociopolitical setting of Roman conquest and domination allows for readings of Mark in which children and women (to a lesser extent) appear incidental to the story and its communication of the reign of God.[15] Such readings treat child characters in the narrative as unimportant, either by virtue of their being taken as "merely" symbolic/figurative, or as superficial background devices for the text to make a more important point unconnected to children per se. Taking the sociopolitical context of this gospel seriously leads me instead to view Mark as a story of the Jesus movement told from the perspective of subjugated people.[16] Mark thus operates as a counter-narrative to the dominant story of the imperial regime, and children and women become crucial to the sense of the story as those persons most deeply disenfranchised and oppressed under imperial rule, and as those who therefore stand to experience the greatest sense of hope and joy in manifestations of oppression's transformation.

As such, Mark, in telling the story of the Jesus movement from a counter-imperial perspective, asserts a different version of reality from that of the empire.

1. God's rule brings life, marked by the throwing out of destructive spirits, manifestations of healing and wholeness in the concrete lives of people, and renewed hope as well as restored forms of community and social relationships that allow even the most vulnerable to thrive amidst continuing hardships;

2. the last, least, and littlest matter the most, while the power of the rich,

powerful, and elite becomes relativized in overturned hierarchies and unsettling of social relations between groups and persons;

3. serving and following in the way of Jesus become primary practices by which life is valued, while the usual positioning and status markers between people become irrelevant;

4. social relationships including kinship networks are rearranged under a norm of radical solidarity with those doing the will of God, a move that supports persons like sick women, demon-possessed children, and widows, those most unable to withstand the difficult economic and social conditions of life under empire;

5. faithful walking in the way of Jesus (discipleship) ultimately means engaging in conflict and struggle against the forces of empire, which likely involves suffering and may even bring death; and,

6. following in this way brings persons both into new life here and now and into the new resurrection life of Jesus.

As I turn now to consider several specific stories from Mark's gospel, my focus is not on the question, "What does Mark's gospel say about children?" but instead asks, "How do children appear in the story of Jesus as told by Mark?" As I will show, the children in Mark's gospel are multifaceted: affirmed and blessed, they are also dirty, sick, and spirit-possessed. Ultimately, they are the ones who embody the reign of God and faithfulness in their walk with Jesus to the end.

A Child in the Midst of Them: Mark 9:33–42

Mark 9:33–42 taken in isolation and rendered as it often is in artistic interpretations, paints a beautiful pastoral scene in which Jesus blesses a child. Its emphasis on the welcome of children as the way to welcome Jesus himself certainly shows how central children are to Mark's story of the reign of God, and interpretations of this story as affirming the worth and importance of children are certainly appropriate. At the same time, though, read in its immediate literary context, this story appears in the midst of some ugly "adult" realities. It comes on the heals of Jesus' efforts to explain to the twelve male disciples the coming conflicts he will face, culminating in his death and resurrection. Unable to grasp what Jesus is telling them, or the deeper meaning of his ministry of healing and exorcism, the disciples argue about their status positions.

Mark 9:33 sets up the action with Jesus asking the disciples what they are arguing about. He then explains to them what makes for greatness in the reign of God: "If someone desires to become first, that one will be last of all and a servant of all" (9:35, AT). The narrative tells of Jesus then taking a child, setting the child (Greek, *auto*, "that same one") in the midst of them. Taking the child into his arms (the sense of the verb *enagkalizomai* is that of a protective and tender embrace[17]), Jesus then says to them, "Whoever welcomes/receives (*dexetai*) one such child in my name welcomes me. And whoever welcomes me welcomes not only me but the one who sent me" (9:37, AT).

The sense of the Greek verb variously translated as "welcome" or "receive" concerns hospitality. It points back to the language of 6:7–11 in which Jesus sent out the male disciples in a state of absolute dependence on and vulnerability to the hospitality of strangers. In essence, they were sent out to be like children, helpless save the protection, care, and welcome of those who received them. The practice of hospitality in the context of Israelite religious tradition thus referred not to superficial activities in the domestic sphere but to a deep tradition of welcoming strangers. It had a particular connection with children, of welcoming and providing for those who were the most vulnerable of the vulnerable, orphans (cf. Ex. 22:20–23 and Isa. 1:23). Ultimately, the God who brought Child Israel out of Egypt in care (Hos. 11:1–4) protects the orphans, so the failure to receive them with hospitality is tantamount to turning one's back on God, who similarly provided hospitality to Israel.

In Mark's story, the child becomes the occasion for Jesus to explain (yet again) the reordering of social relationships and power made real under the reign of God, a concrete way of showing the meaning of "being last of all" (*panton eschatos*, Mk. 9:35). Horsley describes the issue in terms of children's social status:

> In ancient Palestine, as in most any traditional agrarian society, children were the human beings with the lowest status. They were, in effect, not-yet-people. The [language that] 'the kingdom of God' belongs to children sharpens the agenda of the whole Gospel story that the kingdom of God is present for the people, the peasant villagers, as opposed to the people of standing, wealth, and power.[18]

In the patriarchal honor/shame society being described, children were quite literally the possessions of their fathers. Thus in this story the child's low social standing accentuates Jesus' message that "kingdom politics" lift up the lowliest, unlike imperial politics revolving around patron/client relationships that simply apply more pressure to keep the lowliest ones down.

What is most remarkable about Jesus' teaching here is the connection he draws between the divine reordering of power in social relationships (like a child, last and servant of all) and the social practice of welcoming children, a practice directly linked to Jesus and to the God who sent him. Welcoming God means welcoming and embracing those who are "last and servant of all." Or, in the mission of Jesus, the practice of welcoming children stands alongside other practices (e.g., healing and exorcism) as manifestations of the reign of God. If these (or other) disciples seek God, they must welcome children. When they do so, they welcome Jesus and the one who sent him. Ironically, of course, the disciples miss Jesus' teaching that to welcome him and walk with him means to go with him into the struggle against empire in all its manifestations, including the creation of new lines of exclusion. John immediately launches into comments about who should be permitted to cast out demons in Jesus' name, in response to the disciples arguments to restrict membership in the Jesus movement to those "following us" (9:38).

Mark 10:13–16

As if to reiterate the previous story, Mark 10:13–16 provides another instance in which Jesus takes children in his arms. Judith Gundry-Volf notes parallels in Hellenistic texts of the same time period that use the term *enangkalizomai,* "to take in his arms." She contends that Jesus' action takes on special significance in that the Hellenistic texts depict women taking children in their arms. Mark, in contrast, shows Jesus taking children into his arms: "Jesus thus redefines the service of children as a sign of greatness for all disciples. What appeared to be an undistinguished activity–care for children, belonging to the domain of women, similarly marginalized people–becomes a prime way for all disciples to demonstrate the greatness that corresponds to the reign of God."[19]

In the case of Mark 10:13–16, though, Jesus performs this embrace after his disciples "rebuke" (*epetimesan*) those bringing the children to Jesus for his touch. "Rebuke" translates the same Greek word that describes how Jesus casts out demons (Mk. 1:25; 9:25), a parallel that underscores it as a strong (here, negative) action. Seeing this, Jesus becomes angry (the Greek verb means "aggravated" or "indignant") with them, saying, "Let the children come to me. Do not hinder/stop them, for of such as these is the kingdom of God. Truly I say to you, whoever does not receive (welcome) the kingdom of God as a child may by no means enter into it" (10:14–15, AT). Then Jesus took the children in his arms (as in 9:36), placed his hands on them, and blessed (*kateulogeo*)[20] them.

Numerous interpreters dwell on the ambiguities of meaning in the notion of "receiving the kingdom as a child" (10:15). Some make sense of this phrase and the story from which it comes by referring to an essentialized notion of a child as one who naturally, spontaneously, and passively accepts the kingdom of God.[21] Others read the story through its Matthean version, identifying supposedly childlike qualities such as humility as the requisite characteristics for entering the kingdom of God. I find both of these options problematic because they uncritically assume certain emotional and expressive qualities as essential to childhood and identify participation or membership in God's *basilea* with the assumption of such features.

Interpreting Mark's gospel as a counter-narrative to the dominant discourse of imperial regime leads to a different reading of these stories in which Jesus takes children into his arms, welcoming and blessing them. The oppressive economic policies of the *Pax Romana* and its multiplied impact on Mark's readership as described earlier were policies that necessarily created a material (and, undoubtedly, also a social and psychological) climate of scarcity. In such a context, one possible and humanly understandable response would be for people to become focused on securing resources for themselves and their own kin. From all indications, these children who came to be touched by Jesus were simply children in the crowds who followed him from place to place–they were "other people's children." In Mark 3:31–35 Jesus refused to restrict his own kinship network to his "actual" mother, brothers, and sisters, claiming instead a new definition of family and kinship based on those who are together in doing the will of God. So here also Jesus makes the claim that expands the bounds of membership in God's "family."

Belonging to/receiving/entering the kingdom of God comes from solidarity with–and not separation from–those who are the lowliest and the least, the most vulnerable to the hardships of imperial oppression. Such solidarity displayed itself concretely in welcoming those children left alone by parents enslaved by imperial conquest or debt slavery, or children who were themselves sold into debt slavery, for example. Such concrete show of solidarity could make possible life itself for children on the edge of existence in agrarian Palestine. The empire's economic oppression destroyed the capacity of agrarian households to function as economic units in which family members could contribute to the common livelihood (however basic). As counter-narrative to this, Jesus called on his followers to welcome, touch, and bless those members of the society most precariously positioned, the children; not only "their own," but also the children of others.

The disciples, problematic figures throughout Mark's gospel, appear here as a group of men ready to replace one form of domination with another. They move to restrict access to Jesus by those at the lowest rung of their culture's social status hierarchy. It is a move that Jesus steadfastly refuses. As counter-narrative to the ways of empire, Mark's story makes clear that the renewal of life with a new social order really does mean giving up all forms of domination, and not simply falling back into the same patterns they are trying to overcome. Receiving the *basileia* of God as a little child, then, is "a challenge to relinquish all claims of power and domination over others…The child/slave who occupies the lowest place within patriarchal structures becomes the primary paradigm of true discipleship."[22] At the point at which this gospel story took literary form, that message undoubtedly had a special sting for the emerging male apostolic leadership of the nascent church.

A Spirit-possessed Boy

Exorcism stories in the New Testament, such as the one Mark records in 9:14–29, are miracle stories, and several of them involve children. On the one hand, these are stories about Jesus helping particular afflicted children, in which his actions have material effects on the child portrayed in the narrative. At the same time, as stories within a counter-narrative opposing imperial domination, these exorcism tales also operate as symbolic stories of a struggling people's experience of painful occupation by a foreign power.

Mark's way of telling the exorcism of a spirit that makes a boy deaf and mute (9:25) stands in stark contrast to its parallels in Matthew (17:14–21) and Luke (9:37–43). Mark offers dramatic and detailed descriptions of the boy's condition under possession by this spirit. This detail is made all the more significant by the fact that Mark is normally the shorter, more concise narrator among the gospels. This departure from his normal literary pattern suggests that the vivid description of the boy's condition holds some importance for Mark's communication through this story.

The story begins with a conflict between the Jerusalem-based authorities and the gathered crowd and/or disciples. (The text is ambiguous about who is having the argument here.) When Jesus arrives, the crowd is drawn to him. He asks, "What are you arguing about?" A man from the crowd answers with a detailed description of his spirit-possessed son,[23] whom the father had brought for help but to no avail because, "I asked your disciples to cast it out, and they were not able" (9:18, AT). Jesus expresses annoyance with the twelve (9:19), a milder foreshadowing of the "indignation" or anger (*aganaktesen*) he will express in relation to their later efforts to keep away children who seek his touch (10:14). Jesus tells the father to bring the boy to him. When the father does so, the spirit occupying the child responds to the presence of Jesus by bringing on a seizure that causes the child to convulse, fall to the ground, roll around, and foam at the mouth (the second description of this possession given in the narrative).

Jesus asks how long this condition has been going on. The father replies, "since childhood," and then elaborates further on what happens when the spirit seizes his son: "It has often thrown him into the fire and into the water to destroy him," (9:22a, AT). He asks Jesus to help his son if Jesus is able (*ti dunai*, "if you are able," or "if you have power"). Jesus responds that all things can be done for the one having faith. "I have faith. Help my unfaith," (9:24b, AT).

Jesus then commands the spirit to get out of the boy and stay out. The spirit does so, but not before seizing the boy one final time to convulse him. The spirit leaves the boy as if dead, and many there said he had died. But Jesus takes the boy's hand, lifts him up (the text uses the same verb for resurrection, *egeiro*), and the boy stands up. When the disciples get Jesus alone in a house away from the crowd, they ask why they could not exorcise this spirit. "Nothing is able to cast out this kind except prayer" (9:29, AT).

In this story, Jesus heals a child by exorcising a spirit that possessed him. The spirit apparently caused the boy to be deaf and mute in addition to wracking his body with horrible seizures. The boy's silence and relative invisibility are thus an effect of his spirit-possession, a state signifying an absence both of freedom and of the possibility to be authentically human. At the same time, though, the same might be noted about other, nonpossessed children in the rest of Mark's gospel. They rarely speak or act on their own. Instead they are "spoken into the story" by others. In this instance, the boy's father both brought his child to Jesus for healing and brings him into the narrative as he describes his son's condition. The relative silence of this boy and other children in Mark only underscores the low position children occupied in the social world of Mark's gospel. Mark's choice to narrate Jesus healing children, then, sharpens his overall message about the way of Jesus as a reconfiguring of power in the social relations and practices that structure human lives, such that even (or, especially) children experience renewal under God's reign.[24]

Jesus' exorcism of a child also sharpens the irony of the disciples' ineptness, as the contrast between the lowliness of a sick and spirit-possessed child and the aspirations of the twelve for status becomes poignantly obvious. The male disciples miss the message that the reign of God is in their midst now and is about the restoration of this child to wholeness. They focus rather on why they cannot make a miracle happen. Jesus' answer, apparently obscure to them in light of the episode immediately following it, is simple: this kind only comes out through prayer. Prayer, of course, is an engagement with God. Thus Jesus directs the twelve to see that it is God's reign of restored well-being that takes form in the exorcism of demons from children such as this boy.

As portrayed in this story, the transformation from being sick and spirit-possessed to being in a state of restored wholeness involves considerable struggle and takes the boy to the very edge of death. For Mark's way of telling the Jesus story, this boy mirrors the experience of Jesus and his walk to Jerusalem and death. As Jesus "resurrects" or lifts this boy up, so also will God lift Jesus up–but only after a very costly struggle to the death. In the character of this child and his exorcism, then, Mark offers a picture of what it means to walk in the way of Jesus that makes this child a paradigm of discipleship *not merely as an individual but in the social sense of the community of followers.* As such, this child as disciple appears in sharp contrast to the image of the twelve men named and called as disciples. Interpreters who focus on the father and his faith as the main point of the story underestimate the narrative significance of the parent's fierce love and advocacy for his child that would lead him to risk uncomfortable public attention[25] to his writhing child who foams at the mouth. Such interpreters also underestimate the narrative function of the boy as a character whose lowliness, powerlessness, and healing embody Mark's central theme that the reign of God is here, now, especially for society's "little ones." The boy's father would certainly have experienced shame in relation to his son but nevertheless remained steadfastly with him. Thus in the same way that the boy mirrors the destiny of Jesus, the father appears suggestive of those (women disciples) who witnessed the shame of Jesus' treatment and execution by the imperial rulers and yet remained with him as best they were able.

As counter-narrative to the discourse of empire, Mark's dramatic narration of the spirit-possessed boy provides a clear picture of both the effects of imperial domination on subjugated bodies and of their transformation under the reign of God. The Roman occupation of Palestine renders the subjects of Mark's community mute and deaf, powerless to speak a word of resistance or hear a revolutionary cry of hope, writhing on the ground with the pain of their economic oppression as their rulers stand with feet on their necks. Like this child, those who are the most powerless and vulnerable suffer greatly at the hands of imperial domination. In Mark's counter-narrative, the conflict between the reign of empire and the reign of God becomes a convulsive struggle between the powerful ones who occupy the land and possess the bodies and resources of the people, and the God to whose rule alone these people assent. It is a long-term struggle—since childhood, as the father of the possessed boy put it—that is, involving many years of colonial conquest, reconquest, and occupation. And it is a struggle in which resistance meets with even more deadly reaction by the forces who occupy this body and threaten to destroy it by throwing it into the water or fire.

I read the father's words about destruction by water or fire, with their allusion to the salvation oracle in Isaiah 43, as a kind of turning point in this Markan counter-narrative exorcism story. In these words the father lays before Jesus the exilic prophetic tradition in which God promises to be with and deliver God's people from the waters and fires that threaten to overwhelm them (Isa. 43:2). The father does this at the very point of asking Jesus to free his son from the demon possessing him with its constant threats to be similarly destructive. Freedom from the demon occurs only after a final intense struggle that leaves the child as if dead (hence Mark's use of the resurrection verb), certainly an accurate portrait of the remaining Palestinian Jewish communities of Galilee after their efforts to resist Roman conquest. The story of the boy, lifted up by Jesus, points to what Mark's counter-narrative and the exilic prophetic tradition alike claim for God's people: they, too, will be lifted up, no longer subject to seizures, occupation, struggle, or even death under imperial domination.

Clearly for Mark's narration of the Jesus story, the child in this passage—while not speaking or acting on his own—is far from incidental to the tale. To the contrary, this child's inability to act, his portrayal as one severely disabled and dehumanized, is central to Mark's message as a depiction of powerlessness and struggle, of resistance, and of hope for transformation in the reign of God. Through this child and his healing, through Jesus' raising of him from a living death, God becomes known. This boy *as a child* embodies what it means to walk in the way of Jesus, in the ways his experience mirrors that of Jesus' own destiny. Far from incidental, in Mark's telling of the story God has a purpose for children, giving them to the world and the church so that God and the reign of God may be known.

A Spirit-possessed Girl

Another story of a possessed child, this time a girl, found in Mark 7:24–30, offers interesting points of continuity and contrast with the above story of the boy. If the boy in Mark 9:14–29 is relatively invisible because he lacks a speaking part in the drama of the story, then the girl in Mark 7:24–30 is for all practical purposes nonexistent. While his story is generally known by the subtitle "the healing of the epileptic boy," her story is known as the story of the "Syrophoenician Woman," a title that refers not to the child at all but only to her mother. The story thus occupies a place within an interpretive tradition in which the child disappears altogether in the naming, and frequently in the telling, of the story. Unlike the spirit-possessed boy so vividly described (albeit in terms of his illness/possession), this girl remains narratively invisible, appearing only in the opening of the story as the occasion for the mother's conversation with Jesus, and at its conclusion as the evidence for Jesus' action. Her condition receives no description or attention in the narrative. She is identified simply as one who has "an unclean spirit," later called a "little demon."

The story takes place as Jesus moves into the region of Tyre, a geographical move that takes him into a Gentile area beyond the Palestinian Jewish villages of Galilee where most of the first half of Mark's story is situated. This area was still a part of imperial-occupied Palestine, however, and its people—like the Galilean Jews—were subject to imperial rule. There Jesus encounters a woman who, having heard about him, comes to him and falls down at his feet, asking for help for her "little daughter" possessed by an "unclean spirit." The text notes pointedly that this woman (and therefore presumably her daughter as well) was "a Greek, a Syrophoenician by race" (7:26a, AT). Most interpreters note that contemporary readers miss the offensiveness of the woman's action, not understanding the deep tensions between Jews and their Gentile neighbors and the "gender faux pas" of her actions as a woman of inferior status asserting herself with a man.

Jesus responds to her with an odd and provocative comment: "Let the children be fed first, for it is not good/fair for the bread of the children to be thrown to the dogs" (7:27, AT). She responds to him, "Lord, even the dogs under the table are eating from the crumbs of the children" (7:28, AT). At that point, Jesus tells her that because of this word she has spoken, the "little demon" (*daimonion*) has (already) gone out from her daughter. The story ends with her departure back home where she finds her daughter lying on the couch, the demon indeed already gone.

Several factors contribute to this nameless girl's heightened narrative invisibility.

First is the gender of two of the main characters in the story—two females, a mother and her daughter—interacting with Jesus. I have already described the subordinated position of women in the time span inclusive of the life of Jesus and the composition of Mark's gospel. Even though Mark's story is a counter-narrative to imperial discourse, a story that focuses attention on the most marginal to make its point, it still took shape under the culturally constructed, gendered power relationships of its time. The greater invisibility of the spirit-possessed girl in this story, particularly in comparison to the more visible possessed boy character of the previously considered text, is in part a feature of gender subordination in that social context. The story does focus on an encounter with a rather remarkable woman. She turns Jesus' ministry around, sending Jesus more deeply into Gentile contexts. Still, these laudable ways in which the story positively highlights the reordering of insider/outsider relations based upon gender do not negate the invisibility of the daughter.

Second, this story's producers were most likely Palestinian Jews for whom this woman and daughter's race and cultural were "other." The mother's racial difference stands at the center of the interpretive tradition surrounding this story, from scholarship focused on the theme of the expansion of Jesus' mission to the Gentiles to recent feminist and postcolonial interpretation addressing the woman's status as a colonized person who differs from Jesus by race. This story is "not her story" in the sense that it was not spoken/written by the woman herself. To the contrary, the story is written about her by others who construct her racial and cultural identity in negative terms.[26] When compounded by the extreme marginality rendered by her age as a child, race contributes to the daughter's invisibility in a narrative where she and her mother both exist as outsiders to the Israelite tradition and community, giving shape to the story as it is told here.[27]

Finally, non-Jewish people living in the region of Tyre also would live, like their nearby Jewish neighbors, under the political and social conditions of Roman imperial rule described earlier in this chapter. However, this area apparently stood positioned quite differently in relation to Rome and was able to benefit politically and economically from that position as a port town operating as a middle manager between the poor agrarian producers of Galilean villages and the rulers of the Roman Empire.[28] Following the work of Gerd Theissen, David Rhoads suggests the tension of Mark 7:24–30 depicts an economic disparity between wealthy Tyrians and Galilean peasants, represented in the story by depiction of the woman as a cultural Hellene who was wealthy.[29] It does seem that compared to residents of agrarian Galilean villages, Tyrian residents lived as a relatively better off colonized area.

But would an apparently single woman with a demon-possessed daughter really be among the wealthy? The text does not mention any social or familial network for this woman or for her daughter, unlike some of the other women in Mark who are identified in relation to a male relative (e.g., the mother-in-law of Simon in Mark 1:30). Horsley states that the Syrophoenician woman of this text was "the utterly marginal, poor, single parent mother of a demon possessed daughter," a situation that would place significant limits on the labor or earning power of both mother and daughter.[30] Clearly, Horsley's statement is one of inference, as the text offers no details to this effect. Thus, while we cannot know for certain their social class, we can surmise that diminished economic status might well follow the outcast status attendant upon demon possession. In short, age, gender, race, and class collude to make the girl child of this story a fleeting mention.

Could it not be the case that Mark places the spirit-possessed daughter of the Syrophoenician woman in the far background simply because his agenda in telling the story does not require otherwise? Perhaps. It certainly is possible to read this story closely in relation to its immediate context as a story of the opening of the family of God to include the Gentiles. Indeed this is the dominant interpretation, supported by much good scholarship. But as I interrogate this text in terms of its larger agenda of proclaiming the reign of God that lifts up and liberates the downtrodden, a narrative move that places the figure who perhaps bears so many marks of marginality into utter invisibility seems inconsistent with the story's central message. The daughter in this exorcism text is potentially the most abject one in the story, but also the most absent.

Notice the irony here. The possessed girl's "missing in action" status within the narrative may well be an effect of the interstructuring of multiple forms of oppression marking her identity. At the same time, her appearance in the text at all, along with what happens to her in the story, actually work to make Mark's point more clear. If God's reign can bring about restoration and wholeness for this girl, then surely the children of oppression elsewhere can also take hope. Her low status as a child is, thus, far from incidental to the story, even while it contributes to her near-total invisibility and silence.

In Mark's gospel as counter-narrative, Jesus' encounter with an extraordinary woman who inaugurates a turning point in the gospel, and the subsequent exorcism of an "unclean spirit" from her daughter, involves three people from subjugated, colonized communities. One of them, Jesus, has embarked on a path of freedom and resistance as he makes present the reign of God. The two female characters, although identifying (albeit as outsiders) with the Jesus movement enough to seek the connection with Jesus when he comes near them, still live under the effects of imperial domination, symbolized by the daughter's demon possession. The issue for the counter-narrative concerns whether or not Jesus will treat these women oppressively, using their differences as an occasion to simply substitute or add himself as a new oppressive man to the imperial oppression the two women already experience. This, in fact, is what Jesus' initial response to the mother appears to do, with its claim that the "children" are the only ones who matter and that other people's children are dogs. The tendency of formerly oppressed people to assert their new positions by oppressing others is well known. I understand one of the central issues being addressed by Mark in this story as "re-hierarchalization." As was noted in comments on Mark 10:13–16, part of Mark's narrative agenda concerns the rejection of any form of domination, including moves by the formerly powerless to take on power that dominates others, as inimical to walking in the way of Jesus.

In Mark 7:27, however, Jesus seems to stand guilty of such a move. The mother's reply (v. 28) challenges Jesus' ethnic exclusion as a Jew concerned first and foremost about Jewish children, that draws the lines of solidarity at the point of racial and cultural difference. "Lord, even the dogs under the table are eating from the crumbs of the children," she replies. She speaks as a marginal person who needs something that a higher status person, the male Jesus, may be able to give her.

The fact that she seems to simply accept his designation of herself, her daughter, and their people as dogs can best be understood as an ongoing effect of colonization that needs analysis and critique. Her willingness to accept the designation suggests that she internalizes her oppression and the racism that is so key to this exchange. At the same time, her reply contains resistance to complete acquiescence to being so negatively identified and excluded. In effect, she uses her outcast status in a rather clever way as she calls on Jesus to make a connection of solidarity out of the shared condition of their imperial domination, instead of choosing separation and rejection. I interpret her reply to Jesus as, in effect, saying to him, "Look, Jesus, no one is getting very much to eat around here, whether they are your children (of Israel) or mine (the daughter possessed)." Hisako Kinukawa puts it well. She says that here the Syrophoenician woman makes it clear to Jesus "that Jesus should become Jesus."[31] Jesus should cross over the social and cultural context in which he found himself embedded, a context that may have made him reluctant to extend himself across the barriers represented in this story. Jesus responds by exorcising the demon from the girl, who, like others who benefit from Jesus' healing and exorcisms in Mark, is lying down (as if asleep or dead) but now without the demon in her.

The Markan counter-narrative of a possessed girl and her mother's plea for help ultimately defines Jesus and his *basileia*. Jesus rejects the option of simply substituting a new form of hierarchy and oppression in the form of racial barriers for the old ones, the oppression of being occupied by a colonial power as symbolized in the daughter's possession. Mark uses this story in conjunction with other episodes in which Jesus expresses disapproval of the disciples' efforts to create new power structures that merely place different people at the top of a new pyramid. For Mark, then, the story functions within the larger counter-narrative as a rejection of all forms of oppressive social relations as inconsistent with the reign of God. Jesus' acceptance of the mother's rejoinder has a strong narrative function. It disallows a symbolic idea of children (*tekna*, used to speak abstractly of descendents or progeny, or figuratively as when adults are addressed as "children," e.g., Mk. 2:5; 10:24) to be used as the rationale for nonresponse and nonaction to a "real" child's (*thugatrion*, diminutive form of *thugater*, indicating endearment) concrete needs. Attention to concrete, material suffering takes precedence over abstract principle in terms of social practice.

Finally, Jesus tells the mother that the demon has already gone out of her daughter "because of this word" (the rejoinder spoken by the mother). Feminist interpreters note that in this moment, the Syrophoenician mother becomes agent and coparticipant with Jesus in bringing God's reign to actuality in the restoration of her daughter.[32] In turn the daughter, a child, shares with other children and adults Jesus healed and restored the role of embodying the here and now realization of the reign of God.

Symbolic and Materialist Readings in Tension

In my reading of the two stories of exorcism and healing of children from Mark 7:24–30 and Mark 9:14–29, I place considerable stress on the symbolic features of these stories. I emphasize the ways in which spirit possession operates symbolically in the narrative to describe the situation of colonial occupation by another "body," the Galilean village populations occupied by Rome, a situation marked by the absence of possibility and freedom.[33] Frantz Fanon's pioneering sociopsychological analysis of colonialism considers the way that demon possession operated as a kind of compromise move within persons whose lives were curtailed by colonial occupation. Demon possession provided a way for colonized Algerians to contend with the forces oppressing them without directly engaging and thereby threatening their French colonizers. With Fanon, Horsley contends that

> Demon possession, for example, of the manically violent man among the Gerasenes, can be understood as a combination of the effect of Roman imperial violence, a displaced protest against it, and a self-protection against a suicidal counterattack against the Romans. In becoming possessed and violently crazy, the man sacrificed his sanity, but at least he was still alive.[34]

Under the extremely adverse conditions of colonial occupation, the sociopsychological act of struggling with demons can be seen as bid for life.

With this symbolic rendering, I do not intend to rule out the more materialist interpretation of these stories as narrations of suffering children. Myers's critique of other interpreters[35] for turning the child characters in Mark into psychological archetypes devoid of social reality is apropos:

> Why should not the child represent an actual class of exploited persons, as does every other subject of Jesus' advocacy in Mark? The impure and the poor and the gentile are representations of real social marginalization; why not the child…Indeed, from the narrative world of Mark we have cause to suspect that all is not well for the child in first-century Palestinian society.[36]

Having suffered several years from childhood epilepsy, I am somewhat familiar with the ways that symbolic meaning and direct personal experience can coincide in the manifestation of illness. I have already suggested that there is nothing objective or detached in my method of interpreting scripture. My own interests and social location obviously guide the questions I pursue, the texts that pique my interest, and the particular lenses through which I make meaning of texts. As I write about these stories of children possessed by spirits, I acknowledge that they make sense to me and that I am drawn to them. This is due in part to my own experience of having seizures as I struggled to negotiate difficult gender and class-related dimensions of "coming of age" in the 1960s, in the South, in a complex family system. I grasp their (i.e., seizures') power to operate in both symbolic and materialist levels.

Even in an age pervaded by scientific-medical explanations, the social stigma and isolation that came with seizures is visceral to me as I recollect them. Did the seizures produce these conditions or merely reflect them? Do they come from neuro-biological sources, or might they be sociopsychological in origin, the kind of compromise formation of which Fanon writes, a form of displaced protest against deeply felt oppression too dangerous to address directly? The agonized, fierce love of parents seeking help for their child looms vividly before me as I recall my mother's long hours of sitting with me in hospitals and doctor's offices, and my father's struggle with love, shame, and avoidance.[37] All this generated a certain social disintegration at the level of family that only became amplified with extension into wider circles. The fearful memory of being seized as if by some outside force (yet which came from within) lingers. In an instant this force could dash me to the floor in convulsions and then leave me there looking unconscious or asleep. These memories deepen my sense of the power of these stories in Mark's counter-narrative to symbolize the experience of being occupied by foreign forces and powers that disallow resistance, struggle unremittingly, and then leave the body alive yet seemingly not.

That such stories involve not only adult characters in Mark but also children suggests to me that the reign of God Jesus proclaimed and made real really does extend to the least and last of society. These stories also underline the importance of expanding our pictures of Jesus with the children. Such portraits must include not only bright, clean children playing happily on Jesus' knees and *looking* like gifts from God from most vantage points. We must also include children who are poor and dirty, who soil themselves with seizures and look both frightening and frightened, children who live as if crazed by experiences of exploitation and colonization—in short, children who appear to be anything but divine gifts. In Mark's telling of the Jesus story, these latter children are the only ones we meet! And there, Mark offers them as gifts from God through whom God's reign is manifest. Keeping in mind this interpretive perspective, namely, that in Mark's account people may not be only what they appear to be, I will now turn to the last child-story in Mark, the story of the youth at the tomb.

A Youthful Messenger: Mark's "*Neaniskos*" and the Empty Tomb of Jesus

The second half of Mark's gospel tells the story of intensifying conflict between Jesus and the various religious and political leaders representing imperial interests. These conflicts eventuating in the death of Jesus as a political rebel against the empire come to a head in Mark 14. Here Jesus is betrayed by one of his own followers in an "inside job." He is arrested by Jewish and Roman authorities and then denied and deserted by those who had followed him. Recent interpreters highlight the role of the women in Mark. Only the women remain with him until death. This fact leads to various assessments of the women as models for true discipleship in Mark.[38] Curiously, however, such interpretations ignore the text's clear statement that the women "said nothing to anyone, for they were afraid" (Mk. 16:8). Furthermore, such interpretations ignore the presence of one other at the tomb of Jesus,[39] a certain "*neaniskos*"–a youth or child.[40]

The youth makes a brief appearance prior to the tomb scene, at the height of drama around Jesus' arrest. At that point, Mark 14:50 notes, "having left him (Jesus), everyone fled." But sandwiched in between the tale of Jesus' arrest and of his trial before the Sanhedrin, Mark offers a peculiar little mention of this young person known only as the "*neaniskos*." The text of Mark 14:51–2 reads that "a young man was following along with him, having been clothed with a linen sheet (*sindon*) over his naked body. And they (the ones who had seized and arrested Jesus) seize him. But leaving behind the linen sheet, he fled naked" (AT). Interestingly, Mark presents him as naked, holding only a (burial) cloth. At the point of being seized, he streaks off naked into the night, leaving behind this cloth as a symbolic corpse.

The action of the narrative then shifts back to Jesus' trial and the other events leading up to his crucifixion. Mark 15:40–41 tells of the presence of women disciples observing his crucifixion from a distance. After Jesus' death, Mark tells of Joseph of Arimathea taking a linen cloth (*sindon*) in which he wrapped the body of Jesus before placing it in the tomb (15:46). When the youth appears again (16:5), he is at the tomb, seated on the right hand or side, the place Jesus had told the Sanhedrin he would sit in power with God (cf. Mk. 14:62, where being seated on the right hand is the symbol of power). Now the youth sits dressed in a white robe that recalls the garments of Jesus' transfiguration (Mk. 9:3). To the amazed women, this youth says, "Do not be amazed. You seek Jesus the Nazarene, the one who was crucified. He was raised; he is not here. Look, here is the place where they laid him. But go tell the disciples and Peter of him. He goes before you into Galilee. There you will see him, just as he told you" (Mk. 16:6–7, AT). The story ends with the note that the women fled from the tomb, seized by trembling–expressed as *ecstasies* (Greek, *ekstasis*) or terror and amazement–and they told no one anything because they were afraid.

Against interpretations that treat as two different characters the boy of the tomb and the naked fleeing boy at the scene of Jesus' arrest, I read the two references to be about the same person.[41] The basic evidence for this interpretation lies in the following:

1.   The unique use of the term *neaniskos* to refer to both the fleeing lad and the youth at the tomb

2. The reference to the sheet he left behind when fleeing seizure by the authorities

3. The burial sheet (using the same Greek word as used for the fleeing lad's sheet) used by Joseph of Arimathea to wrap the body of Jesus

This data offers strong textual evidence that these two figures are the same young person. I understand this child, like other young ones written into Mark's version of the Jesus story, to be Mark's way of symbolically narrating the story or destiny[42] of Jesus. Mark also uses these children to mark the destiny of followers in the way of Jesus, as the various children/youth of the story show others the way of Jesus, the way to "receive" the kingdom of God. In that sense, this naked child who reappears at the right hand of the tomb and tells the other disciples (women) what the mission now consists in (i.e., go back to Galilee and look for Jesus) stands for the nascent church or the baptized believer.[43]

Consistent with Mark's portrayal of children throughout his gospel narration, the youth at the tomb appears as a model of discipleship. As the conclusion to Mark's counter-narrative against empire, though, the youth sitting at the right side of the tomb "interprets" all the narrative's earlier passages concerned with seating patterns and status relations: the one who sits "in glory" is a youth. Or, as Waetjen contends, Mark's placement of the *neaniskos* at the tomb signified that such disciples are, with Jesus, "co-enthroned with Jesus."[44] This *neaniskos*, this one symbolically received into the *basilea* of God is indeed "like a child." Through the figure of this child, a disciple figure like the other children in the narrative, Mark shows that the walk with Jesus, while it surely means death, also means rebirth with Jesus.

Mark's counter-narrative thus negates the official story of the empire, in which the terrorist tactics of imperial death define power as the ability to suppress and put down. In Mark's counter-narrative, a naked child seized by the agents of empire can flee and leave behind the body, to be raised up with Jesus on the other side of the tomb and call other disciples to continue the mission of resistance and struggle. Unlike the male disciples in Mark who strive for glory and the position on Jesus' right hand, in the end it is none of these but a mere youth, a child, whose clothing and position at the tomb depict the child as the one exalted with Jesus.

Against empire, the way of Jesus shows that power means blessing and lifting people up. Jesus lifts up even little children possessed by spirits who appear dead. He touches and blesses and takes into his arms children turned away by those who should know better. And he gives the "last word" of the continuing mission of a young church to a young person raised up with him in glory, not in some future by and by, but *now*.

Clues for a Theology of Childhood

What clues does Mark's counter-narrative offer for constructing a liberatory theology of childhood? First and foremost, Mark's version of the Jesus story accords to children a leading role in the struggle between walking in the way of Jesus and in the ways of empire. In Mark's gospel, children appear as persons who embody the reign of God in being healed, blessed, lifted up, and restored by Jesus. Certainly, by his actions of blessing, touching, healing, and lifting up children, Jesus signifies childhood as a time of life wrapped in the grace of God that needs to be well-regarded by adults, even as Mark's Jesus wraps his arms around children and blesses them. There is plenty of room, therefore, to interpret the children in Mark's narrative as exemplars of joy and abundance in the new reign of God. At the same time, however, Mark's version of the Jesus story resists any easy contemporary perspectives of "child as gift." Such perspectives stress the joy or ease adults may experience being around a child as the basis for considering a child to be a blessing from God, or they relate the gift-status of a child to childhood as a "magical" time of awe and wonder. The children in Mark's gospel often are difficult to be around, and not much about their situations seems magical or wondrous at first glance. They are sick, possessed, poor, and "in the way" of adults.

Mark's narrative, then, offers a central clue toward a liberatory theology of childhood. For Mark, children and childhood are gifts from God not because they are carefree, but because God has a purpose for children. God gives children to the church and the world so that God may be known. "When you welcome a child you welcome me. And when you welcome me, you welcome not only me but the one who sent me" (Mk. 9:37, AT). But the hard edge of this clue also lies herein: in Mark, being blessed as part of the purposes of God means being blessed into the struggle and resistance to the purposes of empire. This clue from Mark's story re-situates blessing from simply and only being a positive affirmation of childhood and its gifts embodying divine love and reconciliation, to a way of being named as a participant in a contentious life of resisting injustice and sin. It is a clue about the impossibility in genuine human experience of separating deep joy from struggle, hope from despair, as if the one were innocent of the other.[45]

Second, Mark's counter-narrative asserts that practices with children as the ones reckoned least in status, power, and importance provide keys to understanding and enacting right relationships in God's newly inaugurated reign. After all, those who actually and symbolically are of the least value in the world's terms are the very ones Jesus exorcises and heals, blesses, lifts up, and affirms. The children Jesus blessed include poor children from the crowd, dirty children soiled from seizures, and possessed children whose bodies are not their own. They include "other people's children" along with "our" children. This clue from Mark's version of the Jesus story points to children as symbolic and actual embodiments of "least-ness," which in the divine economy becomes "most-ness." It therefore has to do with children as resources and guides to solidarity with other people experiencing various forms of oppression. And it is a clue about the need to extend the boundaries that delineate *which* children ought be included in our orbs of concern and action: not only those easily recognized as gifts but also those who are sick, possessed, and naked. This *new* reign of God, intentionally configured in contrast to the old reign of empire, is the decisive point of the gospel, and children figure centrally in it.

Third, in Mark's way of telling the Jesus story, a young person (through the figure of the *neaniskos*, as well as the other portrayals of children, especially in Mk. 9 and 10) represents faithful discipleship. In this gospel, children are disciples–in fact, they model discipleship where others fail. A young person speaks the good news and sends the church into mission. In Mark, God gives the gift of children so that the church will know how to live out its vocation as disciples. This clue from scripture, then, concerns children as agents, children as participants, and children as *already* expressive of the purposes of God. It constitutes a clue about the church's need to listen to its children and youth, to take them seriously as already being disciples who contribute to the mission and work of the body of Christ. Childhood is thus a time of vocation, a time of being called to purposive participation in the divine action in the world. In such a perspective, children are not only in the church to be educated for future participation. They are already called to be part of its missional identity in a world that continues to need such clear manifestations of God's reign amidst the struggle to resist the dominating forces of empire.

Finally, through the children in his stories, Mark makes clear that walking in the way of Jesus has no place for substituting new forms of oppression for old ones, or for lifting up some at the expense of others. The clue toward a liberatory theology of childhood suggested in these elements of Mark's narrative concerns the potential to re-inscribe subordination onto the caregivers of children (who continue to be women, primarily) in the name of freedom and advocacy for children. Jesus disallowed the male disciples from using their apparent position of privilege as the "inner circle" to exclude children. In a contemporary milieu of U.S. society characterized as a culture of youth-worship in which children's supposed privileged status can be seen everywhere in the attention to them by politicians, marketers, and media moguls, the needs and interests of women who care for children easily become subordinated. A truly liberatory theology of childhood cannot lift up children by putting down women. Similarly, lifting some children up (e.g., through a "higher standard of living" attained through consumption of goods made especially for children) at the expense of other children (e.g., the ones who work in sweatshops to produce children's toys and clothing) cannot make for a liberatory theology.

I gradually move toward an articulation of a feminist practical theology of childhood. As I do clues such as these, gleaned from my interpretation of scripture with children in the foreground, become primary resources in the search for a theology that welcomes children as openly and plainly as Mark's Jesus did, especially in the face of an imperial regime that oppresses them. With these clues in mind, then, I will now turn to explore a contemporary imperial regime, the *Pax Americana* of our time, with its cultural construction of childhood, the child as consumer.

SOURCES CITED

Betz, Hans Dieter. "The Early Christian Miracle Story: Some Observations on the Form Critical Problem." *Semeia* 11, no. 1 (1978): 69–81.

Chaney, Marvin L. "Systemic Study of the Israelite Monarchy." *Semeia* 37, no. 1 (1986): 53–76.

____. "Debt Easement in Israelite History and Tradition." In *The Bible and the Politics of Exegesis: Essays in Honor of Norman K. Gottwald on His Sixty-Fifth Birthday*, ed. David Jobling, Peggy L. Day, and Gerald T. Sheppard. Cleveland: Pilgrim Press, 1991.

Cooey, Paula. "That Every Child Who Wants Might Learn to Dance." *Cross Currents* 42, no. 2 (1998): 185–97.

Derrett, J. D. M. "Why Jesus Blessed the Children (Mk 10.13–16 Par.)." *Novum Testamentum* 25, no. 1 (1983): 1–18.

Dube, Musa W. *Postcolonial Feminist Interpretation of the Bible.* St. Louis: Chalice Press, 2000.

Fanon, Frantz. *The Wretched of the Earth.* Translated by Constance Farrington. New York: Grove Press, 1963.

Fiorenza, Elisabeth Schüssler. *In Memory of Her: A Feminist Theological Reconstruction of Christian Origins.* New York: Crossroad, 1985.

Fleddermann, Harry. "The Flight of the Naked Young Man (Mark 14:51–52)." *Catholic Biblical Quarterly* 41, no. 3 (1979): 412–18.

Gundry-Volf, Judith M. "The Least and the Greatest: Children in the New Testament." In *The Child in Christian Thought*, ed. Marcia J. Bunge. Grand Rapids, Mich.: Eerdmans, 2001.

Horsley, Richard A. *The Liberation of Christmas: The Infancy Narratives in Social Context.* New York: Continuum, 1993.

_____. *Archaeology, History, and Society in Galilee: The Social Context of Jesus and the Rabbis.* Valley Forge, Pa.: Trinity Press International, 1996.

_____. *Hearing the Whole Story: The Politics of Plot in Mark's Gospel.* Louisville: Westminster John Knox Press, 2001.

Isasi-Díaz, Ada María. "Solidarity: Love of Neighbor in the 1980s." In *Lift Every Voice: Constructing Christian Theologies from the Underside,* ed. by Susan Brooks Thistlethwaite and Mary Potter Engel, 31–40. San Francisco: Harper and Row, 1990.

Jackson, Howard M. "Why the Youth Shed His Cloak and Fled Naked: The Meaning and Purpose of Mk. 14:51–52." *Journal of Biblical Literature* 116, no. 2 (1997): 273–89.

Kinukawa, Hisako. *Women and Jesus in Mark: A Japanese Feminist Perspective.* Maryknoll, N.Y.: Orbis, 1994.

Kwok, Pui-Lan. *Discovering the Bible in the Non-Biblical World.* Maryknoll, N.Y.: Orbis, 1995.

Malbon, Elizabeth Struthers. "Fallible Followers: Women and Men in the Gospel of Mark." *Semeia* 28 (1983): 29–48.

Malina, Bruce J. *The New Testament World: Insights from Cultural Anthropology.* Revised Edition. Louisville: Westminster John Knox Press, 1993.

_____. *Windows on the World of Jesus: Time Travel to Ancient Judea.* Louisville: Westminster John Knox Press, 1993.

Munro, Winsome. "Women Disciples in Mark?" *Catholic Biblical Quarterly* 44 (1982): 225–41.

Myers, Ched. *Binding the Strong Man: A Political Reading of Mark's Story of Jesus.* Maryknoll, N.Y.: Orbis, 1988.

Patte, Daniel. "Jesus' Pronouncement About Entering the Kingdom Like a Child: A Structural Exegesis." *Semeia* 29 (1983): 3–42.

Rhoads, David. "Jesus and the Syrophoenician Woman in Mark: A Narrative-Critical Study." *Journal of the American Academy of Religion* 62, no. 2 (1994): 343–75.

Sawicki, Marianne. "Crossing Galilee: Architectures of Contact in the Occupied Land of Jesus." (Harrisburg, Pa.: Trinity Press International, 2000).

Schottroff, Luise. *Lydia's Impatient Sisters: A Feminist Social History of Early Christianity.* Translated by Barbara Rumscheidt and Martin Rumscheidt. Louisville: Westminster John Knox Press, 1995.

Scroggs, Robin, and Kent L. Groff. "Baptism in Mark: Dying and Rising with Christ." *Journal of Biblical Literature* 92, no. 4 (1973): 531–48.

Segovia, Fernando F. *Decolonizing Biblical Studies: A View from the Margins.* Maryknoll, N.Y.: Orbis, 2000.

Taylor, Mark Lewis. *The Executed God: The Way of the Cross in Lockdown America.* Minneapolis: Fortress Press, 2001.

Via, Dan O., Jr. *The Ethics of Mark's Gospel in the Middle of Time.* Minneapolis: Fortress Press, 1985.

Waetjen, Herman C. "The Ending of Mark and the Gospel's Shift in Eschatology." *Annual of the Swedish Theological Institute* IV (1965): 114–31.

———. *A Reordering of Power: A Socio-Political Reading of Mark's Gospel.* Minneapolis: Fortress Press, 1989.

Weber, Hans-Ruedi. *Jesus and the Children: Biblical Resources for Study and Preaching.* Atlanta: John Knox Press, 1979.

CHAPTER THREE

A Problem of Ambivalence

Children as Consumers in America

Children's Relationships to Consumer Culture

Leslie, an active member of her church, is especially interested in the church's social justice ministries. She was tired but excited from her work with a committee of the congregation planning for ways to educate the congregation about economic justice issues. The committee had discussed the recent lengthy strike by grocery store workers in Southern California, along with news headlines about various factory closures in the Northeast that were occurring as the parent companies took their production facilities overseas in search of cheap labor.

The pastor leading the meeting offered biblical and theological resources for thinking about the connections between human worth, work, and faith. And the group unanimously affirmed its sense that issues such as the fair treatment of workers and the country's growing unemployment were theological issues that they needed to address as a faith community. They also talked at length about the increasingly central place of consumer behaviors–thinking about purchases, looking at advertising, and making purchases of various goods–in structuring their day-to-day lives, an issue that somehow seemed connected to the other issues in their discussion.

"It seems like everyday I get five new catalogues in the mail, advertising products for me to buy," remarked one man. "I don't even mean to, but somehow I end up spending time looking at them just to see if there's something I might like."

"I feel caught. I need to get the best prices on the things I buy, because I am a single mom supporting my kids on a limited income. But I've heard that the big chain stores put our small local stores out of business and help send our factories overseas, so that what we buy so cheaply is made by somebody who works long hours for practically nothing. I feel bad about it. But I just can't afford to shop at more expensive places. Besides, those overseas sweatshops aren't going to shut down just because I stop shopping at Wal-Mart™. What should people like me do?" a mom in her mid-thirties lamented.

"Maybe that's where we need to start," suggested Leslie. "Maybe we need to start by learning about the connections between our own everyday buying habits and the big questions about Christian faith and economics." The group ended its meeting with an agreement that each member would keep a "consumer diary" for a week, keeping track of all the activities they engaged in that related to consumption of goods. That evening, as Leslie came to the door of the childcare room of the church to pick up her daughter, Megan ran to her saying in an eager voice, "Mom, can I have a play date with Taylor? She has the Teacher Barbie™ and the Malibu Barbie™, and I told her that I am getting the Easter Barbie™ for my birthday. We'll each have eight Barbies™ from our collections, and it will be really fun!" Leslie sighed as she turned to the other parents from the committee who were also picking up children there. "It looks like 'economic justice' just came home. What am I supposed to say—'No, you can't because at eight years old you are engaging in excessive consumption?'"

Within the larger questions about economic justice, consumerism in America, and its global reach lies the issue of children's relationship to the market. I interpret Leslie's sigh as her sad flash of recognition that the consumer desires of her own child and the exploited labor of other children stand deeply intertwined in the postmodern global marketplace. The connection is so strong that she no longer has the luxury of simply thinking about such concerns in the abstract. Leslie knows, too, that it is not enough for the adults in the congregation to think about and reorder their own practices of consumption as an aspect of faithful Christian living, if they do not also address the roles, positioning, and practices of their children in a consumerist society. But what practices will they teach their children about consumption and Christian faith? And how can they best educate their children in Christian faith, including its practices for just living, while those children simultaneously are schooled in a pedagogy of consumption across virtually every sphere of their lives?

In short, Leslie's problem and that of every contemporary faith community that intends to nurture its children in Christian faith, concerns how to educate its youngest members in the alternative meanings and practices of justice, hope, and neighbor-love. How do our daily practices evidence the reign of God amidst the imperial practices of individualism, hyper-consumption, and despair that structure consumerist culture? These are questions of identity. They become especially complex because of the positions North American Christians like Leslie and her children occupy. And I must include myself and my children, who are part of dominant culture groups benefiting substantially from the consumer empire. How do we form our children in a Christian identity, teaching and engaging in practices of resistance to an imperial regime of which we are so thoroughly a part?

In this chapter, I examine the remaking of childhood in relation to contemporary economic and cultural movements variously known as late capitalism, globalization, and postmodernism. As a practical theologian, my interest lies not in explicating various historical constructions of childhood or the nuances of cultural and economic changes for their own sakes. Instead, my concern is to explore the global economic and cultural processes currently at work in the transformation of childhood because the thriving of children is at stake. This concern brings with it a sense of urgency, grounded in a conviction that walking in the way of Jesus means attending to the well-being of children. This urgent concern requires me to analyze and deal with the complex cultural realities that shape children's lives. The urgency also comes about because, for the most part, theologians have offered little assistance in making connections between children's lives and these complex social and cultural processes. I will begin, therefore, by exploring some of the cultural and economic conditions at work in the contemporary reconstruction of childhood as a commodified domain within a consumerist society.

What Counts as Consumerism

"Consumerism" refers to a way of life structured by and around various practices of consumption and accumulation. In a consumerist society, consumption dominates social practices, such that relationships, activities, space, work, and leisure come to be structured around various practices related to consumption. Consumption becomes a way to achieve social solidarity–relational connections with others, even as it also marks identity and status. The activities of consumerism are not limited to the moment of purchasing an item. They also include viewing advertisements, thinking about and planning for purchases, shopping and the acquisition of goods, and the use and disposal of consumer purchases, all of which take a central place in the lives of people in a consumerist society.[1]

The United States is unarguably a thoroughly consumerist society. In the United States, alongside other affluent nations, many children relate to consumer culture primarily as purchasers of goods that they attain at very inexpensive prices as a result of the manufacturers' use of cheap labor to keep costs down and profits up. Even within affluent societies like the United States, though, some children have identities tied to various forms of social inequality (race, immigrant status, gender, class) that differently structure and limit their participation in a consumer culture. These children often occupy a very different role within consumer culture: that of social scapegoats, held responsible for various social and economic ills. Poor children's ways of engaging in consumerist practices may be pathologized and scapegoated, for example. We find one example of this in the many urban African American youth who encounter extensive negative stereotyping by the media about their wasteful spending of limited resources on nonnecessity items such as sound systems or video players. Such media reports give little analysis to who benefits from the ways these youths' identities and desires are shaped. Their ways of participating in consumerist society then are deemed responsible for society's problems by those whose identities and incomes allow other forms of participation (which may also include spending money on sound and video systems, but in whose case such spending is not pathologized).

Children as Producers

In some countries (and in some sectors of the United States), children's primary relationship to the consumer culture of North America is as agents of production: children are the ones providing the labor that produces the goods for consumer purchase. Child labor allows for lower cost in the manufacturing of goods. Through the forces of globalization, however, the marketing of consumer products worldwide creates contexts in which children of the so-called "Third World" also find their desires kindled for the goods their labor produces; but their poverty prevents them from ever acquiring the desired goods. In other words, just because a child does not or cannot participate equally as a middle-class consumer of goods involved in continual acquisition does not mean that such a child remains uninfluenced by consumerism. Consumer culture produces effects upon the lives of these children positioned quite differently in relation to consumptive practices.

Are North American children innocent or implicated in relation to consumer culture and its imperial ways? Perhaps this binary opposition is not the most helpful way to frame the question in a context in which children and adults do not really have the option of nonparticipation in consumerist practices. At the same time, though, it does raise the issue of how children in the United States occupy multiple positions within our consumerist society, positions that sometimes are at odds with prevailing notions of childhood. For example, discussions about the cost of bearing and raising children today often place dollar figures on the expenses involved in caring for a child.

Children as Innocents

Such discussions suggest that monetary amounts can be attached to the worth of a child. Some of the discomfort I experience over the connections between childhood and the economy come from cultural notions of childhood as a "separate sphere" from monetary matters. Such notions arise from the cultural inheritance of a mid-twentieth–century modernist attitude that children are innocent and best kept apart from the mundane, ostensibly polluting associations with money.

Ultimately though, the view of children as innocents is one that deprives children of agency, able to make choices and purposefully engage in practices, including consumer-oriented ones. This "innocents" view also tends to see children as mere victims of social forces that beset them. I am not altogether ready to move into an acceptance of the full-scale invasion of childhood by market logic that sees no appropriate or necessary separation between children and their thriving and the agendas of consumer capitalism. I and many other people react with discomfort to both extremes in this dichotomy. Our discomfort leads us to believe that we are "in between constructs" of childhood. An earlier era's notion of an innocent and pure childhood unpolluted by market forces has not given way entirely to the more contemporary idea that children are just as much fair game for advertisers as any other group within the population.

Let me explain this issue in relation to constructions of childhood as they relate to advertising. In some ways I stand with those who view children as needing and deserving special protections from a market that can abuse their vulnerability and harm them. According to this reasoning, children who still lack fully developed rational thinking capacities may be particularly vulnerable to advertisers' manipulations, unable to see through the rhetoric to the advertisers' true intent to profit from children. Children can be vulnerable to such manipulations. Thus, for instance, I am outraged by advertisers' grossly unapologetic insertions of market agendas into children's education. This takes place in a variety of forms, including company-sponsored textbooks selected and purchased by a business for a school, computer equipment, and food items. My outrage takes shape in part because I stand with one foot in a modernist construction of childhood largely formed around notions of childhood as a separated and protected space of innocence. I do not want to see ads for children's products on the benches of the playgrounds where my children run and climb. I resent marketers' blatant taking advantage of children's "naïveté" at the breakfast table with captivating product advertisements on their cereal boxes. I want my children to play and eat and learn in spaces "unpolluted" by market influences.

At the same time, though, I stand with my other foot firmly planted alongside those who grow increasingly critical of such a modernist construction of childhood as an innocent, untarnished life space. The "innocent child" image simultaneously misrepresents children's identities (psychologically and theologically), treating children as helpless victims without agency, whose very beings somehow manifest the antithesis of that which characterizes market culture. It lumps all children together as persons unable to take any degree of responsibility for their actions, unable to be accountable for their decisions and choices. Children are not only vulnerable and acted upon by personal and social forces around them such as those of market advertising. They are also actors and agents. They buy commodities and make choices. They become part of the imperial regime.

Modernist constructions of childhood as innocence furthermore "misrecognize" the presence of the market in shaping meanings of childhood, including this notion of childhood innocence. It is not only children who stand to be duped by the marketing strategies of consumer capitalism. Notions of childhood innocence may falsely portray children as uniquely vulnerable to deception, while suggesting that adults stand outside this vulnerability. In reality, of course, the seductions of the market operate powerfully in the lives of children and adults alike, a fact disguised by the portrayal of children as those needing protection from the market and adults as those who protect. In the process, both children and adults abdicate responsibility.

North American children occupy a "both-and" status—as people both shaped by market culture's influences and implicated in perpetuating its excesses. This status leaves little room for feeling at ease in a time of historical transition from one dominant image of childhood to a new one. In spite of my discomfort from being "in between" constructions of childhood, however, this transition between constructions of childhood as a noncommodified, protected domain and childhood as constituted by market forces does in fact form the location from which I and others engage theology and childhood today. It, therefore, bears more in-depth attention.

Clean Children and Dirty Money: Modernity's Priceless Child

Viviana A. Zelizer studied the changing social value of children in the United States from the nineteenth- to the mid-twentieth century. She explores a shift in children's value within families under the changing economic conditions in the move from preindustrial and farm economies to industrialized and, increasingly, corporate or Fordist economies (i.e., economies organizing labor around mass production and consumption).[2] Children's usefulness, or way of holding value within the family, underwent a transition. Children moved from being persons holding material value (i.e., children as making material or labor contributions to a family's economy) to those whose worth largely was sentimental (i.e., children as noncontributors economically but as bearers of significant emotional value within the family). In Zelizer's language, children, removed from the "cash nexus" of society at the turn of the century and no longer engaged in labor as part of the family's material economy, became "priceless," materially useless but infused with emotional value that could not–and therefore should not–be assigned monetary worth. Zelizer claims that the process by which the shift occurred was "partly a matter of conflicting economic interest but mostly an ideological dispute between two opposing views of childhood. The sacred child prevailed."[3]

With the agendas and politics of the market place deemed as "base" and motivated by less than noble concerns (e.g., greed and profit) and with children deemed as pure and innocent, the economic and sentimental constructs of children were set in opposition to each other, rendering them incompatible. Of course, such a construction of childhood fit best for children of upper- and middle-class families whose protection from the supposed contamination by the market was most affordable. For these families conventions such as a weekly allowance could transform children's dealings with money into an educational event rather than being a necessity for family survival.[4] Alternative constructions of childhood, and the children living out of these differently defined cultural spaces, were marginalized or treated as deviant by construing them as social problems (e.g., migrant farm worker children; child laborers in family-run cottage industries or factories).

Zelizer suggests that as this construction of the "priceless child" gained currency, childhood became a social sphere expected to exist in a protected domain, ostensibly operating outside of the economic marketplace's commodified arena. Zelizer examines the intersections between the emotional and financial value of children through matters such as life insurance policies for children, legal compensations for a child's wrongful death, and adoption payments. Her analysis reveals an inability to achieve a complete separation between childhood and the market. Each of the above activities in some way "puts a price" on a child's life, rendering the protected construction of childhood largely symbolic.

Even though the dominant modernist construction of childhood proclaimed that children's lives cannot be measured in money, their emotional worth packs some kind of exchange value. Many writers on childhood from Zelizer's time forward express concern about the loss or disappearance of childhood. In so doing, they underscore the current state of transition from modernity with its protected child-construct to postmodernity as a cultural movement marked by the thoroughgoing erosion of boundaries between formerly distinctive, separated spaces of childhood and the market.[5]

Zelizer concluded her work with the argument that the next move in the changing social value of children might be to reconstruct the child as once again useful, through a rediscovery and restoration of children's household labor in time-stressed, work-oriented households of two-parent careerists.[6] Such futuring incorporated the likelihood that increasing numbers of mothers would continue to join the fulltime work force. What Zelizer's vision did not account for is how different the conditions of the economy structuring the workforce would be for the next decades in which childhood would be reconstructed.

The Empire Strikes Back: Capitalism and Childhood in a New Century

Daily news headlines across the country tell the economic story. Corporate layoffs reach massive proportions. Employer-sponsored benefits such as health care insurance for workers and their families decline. The volatility of financial markets (not to mention corporate scandal) results in families losing their life savings in an instant. Family-owned "mom and pop" businesses close their doors, unable to compete with giant national chains. U.S. factories and industries shut down as transnational corporations move their production facilities overseas in search of cheap labor markets. Family farmers, bought out by giant agribusinesses, shift from being economic producers in the market to being wage laborers with more limited control over their own working conditions, or even what they produce. Meanwhile, various advice columns offer tips on how persons laid off from their jobs can re-skill to fit the upcoming version of the new labor market with its continually changing demand for high tech abilities and service sector workers with interpersonal relationship skills. Business analysts report that the average adult will work for multiple companies in their employable lifetime and that the notion of a lifelong career with a sense of mutual loyalty between an employer and a worker has given way to expedient decision-making. The end result is that all parties will "do what they need to do" to secure their own interests, regardless of the impact on others.

The above snapshot portrays a starkly different reality than the one anticipated by Zelizer and many others writing about families and economics twenty years ago. While still a capitalist economy with owners, producer-wage earners, and a market with various commodities for sale and purchase, the capitalism of contemporary U.S. and global societies has undergone a radical transformation. The conditions under which families and children now live contribute to a different construction of childhood. Neither the image of a child as productive in a family-based economy nor that of a child as innocent and untarnished by associations with the market quite adequately locates children in the global economy. For the most part in the U.S. context, children occupy a key place in the market, that of consumers. The empire indeed has struck back, this time in the form of consumer capitalism that colonizes children.

Locating Children in American Capitalism

In his account of the transitions leading to the current economic context generally termed "late capitalism," David Harvey divides capitalism into three periods, termed free market, Fordist-Keynesian, and late capitalism.[7] Each of these periods involved certain "structured coherences"[8] between political institutions, cultural aesthetics, capital, urban life, and subjective identities.

Free-Market Capitalism

The first period, free-market capitalism of early modernism prior to and around the turn of the twentieth century, is the classic form of capitalism that Karl Marx critiqued. The term "free market" refers to the absence of any interventions that would shape the market around interests other than those of investors or capital. At some point during the development of capitalism in this period, a perspective arose that certain vulnerable groups, including children, needed protection from the brutality of the unfettered forces of the market with its values of unfettered self-interest and profit motives. Such perspectives on children's vulnerability and need for protection not only drew from an increased sense of realism about the harshness of the workplace and market but also from an emergent understanding of childhood as a natural and innocent state in need of careful tending and protection.

Historians of childhood note that in the nineteenth century, legislation to protect children from labor exploitation meant that children increasingly were excluded from the workplace and relocated into the school as a protected space separated from the world of adults.[9] Concomitant with the relocation of children's home-based or workplace labor into schools, the idea of child nurture took root and became central to education. Along with it came a discourse and a set of specialized professions to aid in assisting child development, as did an array of child-specific organizations and activities (e.g., Boy Scouts and Girl Scouts). As I will describe later in this chapter, in the early twentieth century the rising view of childhood as a separated life space also took place in conjunction with the market-driven development of specialized childhood products, from toys to clothing.

Ford-Keynesian Capitalism

These developments led into the second period of capitalism, often called Fordist–Keynesian economics. This period reached its pinnacle in the mid-twentieth century and centered around alliances between corporate and government interests.[10] In this period of U.S. economics, profit motives of *laissez-faire* capitalism were promoted yet held in check by governmental assumption of a certain amount of responsibility for human social values and well-being. Governments expressed their responsibility in economic goals such as a stable and high level of employment, government supported safety nets for health and retirement, and upholding a certain expectable level of purchasing power among worker-consumers through wage and price legislation.

THE PROMISE OF ACCUMULATION

In a Fordist economy structured around corporate interests, laborers were socialized to accept long hours of extremely routinized work by the promise of wages that would make possible accumulation of commodities in turn made cheaply available to them by mass production. An elite few held positions of greater privilege through less routine forms of work and higher compensation. But to all was held out the promise of life enhanced by a phenomenal range of commodities available to all. As Harvey puts it, postwar Fordism was not merely a system of mass production but a total way of life. "Mass production meant standardization of product as well as mass consumption; and that meant a whole new aesthetic and a commodification of culture."[11] Notions of craft and beauty, what constitutes quality, and the reason one is involved in work to create or produce something all shift in this way of life.

What impact did this form of capitalism have on the shape of childhood? On the one hand, these Fordist-Keynesian economics, coming in the form of Roosevelt's New Deal policies in the wake of the Great Depression of the 1930s, translated into the possibilities of stable parental employment, government intervention through social programs, and food on the table for many children. That was no small affair for those families plunged into poverty during the Depression. Clearly, the way of life associated with mass production in a post-Depression and post-war era meant that some families had access to goods inexpensively for the first time in ways that contributed to both their basic subsistence needs and their potential for an enhanced quality of life. The chief impact of Fordist-Keynesian economics on the shape of childhood to which I point here concerns the structuring of life around the process of consumption itself. The purchase of mass-produced goods became an end in itself, with children as a key part of the rationale for the production-work-consumption nexus.

HOUSE WORK: THE SOCIAL BARGAIN WITH WOMEN AND CHILDREN

The emerging role of advertising in creating a market of consumers to purchase the huge quantities of mass-produced goods cannot be underestimated. I will address its specific relationship to children more fully later in this chapter. The heightened positioning of single-family homes became a key element in the emerging patterns of consumption and production. Homes became places of consumption rather than of production. Industry now depended on reinforcements of a patriarchal division of labor in which homes became separated, private havens from the harsh worlds of work.

Women's unpaid labor and patterns of consumption constituted an important piece of this mass-production/mass-consumption machine. Housework–labor primarily performed by women that includes the care of children in it–though not compensated with wages, could become a source of cultural capital for women. Housework accrued increasing emotional weight as a means to care for one's family, while also accruing aesthetic weight because certain standards of cleanliness and efficiency were associated with status.[12]

In the television advertisements of my childhood, for example, I recall women being swept away with the ecstasy of a (man's) clean shirt collar procured by the use of a particular laundry detergent, or awed by a floor cleaner's power to make surfaces sparkle. I also recall women in my mother's age cohort being complemented for being "such a great housewife." Shiny floors and dustless furniture were their explicit contributions to the family's standing on the social status ladder. My mother, in contrast, refused to treat housekeeping as her primary source for social capital. She probably would not have made the connection I am making in political terms, but from a practical standpoint of her priorities she seemed to understand this issue. She used to say, "I'd rather have a dirty house where kids can play than a clean house that looks like a museum to make other women jealous."

Beginning in the 1930s, the lines between advertising and professional advice blurred. Advertising began to use an "advisory voice" to encourage mothers to purchase mass-produced products as a way to ensure children a proper childhood (one arranged around "natural" foods, good health, and a vision of domestic pleasure).[13] Soap was advertised as "pure" and therefore good for children's delicate skin. Hot cereal was marketed as natural and therefore good for children's digestion. Nonworkers in this economy, children initially were passive recipients of the purchasing power undertaken on their behalf by their mothers. The mothers' consumption, in turn, was supported by the "family wage" fathers earned in the workplace. Increasingly, though, children's supposed well-being became the rationale for the family's buying activity. As Stephen Kline writes,

During the 1920's and 1930's, industrialists began to think seriously about the function of the family, and in particular of women, as a consuming unit. The family made its contribution in the form of demand for goods rather than in terms of labour and its potential for labour. Youth became an element in visualizing the promise of consumption as a wholesome preoccupation of life...Advertising therefore began to configure its discussion of the benefits and uses of manufactured goods within a continuum of domestic consumption that featured the child as central in the dynamics of the household.[14]

Granted, not everyone fit into the patterned relationship between production and consumption converging in home life as the sentimentalized site of escape from the problems of the harsh work world. Not every child had two parents, one of them being a wage earner and the other a "housewife." ("Stay-at-home mother" is the current preferred term. It does not, however, adequately express the cultural meanings present in the situation of the intensification of women's domestic work in relation to Fordist production-consumption patterns in the first half of the twentieth century with which I am concerned here.) But as a dominant image replicated in media representations and undergirded by workplace and market advertising norms, this economic system shaped children into roles as consumers for which advertising soon began to target them directly.

Late or Global Capitalism

The next economic period, variously known as late or global capitalism, has perfected that role of children through its furthering of the development of a consumerist society in which children are colonized and co-opted to assist the market. This post-Fordist era, marked by the coherence between postmodern cultural forms and globalized structures of capital, began in the 1970s and continues into the present.[15] Harvey locates the transition from Fordist capitalism and modernity into late globalized capitalism and postmodernity in part in relation to a level of discontent about inequalities in access to the benefits of Fordism.

CAPITALISM'S DISCONTENTS: ACCELERATED CONSUMPTION AND THE CULTIVATION OF DESIRE

Put simply, particular segments of the population, such as women and racial-ethnic minorities, experienced exclusion from and lack of access to both privileged employment and the supposed benefits of mass consumption. Their discontent found social expression in the civil rights and feminist movements, among other populist expressions of the need for change. Says Harvey, "The inequalities were particularly hard to sustain in the face of rising expectations, fed in part by all the artifice applied to need-creation and the production of a new kind of consumerist society."[16]

Meanwhile, in the high-modernist period of Fordist-Keynesian capitalism, the owners of capital depended upon continued production and consumption on a mass scale for continued profits. But owners faced a major problem. The ultimate user of whatever goods they produced needed only a limited amount of the particular good. To deal with the perennial tendency of capitalism toward overaccumulation, owners needed to stimulate new consumption. This they did through several mechanisms:

1. stimulation of public appetites for new goods
2. establishment of new markets overseas and domestically through niche marketing
3. by shortening the life spans of durable products so that they would need to be replaced more frequently

Acceleration of consumption takes two primary forms in the new market. The first is the mobilization of the concept of "fashion" in mass consumption. Creating the urge to have the latest style accelerated the pace of consumption not only of clothing but also of videos, children's games and toys, and various forms of leisure and recreation. One way this occurs is through the development of different age groups as discrete market niches. Daniel Cook suggests, for example, that the stage of life termed "the toddler" arose in conjunction with the marketing of products specific to that age group as distinctive from other ages.[17] By increasingly segmenting human life into discrete age groupings, each associated with different consumer products that display a person's identity status in a particular segment, ongoing consumption of goods is assured. Changing fashions and constant repositioning of people into various age group niches insured the "need" for continual new purchasing as these changes are key to the expression of identity. The connection between fashion and identity is not casual in a context in which traditional signifiers of collective identity and belonging give way to commodity display as a means of identity expression.

The second form of accelerating consumption is the shift away from consumption of goods to consumption of services and experiences (entertainment, travel). These have a shorter lifetime than durable goods. Several important social consequences adhere from this acceleration. First the volatility and ephemerality of fashions, products, and ideas creates a context for the "instantaneity and disposability" of commodities—and not only commodities but also lifestyles, stable relationships, attachments to things and places, and received ways of living.[18] In such an arena of continual change, advertising and marketing move to the foreground as the ability to "intervene in the production of volatility by manipulating tastes and opinions"[19] becomes more important than the ability to engage in long-range planning that will direct labor and production.

Sociologist and culture critic Zygmunt Baumam aptly names as "seduction" the situation in which a seemingly unending series of "fetishized" goods are held out to consumers who fantasize the fulfillment and satisfaction they will experience upon attainment.[20] The fantasy experience of yearning and longing for the commodity becomes more rewarding than possession of the thing itself, since the object ultimately will always disappoint because it cannot actually fulfill its fetishized promises. Bauman argues convincingly that the seductions of consumerism actually comprise a means of social control.

Several years ago I might have viewed such an assertion as mere paranoia, dismissing it as just another conspiracy theory. But Bauman's assertions appear valid as I watch the way my children's media- and peer-evoked desires to collect a particular set of stuffed animals or particular brand of building blocks involve them in repeated acts of consumption that support market interests. I see how often the excitement and interest in the future purchase hold greater intensity than the purchase of the item itself, which, once obtained, will all too soon be relegated to the bottom of the toy box. The promise of pleasure, however, is so much greater than the pleasure these mass-produced commodities can deliver that it effectively reproduces itself by creating the hope that the next purchase really will be as satisfying as its advertisers claim. Thus advertisers insure ongoing participation in the market processes of repeat consumption.

CHILDREN'S POSITIONS IN GLOBALIZED CAPITALISM

How are children positioned in this third era of capitalism with its restructuring of labor markets and accelerated consumption? Besides their positioning as "consumers *par excellence,*" children are also deeply affected by the changes in the labor market. Parents who might have had some measure of job security in the past can no longer count on long-term employment. With the shift to less stable and less permanent patterns of employment, a huge amount of social and personal anxiety comes into family life, and thus into the lives of many children. For some children in immigrant families, restructuring of labor markets has the effect of moving production back into the home. This move can best be understood not as some nostalgic recovery of a pre-industrial integration of labor and domestic life, but as a symptom of diminishing protections for particular groups of children within the new economy that depends on their labor and/or that of their families. In the new capitalist regime of flexible accumulation, producers have moved to systems of small batch or "just-in-time" production, producing quantities of a good on demand rather than amassing large inventories without certainty of their sale to consumers.

Such systems in turn stimulate an underground production economy of sweatshops and immigrant family-based production shops. These shops can rapidly switch products on demand (or, alternatively, be replaced by other workers who can make the new product). This new underground system makes it difficult for organized labor to operate or to influence work and wage matters and for government regulators to enforce accountability to fair labor practices. Thus the very conditions of consciousness formation and political action have changed with these alterations in the composition and nature of the global working class.[21]

Previous arrangements of power relations between capital and labor in which the power differences could be somewhat mediated by the strength of organized labor do not work in an economy of dispersed workplaces. This situation turns the clock back on a veritable century of struggle to win protections for children from direct oppressive exploitation in the labor market. Children today experience less protection, whether directly in relation to their own experiences as easily exploited workers, or in relation to their dependence on other family members impacted by these labor arrangements. Perhaps one of the negative by-products of the shift away from the modernist construction of childhood as a time of innocence may be seen here. Children understood as fully knowing, competent agents may be seen as having little need for special protections, a construction that only stands to benefit the market's need for inexpensive and expendable workers.

For the most part, however, today's changed labor market impacts children primarily by its larger social effects. To state the case more generally: at the same time that local contracts began to replace collective bargaining, employers began to change the way they structured labor in the workplace. This restructuring made possible a greater responsiveness to the often fickle, rapidly changing demands of consumers. This happened by reducing the number of "core workers," those permanent workers with relative job stability and benefits. In their place corporations placed greater reliance on a workforce that can be easily and quickly laid off through the use of subcontracting, temporary employment, and the replacement of full time jobs with multiple part-time positions. Importantly, such restructuring in the workplace has a differential effect upon women:

> The effects (of the restructured workplace) are doubly obvious when we consider the transformed role of women in production and labour markets. Not only do the new labour market structures make it much easier to exploit the labour power of

women on a part-time basis, and so to substitute lower-paid female labour for that of more highly paid and less easily laid-off core male workers, but the revival of sub-contracting and domestic and family labour systems permits a resurgence of patriarchal practices and homeworking.[22]

In such an economy, a huge gap opens up between a proliferation of low-level service sector jobs requiring de-skilled workers on the one hand (often termed "McJobs") and a diminished number of high-level jobs held by an increasingly elite few. This has the effect of widening the income gap between a few very wealthy persons and a large number of persons living on marginal incomes or in poverty. It also makes enforcement of protections against the exploitation of children and youth labor extremely difficult, especially among immigrant populations and people of color, as the kind of temporary and family-based jobs to which their children have access fall between regulatory and legal cracks.

Similar to the shift toward a more flexible workforce, businesses in the era of late capitalism changed their modes of holding capital. No longer did they accumulate fixed capital in the form of machines that only make one product, which might be obsolete tomorrow (e.g., a particular kind of videocassette). Nor did they accumulate fixed capital in the form of buildings in a fixed location subject to the whims of local politicians' tax codes. Instead, businesses began restructuring in patterns of "flexible accumulation." Flexible accumulation refers to smaller-scale, geographically mobile processes of organizing production, labor, and marketing. Flexible accumulation makes it easier to relocate quickly to places around the globe with the most favorable conditions for producers or even to alter their product with the whims of the consumer market.[23] In the United States, low wage service sector jobs that most often do not include benefits have replaced high wage manufacturing jobs. Such a situation holds obvious advantages for corporations that can "outsource" their labor and manufacturing requirements cheaply in overseas and foreign labor markets.

As was the case in the earliest form of capitalism critiqued by Marx, the labor conditions through which this flexible accumulation becomes possible remain invisible in the products themselves. Ultimate users can hardly imagine the exploitation of and inhumanity to countless faceless workers who produced the products we use. We never stop to think about hazardous working conditions and low pay that allow us to pay low prices. Consequently, when eight-year-old Megan buys her new doll, nothing about it (including the price) indicates anything about the Indonesian factory in which other children work for pennies in fire traps to produce the doll. A key difference between earlier capitalism critiqued by Marx and current global capitalism, also critiqued for the way commodities hide the conditions of labor that produce them, is that the exploitation is likely to be further removed. Global export of manufacturing means that, increasingly, child and adult workers of other nations are exploited for the sake of commodity accumulation by the child and adult consumers of the United States.

WELFARE DISMANTLING AND THE FAREWELL TO CHILDREN

Not unrelated, in the United States these changes in the structure of the market and of labor also brought about restructuring in the social bases for caring for persons whose basic needs were not being met. The alliance between business and government under high modernity's capitalist forms created a welfare and social securities entitlement system that no longer finds a home in late capitalism. In the Fordist-Keynesian era, businesses essentially agreed to certain fetters on their otherwise unrestricted pursuit of profits. These fetters included providing employment-related health insurance, paying a legislatively enacted minimum wage, and maintaining certain standards for working conditions. In exchange the government bolstered the economy and maintained a certain level of economic growth along with the provision of a safety net for the unemployed.

Welfare dismantling can be understood in part as the restructuring of this alliance between business and government in the shift to late capitalism. Elizabeth Bounds puts it well: "Globalization has made it impossible for the national welfare state to provide the employment and the protections that were part of the consensus over its formation and legitimation."[24] Other commentators note the rising gap between the few wealthy and the many poor, alongside a willingness to scapegoat and stigmatize welfare recipients, as a systemic way to deflect attention from the structural sources of inequality in globalized capitalism.[25]

The dismantling of welfare has a vast and differential impact on women and children, such that so-called "welfare reform" has led to increases in the number of poor women and children at the very time employment is most difficult and carries fewer of the benefits most needed. What was formerly a state-legitimated sanctioning of support for the welfare of children has now turned into a state-sanctioned farewell to children. Government statistics obscure the human realities of this situation as they report fewer people on welfare, with the assumption that those people removed from welfare rolls now constitute part of the nation's productive work force instead of being "charity recipients." In actuality, aid organizations report huge increases in the numbers of working poor persons seeking basic assistance such as food aid or shelter from nongovernment aid sources such as churches.

Bounds, Brubaker, and Hobgood, reporting on a 1998 survey of the International Union of Gospel Missions, note a huge increase in the number of homeless women with children, up from 46 percent of homeless families in 1991 to 66 percent in 1998. One fifth of these families report the loss of AFDC benefits or food stamps in the past year. Current welfare policies require participation in the labor force without attending to what actually is required for these women and their children to be economically self-sufficient in the present economy. Such policies simply move persons from one category of poverty (state supported as welfare recipients) to another (unsupported persons seeking aid elsewhere).[26] The National Center for Children in Poverty stresses that "After a decade of decline, the rate of children living in low-income families is rising again, a trend that began in 2000."[27]

According to the Children's Defense Fund[28] the United States has some 11,746,858 poor children, or one in every six children. The government hopes to solve this math problem by simply moving the numbers to a different ledger as it celebrates the reduction of welfare recipients rather than the reduction of poverty. Requiring poor women to enter the workforce with no possibility for adequate and affordable care for their children hardly constitutes genuine welfare reform. But one structural effect of this mode of welfare dismantling is that it creates and maintains a class of de-skilled workers necessary to fill the increasing numbers of bottom-tier "McJobs" created by the new economy. When the empire of global capitalism strikes back, it is very thorough, so that even processes of dismantling social supports for the poor work toward the interests of market forces.

Obviously this new, restructured economy creates a rather different world for families today. In this new world an increasingly elite few have job security or protected long term employment. The collusion of state and corporate interests in the form of employer-provided health care or other benefits no longer operates to guarantee those benefits to a large segment of the work force. But nostalgia for Fordist-Keynesian capitalism with its ostensible supports for family through the so-called "family wage" and other provisions masks the way in which this arrangement actually operated. It depended greatly upon structured inequalities of gender, race, and class and upon the isolation of families into single-family households highly dependent upon the organization of domestic life around women's work defined as consumption. For persons working in underground economies such as day labor, domestic labor, and child care these purportedly secure wages and health care benefits were not part of the picture even in the 1950s.

This is not, therefore, an argument for turning the clock back. In giving my reading of the transitions into the latest phase of globalized capitalism, I do not seek to invite nostalgic lament of a better bygone era. I give these readings because I see an understanding of the new economy and its consequences in the lives of families and children as critical to contemporary reconstructions of childhood. One last piece remains in putting together multiple factors contributing to this construction, namely a consideration of the connections between the economic conditions described and cultural forms of postmodernity. These connections form the nexus for a consumerist society and the contemporary forms remaking childhood in terms of consumption.

Postmodern Cultural Forms and the Economics of Childhood

Postmodernity, though variously defined, emphasizes a complex of cultural transformations in relation to the period of modernity. Sometimes expressed as a preference for that which is particular and local over the universalizing and totalizing tendencies of "grand theories" associated with modernity, postmodernism is less about an era in time per se than it is about cultural conditions of knowledge.

Market Forces as Colonizers

The most prominent characterization of postmodernity in relation to the economic form of late capitalism is the interpenetration or "colonization" by market forces of various life domains previously separated from the market. For example, in earlier times childhood education stood as a protected and separated space from market promotions. Today, however, public education is thoroughly enmeshed with these market interests as various corporations provide monetary and in-kind support that places their names and products (from soft drinks to computers) prominently in school settings across the nation. Parents, faced with an education system no longer adequately supported by public funding, engage in all sorts of market-related activities–from collecting product box tops to using computerized "e-script" in order to channel corporate resources into the support of schools. "E-script" is an electronic means by which parents grant businesses the right to an electronic record of all their purchases in exchange for the business contributing a small percentage of the purchase amount back to the schools. Businesses use the information they get for marketing purposes, and their giving to the schools becomes a public relations platform. Meanwhile, parents remain too busy collecting product box tops to engage in political organizing around the underfunding of public education.

Some see this colonization of formerly separate life domains by market agendas as the logical extension of market power over the whole range of cultural production. As Fredric Jameson puts it, postmodernism is "nothing more than the cultural logic of late capitalism."[29] Jameson's point, of course, is that late capitalism, with its needs for accelerated consumption, flexible capital and labor markets, and just-in-time production processes gives rise to cultural and knowledge forms known as postmodernity that support and enhance it. Put differently, the market effectively colonizes various life arenas formerly separated from or seemingly impervious to it. The effects of this colonization on different groups of persons in a given society such as women and children need to be evaluated. It is clear, for instance, that a mutual relationship of support exists between postmodern cultural forms and the interests of global capitalism, but how such an arrangement supports the thriving of children remains in question. Some persons might claim that the advantages of corporate involvement in public education far outweigh any disadvantages, because business involvement in the schools provides crucial educational resources for children that otherwise would be missing from schools in a time of declining governmental and public support for children's education. At the same time, though, this situation tends toward the structuring of education around corporate interests in ways that threaten to diminish education's important role within a democracy of cultivating persons with capacities for critical thinking in relation to business, government, religion, and public life.

Among the clearest examples of the colonization of various social spaces of everyday life by market forces, and one that particularly impacts the lives of children, is the eclipsed boundary between advertising, art, and entertainment. Under conditions of postmodernity, advertising (a product of market interests and forces) becomes art (as in the example of Andy Warhol's Campbell Soup Can painting, but also in countless film and print productions), such that the cultural form called art is now "produced" by market forces. As they market their products, commercials now constitute a form of entertainment and thereby become features in the social bonds between people as they constitute commonly shared experiences. Toys become characters in animated feature movies. Then toys also decorate cereal boxes and appear on playground equipment in public parks. Children's play spaces and breakfast tables are as infused by market forces as is their Saturday morning television entertainment.

Preference for "Seems Like"

Analysts of postmodernity often mention as another cultural form that dovetails with market interests the subjective preference for the virtual or for reproductions and replications over genuine objects or experiences. As persons come to prefer that which "seems like" the real thing–what Baudrillard aptly talks about as "simulacra"–they substitute an image or replication that simulates the presence of the real, as opposed to being or having the thing itself.[30]

Disneyland and Epcot Center offer perhaps the quintessential example of this. There persons can "tour" other countries, for example, without actually experiencing the dissonant aspects of encountering real people from other cultures or the unpleasant aspects of travel. A friend of mine tells the story of a man who, while observing the changing of the guard at Buckingham palace, discovered that his video camera had no more recording space remaining on it. Disappointed, he walked away before the event started, apparently placing more importance in the ability to make a videotape of the event than in experiencing the event itself. In terms of children, preference for the virtual over the real may have its greatest impact in the way it reshapes social relationships. Children's real-time relational worlds shrink, replaced by virtual teachers, store clerks, and even preachers. Interaction on playgrounds and in neighborhoods gives way to virtual interaction in electronic games.

Intensifying Experience through Spectacle

A final but important feature of postmodernity's cultural forms as they impact the thriving of children concerns the intensification of experience (particularly the visual) in the form of spectacle. One aspect of spectacle may be seen as postmodern aesthetics and architecture place side by side elements that seem discontinuous or even opposed to one another. This proliferation of symbols and images expresses a kind of dislocation, fragmentation, and chaos. Harvey cites an example of a magazine ad picturing naked bodies. The item for sale is an expensive wristwatch. There is no text other than the single word of the manufacturers name in small print at the bottom of the page. Time pieces and naked bodies, perhaps incommensurable in a previous generation of advertising, are put together here for the creation of an intense image, a spectacle. In other ads, women clothed only in bras and panties appear in office settings or other locations where they appear obviously incongruous, creating a sexualized spectacle within the advertisement and the gaze of the viewer.

"The collapse of time horizons and the preoccupation with instantaneity have in part arisen through the contemporary emphasis in cultural production on events, spectacles, happenings, and media images,"[31] leading to what Fredric Jameson terms "contrived depthlessness."[32] Time becomes eclipsed into a series of intense, present-focused experiences, pasted together as depthless pastiche. Under these cultural and market conditions, children are constructed as persons who hunger for spectacle, from the excitement proclaimed on the cereal box to the latest, wildest roller coaster ride at the amusement park.

But what impact does such a construction of childhood have upon the everyday lives of children? Seeking the spectacular in everyday ordinary experiences promises to heighten the possibilities of boredom. Consumption of ever-new and more spectacular experiences and products is marketed as the sure relief consumerist children can count on for the boredom that has become the most dreaded of human experiences. The constant stimulation of desire shapes children into a state of perpetual dissatisfaction with previously sought-after objects and experiences and into a never-ending quest for that which is novel. Childhood itself comes to be seen as a time defined by constant access to whatever is amusing, fun, and exciting.

In all of this coherence between market forces and cultural forms, children's identities, like those of adults, are at stake. "Time-Space compression" is Harvey's phrase to express the collapse of temporality and of particular location in postmodernity. The incursion of market forces into virtually every part of the globe depends heavily on new technologies of communication and information processing, important features in postmodern culture, as temporality and actual location in space come to appear fairly insignificant. This, along with the erosion of local cultures through the export of Western commercial/cultural forms around the world, creates a vast homogenizing movement eclipsing traditional markers of identity and difference. Since social and temporal practices are never politically neutral, but express cultural, social, and class positioning, these consumerist practices become sites for struggle over identity. When traditional markers of identity and status no longer operate, commodity display takes on a heightened role in expressing and securing identity and status among children and adults alike.

Such conditions produce and promote social and economic patterns of consumerism. As Bauman notes, "Consumerism puts the highest premium on choice: choosing, that purely formal modality, is a value in its own right, perhaps the sole value of consumerist culture which does not call for, nor allow, justification. Choice is the consumer society's meta-value, the value with which to evaluate and rank all other values."[33] In a consumer society, status accrues from being a skillful, cultivated chooser, such that society becomes stratified based upon the ability to choose. Those with more limited choice-making power are at the lower end of status hierarchies in a consumerist culture in which identity and status are demonstrated by consumptive choice.

Children as Symbolic Capital in Adult Consumerism

In such a commodified culture, children easily become yet another "consumptive choice," themselves functioning as commodities through which their families can demonstrate distinction, gaining access to identity and symbolic forms of capital.

INFANT PURCHASES AS IDENTITY BUYING

One of the easiest ways to recognize children's role as symbolic capital for their families is in the purchase of high-priced designer clothing and baby products for infants. The baby's well-being does not change if the child is clothed in secondhand unmarked cotton clothes, or the latest spring fashion line from Baby Gap™. Facing increasingly fewer options for demonstrating identity, parents, through their consumptive choices for their child, demonstrate status and identity within a consumer culture that places value upon–and attributes status to–fashion, even for infants.

Furthermore, the high price parents (and grandparents) pay for these baby products implicitly confirms the value of the commodities they purchase. While middle-class and affluent children today may not contribute directly to the family economy, remaining "priceless" in Zelizer's sense, they do constitute a source of symbolic capital for their families. Childhood has an exchange value. From the child's earliest infancy, middle-class and affluent parents use their spending power, their participation in the consumer economy, to gain cultural capital for their children and for themselves through their children. That relates directly to the kinds of structured coherences and shifts Harvey and others depict in describing globalized capitalism and postmodernity, in which image and symbol take on a heightened role and in which all life domains– including childhood–become commodified space.

Toys provide a good example both of the power of the market to co-opt resistance and of the use of children and their possessions as symbolic capital through which families acquire status and display identity. Some families, for example, attempt to resist the mawkish consumerism of mass-marketed toys by avoiding certain national retailers. They choose only toys made from "natural" (nonplastic) materials that have no commercial links to the entertainment or children's food industries and that have an explicit educational purpose. As Seiter points out, however, toymakers have been extremely effective in creating a new market niche out of this group of consumers who are willing to pay elevated prices to purchase toys they see as standing outside of the mass market.[34] Many of the smaller high-end toy companies producing these toys are now subsidiaries of the mass production toy giants.

Children's Purchases as Status Buying

Seiter contends that such toys also serve the often unrecognized function of reproducing status hierarchies of social class as they become markers of distinction, bearing the aesthetics and taste codes of upper classes more than they embody different modes of play for children.[35] Similarly, major food processing companies have begun to systematically acquire organic food producers to gain market concentration in these niche markets. For example, consumers buying organic ice cream from a company known for supporting social justice and environmental causes probably are unaware that they are in fact paying the fifth-ranked corporate giant that bought the ice cream company a few years ago. One cannot easily opt out of participating in the system of globalized consumer capitalism.

The above detailing of contemporary economic and cultural conditions underscores the colonization of previously uncommodified domains by market forces. Childhood represents one such domain. I doubt that childhood ever existed in the purely uncommodified and protected form that those most nostalgic about childhood innocence would portend. Still, it is clear to me that under conditions of contemporary late global capitalism, childhood as a construction and children themselves are being transformed into a highly commodified form shaped by market forces. Such transformations can be considered in their more abstract form, at the level of ideas. For example, one could relate postmodernity's attachment to spectacle and capitalism's holding out a seemingly never-ending series of novel goods for consumption to the contemporary production of childhood as a time defined by the constant quest for novelty and "fun." Taken concretely, however, such cultural and economic transformations impact the lives of children, who claim constant boredom as the material result of such a construction. Children suffer in a variety of ways from the constant stimulation of desire and longing.

Consumerism Shaping Orientation to Children

Perhaps a more disturbing implication of the reconstruction of childhood under globalized capitalism concerns the power of consumerism as a way of life to shape adults in an orientation to children. Consumerism leads adults to view children alternately as disposable commodities (other people's children, "welfare babies," gangs, and "street children") or as objectified sources of social capital. Consumerism as a way of life forms all of us into a certain "habitus" that treats everything in our life world as an object of consumption, an expendable commodity. Consumerist culture invites persons to constantly engage in practices enmeshed in acquisition. As Peter Stearns so aptly notes of consumerism, when people grow up with it from infancy, they come to assume its logic and normalcy, so that relating to children primarily around the acquisition and use of commodities comes to seem not only "natural" but also necessary.[36] Habituated into relationships formed around consumption, consumption comes to structure the identities of children themselves along with adult relationships with children.

Transforming Children into Consumers

In what follows, then, I want to explore the working out of the transformations detailed above in the contemporary North American construction of children as consumers. I do not claim that this is the only construction at work, or that it is uniformly experienced by all groups of children within North America. Obviously, at any given time multiple constructions of childhood exist within any society, particularly in a society such as the United States, where diverse cultural groups live side by side (and occasionally together), each with their own particular nuanced meanings and practices in relation to children. Nevertheless, in any given historical period, amidst multiple available constructions of childhood, particular images of the child rise to the foreground as primary. These images are propelled by various social and economic forces, and by the interests of dominant groups who lend the images legitimacy and use their positions of cultural dominance to eclipse or displace alternative, competing images. In our time, propelled by the interests and power of global capitalism, the preeminent construction of "the child" in North America is that of consumer.

Ignored No Longer

Children's consumer behavior is big business in the United States. James McNeal's 1969 article set the stage for a new generation of marketing studies on children as consumers–people who have desires, who want things to satisfy their needs, and who have the ability to buy.[37] McNeal's later works trace the change in marketing practices, changes that he as a marketing researcher helped to create. Beginning in a time when children were ignored as insignificant to the goals of advertisers and sellers, McNeal brings us to the present context in which children constitute one of the most significant–meaning profitable–market niches in existence.[38] This transformation has taken place in a relatively short time. In the 1930s advertisers first started to focus upon children directly, instead of assuming that their mothers alone constituted the main target.[39] McNeal paints the shift in dollar terms, from the mid-1980s when only a third of major retail chains targeted children as a market, to the present when such companies each year spend over a billion dollars on media advertising to children, alongside another three billion dollars on packaging designed for children.[40]

Picking up on a formula present in the marketing literature at least since 1923,[41] McNeal offers as his mantra the idea that businesses today cannot afford to ignore children because children actually constitute three markets in one.

Three Markets in One

First, they are a primary market, spending some $35.6 billion of their own money annually. They spend more than $6 billion each year on soft drinks and sweets, over $6 billion every year on toys, and $3.6 billion of their own money goes to clothing purchases. Another $2 billion annually goes for children's movie admissions, not including what they spend on snacks and drinks at the theatre.[42] Obviously these figures show that children between the ages of four and twelve spend a sizable amount of money that marketers would like to count as profits for their companies, making child-consumers extremely valuable in the eyes of marketers.

Second, children constitute an influence market, often referred to as "kidfluence."[43] That is, children directly influence the spending of another $187 billion each year by their parents and indirectly influence another $300 billion in purchases. Indirect influence refers to purchases for which parents take account of the children's preferences as they buy goods even though the children are not directly or actively involved in influencing those particular purchases.[44] Being part of an influence market opens up the new possibility of "marketing to and through kids," as the title of one marketing text unabashedly expresses it.[45]

Third, children constitute a future market, a group of people with purchasing power in the future who as children are ripe for the establishment of brand loyalty and the development of consumer behaviors that will shape how they spend money as adults. "Children are consumers in training…born to be consumers, at least in the United States, and they begin their consumership early in life."[46] Deborah Johns reviewed twenty-five years of research on advertising to children. Studies show that between preschool and second grade children "begin to make inferences about people based on the products they use…Inferences about people based on the brands they use also develop during childhood."[47] By the sixth grade, children possess a strong sense of the status associated with ownership of certain products, as well as a product's capacity to function as a symbol of group belonging and identity.[48] McNeal's research shows that children develop awareness of product brands early (before age 2) and begin to attach certain meanings or attributes to specific brands at an early age as well, having a working knowledge of some two hundred brands by the age of six.[49] Such equations between commodities and persons in the consciousness of children happen as increasingly children and adults in a consumerist society express identities through consumption.

Marketers' Utilitarian View of Children

Of course, from the perspective of market researchers, such findings are cause for glee since they indicate that children are indeed a ripe and profitable target for advertising. The language of McNeal and other researches is unselfconscious and completely unapologetic about its utilitarian view of children as the means to selling commodities. The unapologetic tone of marketing research on children comes in large measure as a result of its reliance on a construction of "the child" whose innate needs and desires are satisfied by the goods advertisers offer. In other words, as Daniel Cook so aptly demonstrates, across the twentieth-century history of advertising directed to children, children are increasingly portrayed as individualized consumers for whom purchasing represents an avenue of self-expression and agency as the child acts autonomously to satisfy innately held desires.[50]

In such rhetoric, the self-interested status of market research remains masked behind an ideology of children's "needs" and consumption as an expression of their identities. In this rhetoric, marketers see themselves as providing a service that benefits and empowers children. Where market interests do surface, there exists little sense that those interests might conflict with the well-being of children. As Cook writes, market research analysis like that of McNeal constructs a notion of "the child" as "a being who possesses presocial, naturalized desires for consumer goods...the view of the child as an 'autonomous consumer.'"[51] Children's desires for consumer goods are construed as preexisting and natural, so that marketers who study children to better understand their consumer behaviors are only trying to do a better job of satisfying those desires. In reality, consumption is not only a practice undertaken by individuals with natural desires. It is a social process in which children and others participate in ways mediated by the particularity of culture.

Cultural Capital and Cultural Reproduction

Pierre Bourdieu's concepts of cultural capital and cultural reproduction are helpful here. He argues that various practices people engage in, from consumption to gender-based forms of bodily comportment, have a way of appearing to be the result of individual choices when they are in fact the result of lengthy apprenticeship in a particular culture and its "habitus."[52] Growing up in a certain habitus socializes children into the specific practices and forms of knowledge they need to function appropriately as members of their society (including their race or class or gender group). A person has cultural capital when they possess such necessary knowledge and experience.

For Bourdieu, the term "capital" refers not only to economic value but also to whatever is at stake for persons in a given social context. In that sense, membership in a particular group such as a social class is not simply a function of financial status or education. It also comes from the ways preferences, abilities, and actions of individuals are shaped by the habitus in which they gain the knowledge of how to be a "person who belongs" to their social class or other group. People who have the cultural knowledge to belong are those with cultural capital. In a society structured around consumption, knowledge of the practices of consumption, such as shopping for bargains, knowing how to express the value of an item without appearing to engage in conspicuous display, or choosing the right products to enhance identity and status, comprises practices related to cultural capital.

Cultural *reproduction* works by disguising the ways in which various elements appearing to be individual preferences and choices (such as musical tastes or interests in discussing world affairs) actually are learned practices, the products of lengthy apprenticeships within a particular habitus in which those activities were valued. Such activities come to be viewed as a matter of innate tastes ascribed from birth ("genesis amnesia") when in reality they are arbitrary.[53] Not only is the content of culture arbitrary (i.e., a preference for the music of Beethoven over that of rap artist Eminem) but also its imposition is arbitrary (i.e., involving whatever groups inhabit a particular social space). As such, "cultural arbitraries" become the basis for distinction between groups. By treating the consumptive desires and behaviors of children as presocial or elemental, the behaviors' arbitrary status as learned, socially constituted practices remains hidden. Consuming children seem only to be doing what is natural.

The process of cultural reproduction happens as dominant groups, able to disguise the power relations in such impositions of cultural arbitraries, thereby set the agenda for what other groups aspire to as they seek to alter their status and power positions. In effect, a particular way of doing things comes to be seen as commonsensical, natural, and self-evident. Even though no physical coercion is involved, says Bourdieu, the mechanism of cultural reproduction is one of what he terms "symbolic violence" because it enforces and reproduces cultural dominance as a mechanism of social order.[54]

The Market's Definition of a Child

In the case of childhood, marketing and advertising have been highly successful in establishing the legitimacy of corporate capitalism's definition of the child as consumer, making this arbitrary definition appear to be fixed, natural, and necessary, while disguising consumption's existence as a social process. Various cultural artifacts, including intense medicalization of childbirth, the existence of specialized infant foods and furniture, and the burgeoning market in children's designer clothing, all form part of a dominant social ideology of the child as one who needs things–things that can be supplied by the marketplace in corporate America.

Parents, schooled by advertising and popular education on childrearing practices, "learn" that to be happy, well-adjusted babies and children, children "need" special disposable diapers for each supposedly distinctive age segment of their diaper-wearing months, or expensive baby foods, toddler beds, and kiddie computer games. Such schooling invites parents to misrecognize[55] the interests of market forces in representing products as beneficial to children's education, safety, or growth.[56] Marketers, segmenting childhood by age and gender, create ever more specialized groups of children with ever more specialized "needs." Under the guise of legitimate needs, which are treated as "natural" and necessary aspects of childhood, the construction of children as consumers imposes a definition upon children even as it masks the power relations funding that arrangement in which children's interests become subordinated to the interests of global capitalism.

The shaping of children into excellent consumers is problem enough on the personal relational level, as anyone can attest who ever attempted to move with a child through the checkout line of a grocery store, alongside the open shelf of sweet tempting chocolate bars and bubble gum positioned just at the child's eye level. But this issue has critical social dimensions. Our society appears to value children highly on the basis of the consumerist practices involving them. Nevertheless, our society continues to have a shortage of spending practices that in actuality value children by contributing to their thriving. The child consumer stands as a highly ambivalent image, combining what the market most wants (a child who will buy to satisfy needs) with what the market most disdains (a child who has needs, some of which cannot be addressed through consumption).

The prevailing construction of children as consumers functions to secure the subordination of children's needs and interests to those of market forces in the United States by reproducing the ambivalence contained within this image. The child as consumer stands simultaneously as one who is apparently highly valued by corporate America for having needs that only corporate America can fulfill, but, paradoxically, also as one whose neediness is cause for devaluing children in a market-defined culture where self-sufficiency and autonomy are normative. Of course, this problem is also one that the market purports to "solve," as the child's consumption of particular products (e.g., developmentally stimulating infant toys; educational games, etc.) promises her/his eventual development out of a state of dependency. Children whose caregivers fail to take advantage of these products so "necessary" to healthy development stand condemned to remain in the lesser-valued status group of dependent, needy persons.

The Discourse on Children's Needs and Mothering

An important but often overlooked element of marketing to children concerns the positioning of parents, particularly mothers, in relation to the satisfaction of children's needs. In the 1990s marketing researchers began to write about ways for advertisers to take advantage of the situation in which overstressed working mothers would rather give in to their children's demands for purchases than to struggle with or set limits on children's consumption. Advertising guru Gene Del Vecchio coined the term "pester power" to refer to the potential business dollars to be had from children nagging their parents to buy things.[57] Beyond that are numerous descriptions of how children with working parents end up taking more responsibility for running the household. They even purchase groceries for the family, thereby legitimating the new practices of creating advertising for all products (not just those traditionally purchased by children) with children's purchasing power in mind.[58] Marketing writers blame the changing social institution of the family (a less politically charged way to talk about changes in women's social roles) for parental inclinations to substitute buyable goods for parental involvement in the lives of their children. Of course, the advertising industry is then happy to exploit this regrettable condition:

> Mom and Dad are working late again. Both parents are working in more two-parent families, and many work longer hours, requiring more household participation (read responsibility) on the part of children. Mom may call home in the afternoon and ask her child what he wants to eat tonight. When the child suggests ordering a pizza for supper, it simultaneously simplifies things for parents and satisfies one of children's elemental desires...The guilt factor has grown among some working parents. Their focus is on "quality time": a term that can translate into giving kids a lot of what they want in an effort to make up for time not spent with them.[59]

To tell it the way the advertising pundits do, marketers are merely trying to make up the difference for children left unattended by their working mothers, by satisfying the "elemental desires" of children through consumable products. Note that although McNeal's above comments start out mentioning that both "Mom and Dad are working late," Dad quickly exits the scene as Mom's working late becomes the real problem. *She* is the one who calls home and has to solve the "what's for supper?" problem. It is her altered role in the domestic sphere that advertisers capitalize on, making the language of marketing of goods in relation to changing family structures a highly gendered discourse.

In addition, this rhetoric carefully conceals the power of the market to create desire, to construct so-called "elemental desires" of children precisely along the lines that will benefit sellers, and to mingle the desires created with nostalgia for gender-related household arrangements. Marketers rather skillfully manage simultaneously to negatively cast blame upon women and to affirm women. Blame comes for the social changes resulting in children's elevated consumer role with its socially undesirable effects of childhood materialism and forced loss of innocence. Marketers affirm women who at least attempt to rectify this unfortunate situation by making purchases that satisfy their children's desires and needs.

A contemporary example of the market's reconstruction of both childhood and parenting is published in a December 2003 ad for a canned "sloppy Joe" sandwich product. The ad appeared in probably the most widely read parenting advice magazine in the nation. The ad pictures a young European American girl dressed in pink with curly red hair, rosy cheeks, and a big smile, eagerly grasping a sandwich. "I want some FUN piled on a bun," reads the caption. The child appears off to one side of the photo, while the sandwich takes center stage. Only the sandwich and the girl's grasping hands are in sharp focus. The child's facial features take on a blurred, slightly dreamy quality, as they constitute the background for this ad's attempt to market a food product to parents by appealing to parental desires to provide their children with pleasure. The child's wistful happiness is tied to her anticipated consumption, which, in turn, is tied to parents with purchasing power who will buy this product to provide the child with a "fun" experience.

On the one hand, the advertisement banks on a timeless and fairly transparent marketing ploy to associate pleasure with the purchase and consumption of a product. On the other hand, though, this ad and the countless others like it found in parenting magazines, daily newspapers, and twenty-four–hour-a-day television advertising, less transparently put forward particular understandings of childhood and parenting on which such ads depend for their effectiveness. This ad portrays childhood as a state of dreamy, innocent pleasure. Here, children are by nature pleasure seeking and in need of novelty. In ads such as this one, children appear content in the imminent fulfillment of their desires. At the same time, the grasping hands make consumption the defining feature of the child.

The ad assumes that parents view providing fun experiences to their children as an important and legitimate task of parenting–at least important enough to motivate the product's purchase. Furthermore, the ad makes the claim that its product can deliver something far more wonderful than its face-value purpose, the mere fulfillment of a nutritional need. Most advertising today relies on commodity fetish, making implicit claims that an ordinary product like toothpaste or soap will magically bring virility, prosperity, success, and popularity. The product's maker claims in the ad that the food will supply the user with fun. At base, then, the ad evokes a situation in which it is not enough for children's meals to nourish their bodies. Eating must also be an event, even a spectacle, and an intensely pleasurable one at that.

What the ad does not contain, of course, is any indication of the transnational corporate interests involved in producing this product. Nor does it hint at the threat to the environment and to "other people's children" embedded in that production. The producer of the sandwich sauce is a $20 billion corporation estimated to be among the top three food-producing corporations internationally. The company gives generously to a number of efforts targeted to help hungry children in the United States. Thus it presents itself as being "pro-children" through its public relations material and its marketing campaigns. Unfortunately, though, the same food conglomerate also has been indicted in several environmental lawsuits claiming that its meat production facilities dumped animal waste into rivers and waterways. A news report in 1997 carried a story of the company being among several companies using products for manufacturing its goods that were traced to illegal child labor.[60]

In 2002 the USDA, a government watchdog group charged with overseeing food safety, took more than three months to investigate e-coli contamination of one of the company's beef plants. The investigation resulted in the largest recall of U.S. beef ever, but the delay of the investigation prompted questions about whether business interests interfered with concern for public safety.[61] The company has been cited by various labor- and human rights-watch organizations for unfair labor practices, a matter that surely impacts children as it affects families of wage earners employed by the company.[62] Yet most mothers targeted as product consumers by the ad in the parenting magazine will never come into contact with this side of the company. Potential customers have no easy access to the complex interfaces between the company's business practices, government groups, child workers in the United States and abroad, and public relations efforts to elide media coverage of matters related to the company's corporate image. Most of these mothers will encounter only the advertising images of pleasure in a can offered to romantically content children on the brink of having their desires satisfied.

Clearly, marketers stand poised to capitalize on contemporary women's conflicted and complex positioning in relation to their own children's needs and desires. These marketers are ready to take advantage of the general inability of consumers to hold producers accountable regarding issues of social responsibility in relation to poor children, child laborers, and the environment. At a time of considerable backlash against feminism and of global economic conditions unfavorable to women, women's lives are especially vulnerable to problematic reconstructions of motherhood in terms of consumption for their children. This reconstruction obviously goes hand in hand with that of the child-as-consumer and is highlighted by the development of vast numbers of specialized products deemed necessary for the well-being of babies and children. Such products, especially in a child's infancy, depend on the presence of a mother-who-buys for their success in the marketplace.

Educating Children to Be Good Consumers

Early in the development of children's advertising, however, some mothers posed a counter-narrative of their own identities and those of their children, one stressing children's innocence and their vulnerability to exploitation, in which mothers were their protectors. In her critical study of children's advertising, Ellen Seiter notes that in the early history of television advertising to children in the United States (e.g., the 1950s), networks created programs without commercials. Thus in an effort to promote the purchase of televisions they engaged in a rhetoric of family entertainment that would enhance bonds within the family. As a pattern later developed in which networks produced programming to be sponsored by marketers who paid for commercial time, the power of television advertising to effectively market products to large numbers of potential consumers became obvious.

FOCUSING ON CHILDREN

When animated programs gained popularity and showed a profit for marketers, giving birth to Saturday morning children's television, marketers had an amazing and unprecedented opportunity to focus their advertising to a very specific audience, namely children. Unlike print advertisements that depend on reading ability, television ads could extend the scope of the target group of potential consumers to include even the very youngest household members.

However, direct advertising to children soon met with opposition from those concerned about the possible exploitation of children by marketers. Advocacy groups such as Action for Children's Television (ACT) developed out of concerns that children constitute a vulnerable group in relation to television marketing. Such groups sought, and in many case won, legislative restrictions on marketers. The cases involved marketers who focused particularly on deceptive advertising practices with children such as making a toy appear larger in an advertisement than is actually the case, or suggesting with visual image or text that a toy can move on its own when in fact it requires the player's action to make it move.

Many of the arguments about children's vulnerability to media advertising took the form of a concern that children's more limited cognitive capacities gave marketers an unfair advantage over children. This assumed that children's developmental limitations prevented them from "protecting themselves" from the persuasive intent of sellers. Such concerns, in part, reflect a highly rationale and cognitive understanding of how advertising works. In this view, advertising provides information about products and attempts to persuade buyers through conveying information. Logically then, if buyers can understand the information and are aware of the persuasive efforts of the seller, they will be able to make informed decisions about their purchases and avoid manipulation by sellers. Along these lines, in the early debate over television advertising to children, children were represented as vulnerable and innocent ones who could not possibly understand the intentions of sellers. Marketers appeared as potential rapacious exploiters of children who possessed an unfair advantage in being able to manipulate children to buy against their will or best interests.

DEBATING CHILDREN'S COGNITIVE LIMITS

Since the problem of advertising's influence upon children was attributed to cognitive developmental limitations of children (with some legislative nods to the potential culpability of unethical marketers who intentionally misled children with their ads), that became the primary focus for the supposed solution as well. In the 1970s, marketers began to apply the cognitive developmental theory of Jean Piaget to understanding children's interactions with advertising.[63] At the outset, marketers' use of developmental theories came as responses to critics of children's advertising, with justifications that the theories would allow them to be more ethical. Advertisers could avoid the creation of advertisements that took unfair advantage of a child's inability to operate beyond a developmentally determined range of information decoding. For example, Ward et al.'s study addresses the tendency of younger children to value a pictured product exclusively in relation to concrete qualities. The child would value larger size or brighter color rather than making a more complex evaluation of how the product might perform its advertised functions, which could be expected at a later stage in a child's development.[64] The authors suggest that such knowledge can help advertisers create appropriate ads for young children.

In this debate, the question focuses solely on appropriate and ethical means of advertising to children, based on the assumption that making them good consumers is a worthy goal, and this assumption is never called into question. The now taken-for-granted understanding that children are consumers, therefore they may as well be good ones, reflects the extent to which late capitalism's construction of children as consumers had taken hold by the time of this debate in the 1970s.

The debates on advertising to children continue, nevertheless, with proponents of an understanding, knowing child squaring off against those who assert children's essential innocence and naiveté. One obvious problem in setting up the conflict between children and marketing as an issue of an individual child's limited rational thinking ability lies in the assumptions that advertising consists principally of conveying information about a product and that a rational individual is free to act on received information. This perspective ignores the multivalence of symbol and image in advertising, along with the variety of ways in which persons experience a commercial–e.g., as information, as persuasive rhetoric, as entertainment, as a shared point of reference creating a social bond between people. It also ignores the power of social relations and social forces (such as consumerism) to shape individual behavior.

Such high faith in the power of rational thought, devoid of awareness of social forces framing a person's actions, still can be heard in the comments of current marketing scholars such as Adrian Furnham. He claims, "You can't be coerced into doing something you don't want to if you know and understand the process."[65] Interestingly, this line of thought necessarily leads to the goal of teaching children the skills of being good consumers so that they can protect themselves from the inherent coercion of the market. A comment by Debra Goldman in *Adweek,* a journal of the advertising industry, suggests that not everyone in the business sees the situation from Furnham's perspective. "Marketers covet young customers for the same reason child advocates want to protect them: the belief that the young are vulnerable to marketing in a way that adult consumers are not."[66]

DEVELOPMENTAL THEORY AS A MARKETING TOOL

Once marketers began to apply developmental theory to their work, they discovered that they had a potent tool for furthering the promotion of their products. They could use developmental theory as a scaffold for educating children into consumptive practices. As one study put it, cognitive-developmental theories "portray the processes by which young children develop from what might be characterized as 'perceptual, narrow information decoders' in their earliest consumer acts to 'abstract, flexible, broad information processors' by early adolescence."[67] Rather than viewing development as a barrier for marketing, these authors note that "a child's stage of cognitive development does not necessarily restrict his [sic] capacity to learn various consumption-related skills…Certain consumer-related skills can be taught early in the life cycle."[68] Marketing literature in the 1970s began to refer to the processes of "consumer socialization" and to the importance of studying children and their socialization into the consumer role.[69]

Perspectives such as this one, common in the literature of children's advertising, involve a particular construction of childhood. As Seiter, Cook, and others points out, advertisers construct children as those capable of understanding and possessing a sense of agency beyond the innocent vulnerability described by ACT and other children's television advocacy groups. In this construction, children share with adults the ability to express their agency through consumption, and in the logic of marketing experts ought not be prevented from opportunities to do so:

> Consumption is as legitimate an activity for children as it is unavoidable. Rather than making cumbersome attempts to protect children from all marketing stimuli, which is in all probably futile, efforts should be made to prepare children for efficacious, satisfying consumer behaviors.[70]

EXPORTING CHILD CONSUMERISM

In this 1970s report appropriately entitled *Children Learning to Buy: The Development of Consumer Information Processing Skills,* children exist as consumers-in-training. McNeal's work some twenty years later expresses his hope that this construction of childhood as consumerism's dress rehearsal can be exported to other countries: "Is it possible to direct marketing activities to children worldwide much in the same manner as in the States?"[71] The dollar amounts he goes on to cite in relation to children's spending in countries outside the United States signals an affirmative answer to the question. He asserts that "Many countries offer more growth opportunities in children's products than does the United States,"[72] since those markets may not already be flooded with an excess of children's products.

> A multinational marketing strategy to kids is viable...With satellite-based television broadcasting growing rapidly in Europe and Asia, children can be expected to discover many more things to request from their parents. As U.S. marketers have known for a long time, and as large numbers of them have recently begun to act on, children are a future market that can be cultivated now so that when children reach market age they can more easily be converted into customers.[73]

As if it needs to be said, McNeal later underlined the imperial role of the United States. in turning other nations into consumers for its own goods. "The U.S model of consumption, in general, has become the guiding model of new consumers the world over, suggesting great market opportunities for many existing U.S. products and brands."[74]

Plenty of evidence exists to suggest that McNeal's claim has come to pass. I could cite many examples and give figures for the worldwide market for various U.S. products. I will suffice with one of the most poignant proofs for the successful exportation of U.S. consumerism that I have ever seen, a small comic-book–styled pamphlet produced by an agency of the government of the Philippines. This pamphlet's ostensible purpose is to support families of "overseas contract workers"–Filipinos who live and work in countries outside the Philippines under contract for a few years at a time, mostly as household domestic workers, oil industry or factory laborers, or in the entertainment industry. The pamphlet's agenda is to help families adjust to the absence of parents in the overseas workforce, and its chief target audience is children in these families.

The pamphlet lauds the parents as heroes for helping the nation's economy by being willing to leave their families to work overseas. It expresses empathy toward the understandable grief a child must feel when a parent leaves them to work overseas, while remaining silent about the political and economic agendas that create overseas contract work as an option for Filipino parents. But the main consolation offered to children, and the punch line of the pamphlet, is that although children will miss their mothers and fathers, they now will have televisions in their homes, cell phones in their pockets, and spending money for other things they want to buy. Consumption is the promise held out to children by their government as a worthy exchange for lack of parental presence.[75]

Defective Consumers: Difference and the Child-Consumer Construct

Clearly, some children in Third World contexts and in the United States do not fit the dominant capitalist culture's definition of consumer-children. Rather than critiquing the system that creates these inequalities, however, those who fall outside the construction are themselves pathologized: they take on a deficit identity as flawed consumers.

Being Poor in a Consumer Society

Zygmunt Bauman articulates the different meaning of "being poor" in a consumerist culture:

> It is one thing to be poor in a society of producers and universal employment; it is quite a different thing to be poor in a society of consumers, in which life-projects are built around consumer choice rather than work, professional skills, or jobs. If "being poor" once derived its meaning from the condition of being unemployed, today it draws its meaning primarily from the plight of a flawed consumer.[76]

Like Bauman, Elizabeth Chin focuses on the dilemma of poor children in a society built around consumption, but her focus gives a more positive role to the kinds of consumptive behaviors in which poor children engage. Chin's moving and incisive ethnography on the participation of poor African American children in consumer culture looks at the consumer sphere as a medium for social inequality and explores the variety of ways children from an economically blighted neighborhood in New Haven, Conn., negotiated that sphere.[77] She asserts that the problem with theoretical treatments of consumption as a matter of individual desire is their failure to attend to the myriad ways social inequality structures some groups' consumption, such that the term "poor consumer" appears to be an oxymoron. Chin challenges those who fail to understand any positive agency in the consumer behavior of poor children, whose actions and choices often demonstrate creativity and facilitate their social solidarity with others. In her research, Chin found that children used shopping as a space of creativity and play, a chance to express social solidarity and create connections with family and friends, and a sphere for critiquing the social inequalities structuring their lives.[78]

In the media, consumption among poor children has been unfairly constructed as pathological or deviant. Media gives the lion's share of attention to incidents such as a minority child's willingness to kill to obtain a status brand of athletic shoes, or unmarried black teen mothers buying CD's and potato chips when their babies need milk.[79] Such images stereotype minority and other poor children as crazed by selfish greed, unable to make good choices, and making poor use of limited resources by wasting money on luxury items. Unlike media depictions of the consumptive practices of the poor as shortsighted and self-interested, Chin's research showed the careful planning and "other-regard" demonstrated in both children's and their household's consumption practices. Chin criticizes views of consumption that fail to recognize consumption as a hegemonic force that structures inequality. "American society has, for more than two centuries, shaped and limited the consumption of black communities through a combination of structural factors, everyday social practices, and symbolic means."[80]

Personal Experience

My majority culture location as a European American woman means that I do not have extensive personal experience of the limits of which Chin speaks here, although I have witnessed their impact on individuals and communities. I do have some experience with being treated as a "defective consumer" based on bearing the markings of neediness. In the months around the birth of my twin sons I was unemployed and received public assistance in the form of food vouchers from a nutrition program for women, infants, and children known as WIC. (Some of the recipients of the vouchers jokingly refer to it as the "woman in crisis" program, but it actually stands for "Women, Infants, and Children.") One day at the grocery store I got in line with my basket full of all the things to which I as an anemic new mother of twins was entitled in this program–cheese, cereal, carrots, lots of milk. I decided at the last minute to add a small bag of corn chips to my purchases along with a few other items, such as disposable diapers, for which I would pay cash.

The two women in line behind me, seeing my WIC vouchers, began to talk about my groceries and about me. "Look at that. They just don't know how to spend their money. That's why welfare doesn't work. You give these people money for food, and they buy potato chips with it." Neither of the women said anything like, "Oh look, that good mother has a basket full of fine nutritious foods that will contribute to her health and the health of her babies." Instead, their attention went directly to that which to them evidenced poor choice by a person they deemed poor, relegated to the ranks of "these people." Clearly in a consumerist society two of the most horrific crimes one can commit are, first, to be a *poor* consumer (needy and therefore not in a position to engage in consumption on par with others) and second, to be a poor *consumer* (one who makes inappropriate choices). These consumerist, market-driven values are fast eroding competing social values of extending care and support to children and women who care for them.

Ambiguous Need, Ambivalent Practices with Children

Ironically, a child-consumer is above all a person who "needs," even if the need is one the market itself created. A need represents some kind of lack. And so in the context of U.S. corporate culture, the child appears as one highly valued, particularly by corporations who depend upon and even need children in order to capture and maintain a profitable share of the declining market in an unstable economic time. Such a child lacks certain things that the market can then supply. Marketers create desires masked as "needs" in children through advertising directed to them. They also appeal to their parents/caregivers as persons in a position to satisfy the needs and desires of children (as their own were never satisfied). Thus the child as consumer whose vulnerability and neediness is an asset to the market appears as a person of utmost worth and importance.

On the other hand, though, outside their potential or actual role as consumers of goods, whose neediness can be played upon, the neediness of children represents a source of threat to market profits. Their "lack" is construed in terms of basic material needs (i.e., a minimally adequate standard of housing, food, health care, education, etc.) or nonmaterially in terms of supportive and nurturing care or parental attention. Amidst dominant cultural ideologies favoring strength, competence, and self-sufficiency, a notion of children as consumers that constructs childhood around "lack" hardly seems desirable. The number of children living below the poverty line with little or no health care and diminished educational opportunities continues to increase, while services to poor children simultaneously are decreasing.[81]

These economic patterns clearly constitute an example of a deep ambivalence toward children in North American culture. The society appears to support and affirm children on the one hand with material excess, while on the other hand ignoring and even doing harm through neglect of their basic needs. It is an ambivalence in which children are simultaneously valued and despised on the basis of their needs. And this ambivalence toward children becomes problematically reproduced in contemporary religious conversations (and Christian theology) about childhood, as children are simultaneously portrayed as innocents and devils, the subject of the next chapter.

Resisting the Market Empire: More Clues to an Emancipatory Theology of Childhood

If it seems that I have painted a rather bleak and totalizing account of the pervasive reach of market forces and the impact of global capitalism, then I am only too happy to confess that I am not out to present a balanced picture here. The contemporary construction of children as consumers *par excellence* in a culture over-defined by its patterns and habits of consumption is such a distortion of the meaning of human personhood as to render the idea of balance meaningless. With this statement, I do not claim that children (particularly middle- and upper-class North American children) only experience harm and do not benefit at all from some of the opportunities, technological developments, medical advances, and other goods that may be linked to globalized capitalism. What I object to is the dominant voice of analysis of market forces that sees only the so-called "progress" of globalization and none of its human and cultural costs. I object as the dominant voice claims that the interests of agribusiness really are the same as those of our families. I object when that same voice pontificates that with their global expansion, mega-corporations are bettering the lives not only of Americans but also of poor people in faraway lands who now have computers and televisions and other markers of what is supposedly a better quality of life.

In contrast, it is my intention to notice and analyze the way economic and cultural patterns of our time impact the lives of children—my children and other people's children—as they remake children in the image of globalized market forces. This analysis ultimately moves (as will become more evident in later chapters) toward developing resources and strategies of action with others in Christian communities that can be real and just alternatives to the specter of injustice I paint here, in my efforts to describe what childhood constructed around consumption looks like. Out of the foregoing analysis, then, come more clues toward an emancipatory theology of childhood.

1. In contrast to consumerism, Christian faith claims that a child has inherent and incomparable worth that is not based on their consumptive abilities, but instead comes from their status as children of God. The forces of market capitalism constitute a vast and powerful imperial regime in our time. In the previous chapter I contended that the gospel of Mark is a telling of the Jesus story in the form of anti-imperial counter-narrative, in which Jesus' proclamation of the "kin-dom" of God stands in radical tension to the Roman Empire's proclamations of human rulership. Similarly, in our time the reign of God Jesus brought about through his life and ministry, his death, and his resurrection stands in radical tension to the forces of empire that name North American

children as "consumers in training" and who construct children's lives and identities around a set of practices centered on the acquisition of commodities. In the face of market forces constructing children as consumers, Christian faith offers a radical alternative that locates personhood, identity, and worth not in the display of acquired commodities but in their identities as God's children. Thus children demonstrate in fullness the meanings and significance that the idea of being children of God portends for all people. In this alternative vision of childhood, children have value not because of their purchasing power or their ability to influence the purchases of others; not for their present or future brand loyalty; not for their accumulation of many mass-produced commodities or a few high status ones. Their value comes from their being children of God.

2. An emancipatory theology of childhood emerging from this chapter's analysis points to children as "double agents" in God's hospitality. Seen from one direction, children offer to the world a way to welcome God, through Christ's call to welcome children. This clue sees children in terms of their capacities as "God-welcomers," the ones through whose welcome we welcome Jesus and the One who sent him. The call it issues fundamentally concerns the need to overcome indifference, antipathy, and ambivalence to children that is so charac-teristic of consumer culture. Christ already has unambivalently welcomed children. If the church and world want to welcome Christ and the God who sent him, then the church and the world had best figure out how to welcome children.

Seen from a different direction, children are those who personify the divine embrace and welcome that God has already offered to the world, a welcome that already exists even amidst the domination of imperial market forces, as God in Christ blessed and welcomed children while they were still under imperial occupation and while they were still possessed by demons. Seen from this second direction, this clue fundamentally concerns the need of a society that is held in captivity by the empire of consumerism to understand that true abundance lies elsewhere. It issues in the invitation to see in children the signs of God's abundant welcome of humanity and the urgency of resisting the power of these consumerist imperial forces by constructing new narratives by which to live.

Christian faith constructs children as bearers of the divine hospitality to humanity, a construction that resists the distortions and misrecog-nitions inherent in the market forces' construction of children. This construction stands in tense opposition to the image of the child-consumer who must constantly engage in acquisition and whose acquisitive desires eventually become self- and other-consuming. It stands in contrast to the market empire's rejection and exclusion of children who lack the resources to be good consumers and benefit from the market's abundance. It critiques the market construction of children and globalization's crass utilitarian exploitation of other nations' children as mere objects in the production and manufacture of consumable commodities for the sake of a false abundance in North America. The image of children as bearing the welcome of God, in contrast, beckons even those rendered abject by the globalized empire of late capitalism to come and experience God's abundance.

3. God has created children with vulnerability as small players in a vast imperial game that should never be confused as child's play. Children's vulnerability and neediness, the ease with which they are co-opted into the agendas of the market, and the depth of harm done to them make them signal-bearers and exemplars of the vulnerability of humanity to the power of systemic evil and sin. At least some times, some people who are willing to overlook oppressive working conditions of adult field laborers or cottage industry urban workers will stop to notice that something is wrong when it is children who labor under horrendously unsafe conditions. Sometimes it is difficult to recognize the extent to which we as adults are already co-opted by the forces of the market empire as it shapes our desires, our identities, our relationships, and our everyday practices of living. It can be powerfully jarring, like a wake-up call, to hear a two-year old sing a commercial jingle for beer (especially if one pauses to wonder how old the same child may be before she can sing the Doxology with equal facility). The child sends us a sign of how quickly and invisibly we humans are co-opted by this empire and how hard is the way of resistance.

This third clue to a liberatory theology of childhood is one in which we notice that some groups (e.g., children, women, persons living in poverty) experience a special vulnerability to the effects of imperial domination. This special vulnerability comes because of the way they are positioned within their societies, yet even the most vulnerable to its harms may be co-opted and complicit in the imperial regime's agendas. We thus see that persons, including children, in North American consumerist culture simultaneously can be vulnerable and subject to negative effects of consumerism, and also be complicit in it. This recognition speaks a truth well known within Christian tradition. In baptism we renounce evil and turn from it, knowing that we are freed from evil's grasp in this sacramental enactment and that we already belong to God (even before the physical act of baptism occurs). Still we continue to live under evil's tutelage and within its effects.

Children in North America simultaneously manifest their particular vulnerability to the powers of the consumerist empire and become complicit in its perpetuation in ways that then bring harm to others. (Harm comes most notably to children and others in the Two-Thirds

World whose labors fuel the consumptive machine of North American appetites for commodities.) This clue then is fundamentally about how vulnerability and complicity do not cancel each other out. It calls for Christians to take seriously the reality and power of sin in the world and in our lives. We must notice our participation with it and engage in constructing different narratives by which to live–what Robert Franklin has called "*metanoia* narratives."[82] These are narratives of renunciation in which we join together with others to resist what is evil, harmful, oppressive, and destructive, particularly in solidarity with those for whom positions of vulnerability create situations of deepest harm.

These three clues hint at the importance of overcoming the ambivalence toward children so keenly manifested in consumerist culture and so tied to the indifference in which children's persons outside of their roles as consumers are held. The question is how contemporary Christians can act and live in ways that affirm and welcome children as God-welcomers. Problematically, though, the regime of consumerism is so pervasive that even religious discourse on children and childhood in the United States gets caught up in reproducing the ambivalence toward children so prominent in market constructions of childhood. The next chapter will explore contemporary religious conversations on childhood in North America, looking to uncover further clues for a liberatory theology of childhood.

Sources Cited

Baudrillard, Jean. *Simulations.* New York: Semiotext(e), 1983.

Bauman, Zygmunt. *Intimations of Postmodernity.* London and New York: Routledge, 1992.

_____. *Work, Consumerism, and the New Poor.* Issues in Society, ed. Tim May. Buckingham; Philadelphia: Open University Press, 1998.

_____. *Liquid Modernity.* Cambridge: Polity Press, 2000.

Bounds, Elizabeth M. et al. "Welfare 'Reform': A War against the Poor." In *Welfare Policy: Feminist Critiques,* ed. Elizabeth M. Bounds, Pamela K. Brubaker, and Mary E. Hobgood, 1–22. Cleveland: The Pilgrim Press, 1999.

Bourdieu, Pierre. *Distinction: A Social Critique of the Judgement of Taste.* Translated by Richard Nice. Cambridge, Mass.: Routledge, 1984.

Bourdieu, Pierre, and Jean-Claude Passeron. *Reproduction in Education, Society and Culture.* Translated by Richard Nice. London: Sage, 1990.

Brubaker, Pamela K. "Making Women and Children Matter: A Feminist Theological Ethic Confronts Welfare Policy." In *Welfare Policy,* ed. Bounds et al., 25–46.

Children's Defense Fund Action Council. *What You Need to Know and Do to Truly Leave No Child Behind: An Action Guide.* Washington D. C.: Children's Defense Fund, 2003

Chin, Elizabeth. *Purchasing Power: Black Kids and American Consumer Culture.* Minneapolis: University of Minnesota Press, 2001.

Collins, Randall. "Women and the Production of Status Cultures." In *Cultivating Differences: Symbolic Boundaries and the Making of Inequality,* ed. Michele Lamont and Marcel Fournier, 213–31. Chicago and London: University of Chicago Press, 1992.

Cook, Daniel Thomas. "The Other 'Child Study': Figuring Children as Consumers in Market Research, 1910s–1990s." *The Sociological Quarterly* 41, no. 3 (2000): 487–507.

____. "The Rise of 'the Toddler' as Subject and as Merchandising Category in the 1930's." In *New Forms of Consumption: Consumers, Culture, and Commodification,* ed. Mark Gottdiener, 111–29. Boulder, Colo. and New York: Rowman and Littlefield, 2000.

Couture, Pamela D. *Seeing Children, Seeing God: A Practical Theology of Children and Poverty.* Nashville: Abingdon Press, 2000.

Del Vecchio, Gene. *Creating Ever-Cool: A Marketer's Guide to a Kid's Heart.* Gretna, Ill.: Pelican Publishing Company, 1997.

Douglas-Hall, Ayana, and Heather Koball. *Low-Income Children in the United States (2004).* National Center for Children in Poverty, Columbia University Mailman School of Public Health, 2004. Accessed 8/27/04 2004. Fact Sheet. Available from www.nccp.org.

Ellwood, Wayne. *The No-Nonsense Guide to Globalization.* London: New Internationalist Publications, 2001.

Fesperman, Dan, and Kate Shatzkin. "Taking a Stand, Losing the Farm." *Baltimore Sun,* March 1, 1999, Electronic Archives.

Foreman, Carol Tucker. *Statement of CFA's Carol Tucker Foreman on ConAgra Ground Beef Recall.* Consumer Federation of America, 2002. Accessed Feb. 26, 2004. Statement is available from http://www.consumerfed.org/ 071902conagra.html.

Foster, David, and Farrell Kramer. "Major U.S. Corporations Profit from Illegal Child Labor." *Los Angeles Times-Associated Press,* December 14, 1997.

Furnham, Adrian. "Children and Advertising: Politics and Research in Consumer Socialization." In *Children: Consumption, Advertising and Media,* ed. Flemming Hansen, Jeanette Rasmussen, Anne Martensen, and Birgitte Tufte, 125–148. Copenhagen: Copenhagen Business School Press, 2002.

Guber, Selina S. , and Jon Berry. *Marketing to and through Kids.* New York: McGraw-Hill, 1993.

Harvey, David. *The Condition of Postmodernity: An Enquiry into the Origins of Cultural Change.* Cambridge, Mass.: Blackwell, 1990.

_____. *Spaces of Capital: Toward a Critical Geography.* New York: Routledge, 2001.

Jameson, Fredric. "Postmodernism, or the Cultural Logic of Late Capitalism." *New Left Review* 146 (1984): 53–92.

Johns, Deborah Roedder. "Consumer Socialization of Children: A Retrospective Look at Twenty-Five Years of Research." In *Children: Consumption, Advertising and Media,* ed. Flemming Hansen, Jeanette Rasmussen, Anne Martensen, and Birgitte Tufte, 25–89. Copenhagen: Copenhagen Business School Press, 2002.

Kline, Stephen. *Out of the Garden: Toys, TV, and Children's Culture in the Age of Marketing.* New York and London: Verso, 1993.

McNeal, James U. "An Exploratory Study of the Consumer Behavior of Children." In *Dimensions of Consumer Behavior,* ed. James U. McNeal, 255–275. New York: Appleton-Century-Corfts, 1969.

_____. *Children as Consumers: Insights and Implications.* Lexington, Mass.; Toronto: Lexington Books, 1987.

_____. *Kids as Customers: A Handbook of Marketing to Children.* New York: Lexington Books, 1992.

_____. *The Kids Market: Myths and Realities.* Ithaca, N.Y.: Paramount Market Publishing, 1999.

Migoya, David. "Lawmakers Want Details of ConAgra Meat Recall." *Denver Post,* Friday, September 13, 2002.

Miller, Vincent J. *Consuming Religion: Christian Faith and Practice in a Consumer Culture.* New York and London: Continuum, 2004.

Paine, Whiton S. "Some Ethical Implications of Consumer Behavior: Principles When Kids Are Involved." In *Children: Consumption, Advertising and Media,* ed. Flemming Hansen, Jeanette Rasmussen, Anne Martensen, and Birgitte Tufte, 253–282. Copenhagen: Copenhagen Business School Press, 2002.

Postman, Neil. *The Disappearance of Childhood.* New York: Delacorte Press, 1982.

Seiter, Ellen. *Sold Separately: Children and Parents in Consumer Culture.* New Brunswick, N.J.: Rutgers University Press, 1995.

Sommerville, C. John. *The Rise and Fall of Childhood.* Vol. 140 Sage Library of Social Research. Beverly Hills, London, New Delhi: Sage Publications, 1982.

Stearns, Peter N. *Consumerism in World History: The Global Transformation of Desire.* London and New York: Routledge, 2001.

Stephens, Sharon. "Children and the Politics of Culture in "Late Capitalism." In *Children and the Politics of Culture,* ed. Sharon Stephens, 3–48. Princeton, N.J.: Princeton University Press, 1995.

Sutherland, Anne, and Beth Thompson. *Kidfluence: The Marketer's Guide to Understanding and Reaching Generation Y–Kids, Tweens, and Teens.* New York: McGraw Hill, 2003.

Ward, Scott, et al. *Children Learning to Buy: The Development of Consumer Information Processing Skills.* Cambridge, Mass.: Marketing Science Institute, 1975.

_____. *How Children Learn to Buy: The Development of Consumer Information-Processing Skills.* Beverly Hills Calif.: Sage Publications, 1977

Zelizer, Viviana A. *Pricing the Priceless Child: The Changing Social Value of Children.* Princeton, N.J.: Princeton University Press, 1985.

CHAPTER FOUR

What Child Is This?

Religious Ambivalence toward Children

When Katie, her mother, and her two siblings moved into their neighborhood last year, one of the first things they did was to find a church that "has good programs for kids," as Katie's mother puts it. St. Bartholomew's Episcopal Church (not its real name) has a well-equipped nursery where Katie's baby sister can experience safe and loving nurture, and childcare is readily available at most church events. Katie participates in the Sunday school, and on Wednesday afternoons she rehearses with the children's choir known as the Sonbeam Choir. Katie's mom appreciates the supportive parenting group that meets twice a month and feels that her children get "exposed to good values and have a chance to learn about God" there. She also enjoys the fact that she can get a little break from the constant demands of single parenting, because her children enjoy being part of the church's many activities and generally experience St. Bart's as a welcoming environment.

One Sunday as Katie and her mother entered the sanctuary, they noticed a carefully hand-lettered sign on the inner door that read, "Welcome Families. Parents: Please Control Your Children During Worship. Especially in times of silent prayer, as worshipers seek the Spirit's inbreaking, restless children disrupt. Please remove unruly children to the crying room located outside the narthex. Thank you." The sign

117

appeared a couple of weeks after the financially driven layoff of the congregation's part-time Christian educator, a woman with many years of experience as a professional Christian educator. She had been a major advocate for children in the congregation.

The Church's Ambivalence

Upon seeing the sign, Katie (as a new reader who took the time to sound out each word it contained) asked her mother, "What do they mean about controlling me so the Spirit can 'inbreak'?" At the age of six years, Katie grasps that there is something incommensurate about these two ideas of control and the expectation of the Spirit's presence. She might well have asked in addition about what was intended by the juxtaposition of the idea that families are welcome but that parents should "control" their children and "remove unruly" ones. Like Katie, I find it very difficult to know which of the meanings to follow in this highly ambivalent religious message about children.

Ambivalence Defined

Since Sigmund Freud, psychologists have used the term *ambivalence* to describe the human process of being divided in mind and affect–of thinking and feeling in more than one way at the same time, an experience of being equally compelled in two (or more) different directions. On the one hand, ambivalence is a normal part of human life. It not unusual, nor is it necessarily bad, that persons hold divided feelings and thoughts about various matters.

Last Christmas, for example, I wistfully realized–only after we were putting away the tree decorations and our international collection of crèches, marking the end of the season–that my son Micah no longer referred to the parents of Jesus as "Mary and Jofess." Now he speaks of Mary and Joseph as most other English speakers around him do. Next year, when we set out the crèches and he delights in placing each figure in its space to tell the nativity story, Micah will do so using "grown up words." I revel in the development of his capacities, including those of language and articulation that allow him to distinguish this baby-speech form of pronouncing the name Joseph from its "proper" pronunciation. But I acknowledge a measure of grief as well. I have loved hearing about "Mary and Jofess" from him these few early years of his life, and the change in his language signals the passing of a time in both of our lives that I leave behind only with considerable reluctance. Such is my ambivalence about the growing up of my children, which, put positively, speaks to both the joy I have taken in their infancy years and my deep pleasure in seeing them grow.

On the other hand, though, psychologists tell us that ambivalence can also have problematically negative features. For example, we have heard of parents who take such joy in their children's early years that they have trouble allowing them to grow up. They erect barriers to their development that harmfully infantalize them. Or, persons experiencing ambivalence about a career choice may inadvertently sabotage their own education or experience a kind of vocational paralysis that prevents them from using their gifts and making their contributions in the world of work. Freud asserted long ago that a problematic ambivalence that goes unresolved leads to neurosis or to the unhealthy enactment of symptoms that stand in the way of full and healthy well-being.

What could be a greater expression of cultural ambivalence than North American consumerist society's attitudes toward children? Simultaneously, they adulate children as the key to corporate profits, and despise children when they fail to fit into market agendas or when their needs and experiences press our collective interests in the direction of social goals and norms that conflict with those of the market. The economic and social patterns shaping childhood and children's lives today clearly constitute an example of a deep ambivalence toward children in North American culture. Society appears to support and affirm children on the one hand with material excess, while on the other hand ignoring and even doing harm through neglect of their basic needs.

Children as Innocents and Devils

The market's ambivalence toward children becomes problematically reproduced in contemporary religious conversations (and Christian theology) about childhood, as children are simultaneously portrayed as "innocents" and "devils." As church historian Janet Nelson[1] so aptly states, "The history of Christian, and ecclesiastical, ideas and images of childhood is shot through with ambiguity. Children have been represented as innocent, hence peculiarly apt vessels for the Spirit; they have been seen as weak, hence peculiarly susceptible to sin and diabolical temptation."

In this chapter I explore the reproduction of cultural ambivalence toward children in contemporary Christian religious reflections by highlighting two contrasting voices in religious conversations about children. One comes from academic scholars of theology and religion who use psychological insights to critique Christian theology and the church. In these perspectives, by and large, children appear as innocent victims of an abusive Christian theology and church. A second perspective comes from the evangelical right's religiously oriented parent education resources, in which children appear as willful, wild, and oriented toward sin unless brought under control by parents whose restraining parenting allows the children to become good.

This polarized religious dialogue about childhood in the United States contributes to a confusing theology and to distortions in social and ecclesial practices with children. For that reason, it is important to examine the conversation more closely. Bonnie Miller-McLemore takes up a similar issue in her recent work.[2] She looks, in particular, at the influence of Alice Miller's[3] thought on academic critiques of theology's contributions to child abuse and offers the self-psychology of Heinz Kohut and the object relations thinking of D. W. Winnecott as helpful psychological correctives. Alongside she places theological correctives retrieved from Schleiermacher and Calvin, among others. My interests and analysis address the same bifurcation into opposing voices with which Miller-McLemore is concerned but come from somewhat different directions.

Does Church Replicate Consumerism?

I am concerned with the way such a split in contemporary conversations on childhood in the United States in effect recreates within religion the widespread ambivalence toward children that is so characteristic of the empire of consumer capitalism. I want to explore the ways this reproduction of ambivalence toward children distorts ecclesial practices with them. And in particular I am interested in the results of focusing so much on parenting and so little on children themselves. Such focus in the religious conversation on childhood reduces children to the features of their behavior in relation to adults, a reduction that quickly elides into a wide-scale affirmation of middle-class, Anglo parenting and behavioral norms as definitive of childhood.

In far too many mainline church contexts, faithfulness is conflated with being happy, cooperative, and nice.[4] In such an environment the act of nurturing or educating children into a Christian faith identity means little more than socializing them to be the same kinds of smiling, ever-happy little people who populate television commercials and cartoons. Concomitantly, sinfulness becomes equated with an individual child's unruly behavior in relation to adults, behavior that fails to fit socially accepted middle-class norms for a "good child." Such understandings, rather than offering a vision of childhood and of life together with children that challenges the market's utilitarian self-interested ambivalence, simply recreates it.

Reproducing Ambivalence toward Children in Contemporary Religious Discourse

Until quite recently, persons in search of theological resources about childhood were generally faced with disappointment. While religious educators consistently have focused considerable attention on children, much of that work has taken the form of ideas about how to work with children educationally at different age levels to nurture their faith, rather than offering a sustained conversation about the theological meanings of childhood. Meanwhile, throughout the centuries, other Christian theologians have paid relatively little attention to children, in part because the notion of childhood as a particular form of human life separate from infancy and adulthood is a modern idea.[5]

Even when theologians wrote about children, they usually did so in the form of attention to another issue. For example, several theologians–including Augustine and Calvin–use the situation of unbaptized infants as a sort of case study for working out their soteriology, the doctrine of divine salvation of human persons. That situation has changed considerably in the past decade as a number of scholars have sought through historical retrieval and contemporary constructive theology to focus on the theological significance of childhood. A key part of this theological work on children consists in feminist critical writings implicating Christian theology in the abuse of children. While these critiques of Christianity's complicity in child abuse comprise only a partial perspective within the contemporary religious conversations about childhood, they are also the most dominant voice within academic religious discourse on the subject of children. They tend to be "child-centered" in their focus, offering a view of children as innocent victims and distortions in Christian theology as the problem.

At the same time that the academy raises up voices critical of Christian theology's complicity with child maltreatment, a contrasting voice identified with the evangelical religious and political right represents a diverse collection of groups who have successfully coalesced around a purported "pro-family" stance. This side of the conversation takes place in the less rarified arena of popular culture through radio talk shows and Internet Web sites, parent education programs, and popular literature. Here the focus of critique turns to the evils of popular culture, parents' lack of adequate religious piety, and, most importantly, the problematic "nature" of children as manifestations of flawed and fallen humanity.

These two voices in the contemporary Christian religious conversations about childhood differ significantly in how they understand the issues and where they see the fault lines of problems. At the same time, however, the two depend upon each other, and in their mutuality end up reproducing a kind of ambivalence toward children that mirrors the ambivalence of the market. I therefore will examine each of these voices in turn.

Feminist Theologians from the Academy Critiquing Christian Theology

Academic feminist discussions of children as victims of violence and of a violent theology did not originate in concerns with children but emerged out of an earlier set of critiques about Christian theology's complicity in violence against women. In the 1980s a wave of feminist scholarship relating the battered women's and rape crisis movements to Christian theology began to lift up the possibility that such theologies could be liberatory for women who were victims of violence. In that effort, though, feminist theologians also began a thoroughgoing critique of uses of Christian theology to support and condone violence against women. By the early 1990s these scholars were joined by others (some feminists, others simply persons building on the insights of feminist analysis) who pushed the critique into the arena of child maltreatment.[6]

Atonement and Abuse

Joanne Carlson Brown and Rebecca Parker's groundbreaking article, "For God So Loved the World?" raised the issue of whether the Christian doctrine of the atonement legitimates child abuse.[7] Following Brown and Parker, Rita Nakashima Brock's *Journeys by Heart* focused both upon classic Christian views of original sin and upon the doctrine of atonement, calling the latter "cosmic child abuse."[8] Brock uses Alice Miller's view[9] that all punishment damages children because it requires them to submerge their own true feelings to gain the approval of the adults upon whom they depend. On this basis Brock argues against parental discipline and its religious legitimation.

Unfortunately, because her interest is in a feminist critique of Christian tradition rather than practical life with children per se, Brock tends to lump together all forms of parental discipline. She sees these as a set of methods for adult control of the child that find their justification in Christian doctrines requiring submission to physical or psychological pain. Brock sees a theological justification for child abuse in classical appropriations of Christianity's central symbol of the crucified Son of God, which she counters with a process theology perspective on the atonement involving an interdependent and mutual God.[10] Such views find an echo in Lisa Isherwood's introduction to a 1996 issue of *Feminist Theology*. She states the issue in personal terms:

> It has always struck me as rather unhealthy that we have a symbol of abuse at the centre of Christianity, and that we are meant to glory in the love of a God who would torture and kill his son in order to overcome his own anger at the world...My grandmother, who was not a theologian, would not allow a crucifix anywhere near her or her children as she considered it gave them the wrong idea of how life should be. It also shook her, otherwise considerable, faith in God.[11]

Brock and Parker later continue their critique in an autobiographical mode, in which they argue through the stories from their personal experiences with childhood abuse that

Western Christianity claims we are saved by the execution, that violence and terror reveal the grace of God. This claim isolates Jesus, as violence isolates its victims...Jesus' death was not unique. The torture inflicted on Jesus had been visited on many. It continues in the world, masked by the words "virtuous suffering" and "self-sacrificing love."[12]

Instead, they assert, the presence of God "endures through violence...The power of life is strong. Salvation is sometimes possible."[13] The constructive edge of this critical work, then, occurs as writers such as Brock and Parker move to claim the life-giving and violence-resisting elements of Christianity.

Child Abuse in the Perspective of Other Disciplines

These writings represent some feminist scholarship connecting Christian theology and child abuse that focuses on specific theological doctrines. Other scholars extend these feminist arguments into their own disciplines, heightening the connection between Christianity and child maltreatment. One example comes from historian Philip Greven's *Spare the Child: The Religious Roots of Punishment and the Psychological Impact of Physical Abuse.* Greven traced links between historical American theological perspectives on children and abusive childrearing practices in the United States. He suggests that theological ideas about children as innately sinful and in need of correction that will lead them to salvation may actually lead to theologically justified child abuse.[14] In recent years, the extensiveness of clergy abuse of children has surfaced, particularly within the Roman Catholic Church. Feminist theologians like Mary Hunt have responded with critical analysis of the connections between mandatory celibacy in a hierarchical ordering and the exclusion of women from the priesthood. She sees these two church policies as setting the context for abuse.[15] Others bring feminist insights to bear on pastoral care strategies for the support and healing of victims. An entire issue of *Religious Education* (vol. 89, no. 4, Fall 1994), a major academic journal for the field of religious education in North America, was devoted to the theme of "religious education and child abuse."

Pastoral theologian Donald Capps gave a critique of theological legitimations for the physical and emotional abuse of children beginning with an analysis of Augustine's theology. Capps reads Augustine's theology through his autobiographical and biographical stories of being beaten as a child, eventuating in the crushing of his spirit. The negativity in Augustine's understandings of childhood and human nature in general thus stem from his own experiences as a victim of abuse, which in turn replicates this abuse among other children. Capps claims that religion and child abuse are "perfect together," as "there are certain religious ideas that have the effect of legitimating or normalizing the dissociative process. These are ideas that contribute directly to the tendency of adults to view childhood traumas as detached and neutralized observers."[16] For Capps, shame is at the center of the hidden suffering of children. Well-intentioned adults bring about shame as they crush the spirits of children with religiously legitimated, abusive childrearing practices.

Capps is one among many whose analysis relies heavily on the perspectives of psychiatrist Alice Miller on abusive parenting practices. Miller's now well-known theory focuses upon the denial and repression of children's needs by adult caregivers, leading to the development of a "false (narcissistic) self" by the child. Miller also discusses the justification of violence against children by the religiously undergirded notion that such practices are "for the child's own good." Her work thus lends itself well to Christian theologians' internal critique of Christianity's complicity in abuse. Such critique begins with an understanding of parental discipline as organized around breaking the will of a child, an action that stands in opposition to the real needs of a child who is pictured as innocent and vulnerable. The assertion of childhood innocence and vulnerability constitutes a corrective move to what Miller (and the academic theologians who follow her view) sees as a harmful overemphasis upon childhood's innate sinfulness. References to child abuse as a "betrayal of innocence" follow from the use of Miller as a primary theoretical resource.[17]

Brock's essay, "Ending Innocence and Nurturing Willfulness," offers an interesting departure from the use of Alice Miller's assertion of children as innocent, which funds so much of this theological work. Brock argues that claims of innocence actually disempower women and children in the face of abuse, as they suggest that the main rationale for justice is the victim's innocence rather than the dehumanizing of both the abused and the abuser.[18] Similarly, Bonnie Miller-McLemore views modernity's construction of children as innocents as ultimately problematic because it deprives them of agency.[19] Many thinkers from outside the discipline of theology as well raise the problematic issues accompanying idealization of childhood innocence. Thus we appear to be situated on the back swing of the pendulum on its corrective return from several years of focus on children's innocence.

These are only some of the many critical works constituting a strong, even dominant, voice in contemporary religious conversations on childhood. All these feminist theological critiques hold in common an analysis of unjust power relations legitimated by religious notions of authority and the subordination of women and children on the basis of religiously sanctioned hierarchies. Many, but not all, of them put forward a notion of childhood innocence in their discussions of abused children, alongside an understanding that abuse constitutes a loss of innocence.

Such feminist theological critiques perform a valuable service to those of us in the Christian community concerned about children: exposing the potential and actual links between some previously unexamined theological perspectives and the unjust treatment of children, they invite us to reform, reshape, and reimagine theology. Some offer concrete resources, such as feminist hermeneutics, that allow for a reinterpretation of biblical texts that have been used to sanction the abuse of children, or the retrieval of elements of Christian theology that engage faith as a resource for coping with and offering healing from abuse. Some create liturgical or educational resources as well.

Practical Issues Open to Question

Still, many parents continue to question whether the church is a safe place for children (physically and emotionally). Wrestling with their own childhood experiences of being silenced or stifled, many adults bear memories and associations that connect church with some dehumanizing experience of being disregarded, disrespected, or otherwise made to feel "wrong." Their own childhood memories, alongside their observations of children in the church today engender a situation that is short of the overt abuse critiqued by academic feminist theologians, yet which lies at the heart of their concern that children are being harmed by the church.

Such experiences of harm often happen through the unknowing actions and words of well-meaning adults toward children in the church, actions and words rendered no less powerful in their negative associations by the lack of intention behind them. For example, Devon, one of the five-year-old twins our Christian educator networking group hears about when we meet at the Resource Center, expresses his dislike of church every week. Unlike his twin sister Dana, who readily participates in any and all opportunities there, Devon complains of being bored. He expresses his boredom in restless energy and constant motion as he darts from one briefly held object of attention to another. Devon's behavioral portfolio falls outside the range of acceptable behaviors for children in his congregation, and many people implicitly communicate that to him with disapproving glances or not-so-subtle comments like, "Devon, your sister is being so nice and quiet. Maybe you could join her. Shhh!"

Devon gets the message that he can only be expressive in very circumscribed ways in the church. It is a "chicken and egg" question to ask whether his discontent and acting out lead to, or are the result of, the implicit and explicit criticism and silencing Devon experiences in the church. In either event, what academic feminist theologians rightly lift up in their critiques of Christian churches is that the well-being of children like Devon suffers when one of the main messages received in church is that they are unacceptable.

The Importance—and Limitation—of Critiquing
Christianity's Complicity with Child Abuse

I know firsthand the truth of the connections between violence against children and its biblical and theological legitimations through my experiences as a social worker in an Atlanta children's hospital. There, I was called upon almost every night to assess whether or not a child's bruised skin and broken bones could have been caused by adult abuse or neglect. One's belief in the coherence and reasonability of Christianity is seriously tested when faith becomes the justification for child abuse. I vividly recall the father of a five-month-old baby with skull fractures saying, "I follow the law of God, not the law of men [sic]. The Lord demands that children obey their parents. This child has to learn to listen to me when I tell him to hush up. If he doesn't, he gets punished, just like we do if we don't listen to God's commands."

Responding to Theological Support of Abuse

Clearly, the child-centered critique of Christian theology's potential collaboration with abuse strikes a chord of truth when a father can legitimate the abuse of his infant son through it. As someone who has worked in the area of child protection, feminist theological analysis has been crucial to my ability to keep doing this wrenching work. Such close experiences of religiously legitimated violence against vulnerable children as those I had in the children's hospital threatened my faith and Christian identity. My knowledge that at least *some* theologians *critiqued* the use of Christian faith to justify abuse made it possible for me to continue identifying myself as a Christian in the face of such horror. The feminist theological critique of Christianity's complicity with abuse has been crucial in mobilizing faith communities to respond with ministries of advocacy, justice, and compassion to violence against women and children.

These responses include the annual observance of Children's Sabbath initiated by the Children's Defense Fund and practiced in congregations across the country, attention to the needs of homeless children, and the development by congregations of guidelines and policies to prevent child maltreatment in the church and its childcare or education programs. This critique has raised awareness in many sectors of the church about the unique vulnerabilities of children. The critique is a response to theological perspectives that overemphasize divine judgment and wrath, human sinfulness, and hierarchical valuing of persons in relation to a wholly transcendent/other God.

Over against these views, feminist theological critiques stress divine grace, human life as graced, and the abandonment of hierarchy expressed in the foregrounding of divine immanence or in social doctrines of the Trinity. Feminist theologians, therefore, tend to focus on children's innocence and their more dependent or needy status as grounds for a special ethical claim to care and protection. Still, the main stress in many of these works remains on the critique of religious institutions and theology for their abusive and harmful propensities in relation to children.

The Need for Positive Theology and Practices

I increasingly have become aware that a huge gap exists between the contributions made by this valuable critical work in Christian theology and the positive, constructive theological resources available to the church for grounding its everyday practices with children. One can only go so far in developing coherent, child-affirming practices and thought about children out of the critique of Christian theology's potential to harm children. The constructive turn to affirming what is generous and life-giving in Christian tradition, while present in some feminist theological work on children, is scant and often comes as an afterthought. There are notable exceptions to this lack, welcome voices that move the feminist theological conversation on childhood into a new and more constructive space.

Pamela Couture's work on women's and children's poverty is an excellent example of this more constructive voice in feminist theology.[20] Couture focuses on the constructive retrieval of elements in her own Methodist theological heritage that can support practices of economic justice with poor women and children. She also analyzes the co-occurrence of material poverty with what she terms "the poverty of tenuous connections," moving toward strategies of care for poor children that can transform the church along with society and culture.

Despite such exceptions, the main emphasis in feminist theological work on children remains on the critique of Christian theology's complicity with child abuse. In fact, some theologians and historians make their critical points so strongly as to suggest to Christian educators, pastors, teachers, and parents that Christian theology *inevitably and necessarily* leads to child abuse. These perspectives have in common a view of children as innocent victims with unmet needs. Such perspectives do not allow for a more complex and nuanced notion of childhood and can, therefore, contribute to their being dismissed as unrealistic idealism by parents faced with not-always-angelic children. Some of these critical theologians lump every parental action to guide or discipline a child's behaviors under the same rubric of adult oppressive control. Children are innocent; disciplining adults are oppressive. Sharing and egalitarian decision-making are good; parental decisions against the will of their children are authoritarian. End of story.

But most parents and other adults involved with children day to day cannot view their children in such simple terms. For many of these scholars, claims about the innocence of children and the negative view of authority are basic and necessary to their critique of theology. This means their notions of childhood can, at best, be held only partially and lightly by persons of faith who understand children and parenting in a more multifaceted way, or who view the historically constructed ideal of childhood innocence as problematic.[21]

In addition to the problem of a too-simple notion of childhood, these perspectives linking Christian theology to child abuse present another problem. They appear to assume a direct and necessary connection between a particular Christian belief such as atonement and a particular practice or action, such as child abuse. On the one hand, thinking and acting do relate to each other, so that critical analysis of the connections between Christian beliefs and actions such as atonement theology and child abuse is a valid line of inquiry. I have made such arguments myself and understand such theological work as central to the renewal and reconstruction of more liberatory Christian theology. At the same time, though, as I have argued in the opening chapter of this work, the relationship between beliefs and actions is much more complex and multidimensional. Multiple factors are at work in the relationship between a religious idea and a particular practice or action. More attention to the larger ethos or habitus within which beliefs and practices gain meaningful relationship is needed, particularly the contemporary habitus of market culture. In the meantime, in the habitus of market culture, the posing of children as innocent victims of violent theology constitutes one side in the ambivalent and dualistic religious construction of children as either innocents or devils.

Critiquing Children: Popular Christian-based Child-rearing Manuals

One could argue, of course, that few people in Christian congregations across the United States even have awareness of the feminist critique of Christian theology, which, for the most part, takes place in academic circles between feminist scholars or those who rely on feminist insights for their arguments. Another significant voice in contemporary religious conversations about children, though, operates more at the level of popular culture. Many people–particularly parents–involved with children are aware of this voice.

Obedience and Discipline

This voice speaks through various faith-oriented parenting manuals, magazines, radio programs, Internet Web pages, and parent education programs. These media outlets are enjoying tremendous popularity as the last of the "Baby Boomers" become parents. Some of these manuals and programs explicitly claim a Christian perspective, such as James

Dobson's popular "Focus on the Family" series. Others, such as the "Character First!" program that many schools and city governments use, employ the more neutral language of parenting/educating to nurture spirituality and good values. Their connection to Christian beliefs and practices is more implicit.[22] While voices from the academy critique Christian theology, the voices expressed through Christian parenting manuals give carte blanche acceptance to their particular fundamentalist or evangelical version of Christian theology and concentrate their critique on children, their parents, and the culture, including feminism and the women's movement. From this perspective children are prime exemplars of the universal human tendency toward "willful defiance" rooted in the original sin of humanity.[23]

In these Christian evangelical and fundamentalist[24] portrayals of childhood, children are highly unlikely to appear as innocent victims whose needs have not been honored. Instead, they are sinful, willful young tyrants whose true need is for parental constraint in order that these children might be shaped into faithful and good persons. The programs and books place a strong emphasis on obedience as a key value, with orderliness winning out over spontaneity. Discipline becomes the antidote to a permissiveness linked to later bad behavior or even pathology. Thus the emphasis in this material frequently falls upon parental control and authority, discipline, and the importance of constraining the child for her/his own good, in the face of a selfish rebellion against human authority that mirrors the ultimate human rebellion against God.

The Divine Order

This parallel between the authority of a parent over a child and that of God over humanity becomes the rationale for a mode of childrearing understood as divinely ordained.[25] In fact, hierarchically ordered relationships of authority and obedience constitute the central and defining theme in virtually all the "Religious Right" writers I have encountered. They reflect a worldview predicated on the notion of natural design, the idea that harmonious relations will exist when persons live according to the order God naturally designed for them. This order is, of course, a patriarchal order.

For example, Focus on the Family–Dobson's organization–includes radio broadcasts, counseling services, and parenting curriculum among other elements. It has a Web site on which parents can find aids for bringing up their children in faith, throughout which the parallel between divine/human relations and parent/child relations finds emphasis. One such aid available over the Internet is called, "Calling Godly Parents." It begins, "When it comes to parenting, the Father desires that we mirror Him. So we should always have the 'spiritual Windex' handy to keep the reflection clear. Our kids should see the true and living God directly through us."[26] Through such accessible (though trite) language, Dobson and his organization consistently put forward a specific form of family organization as divinely ordained. Using language evocative of the common identification of some women as "full-time mothers," they go on to say, "God employs parents full-time to do the work of turning a sinful generation into a godly seed."[27]

Stormie Omartian is another writer of conservative Christian devotional books and Christian parenting resources. She places a heavy mantle of responsibility onto parents in ensuring obedience as a reflection of the divine order. Her interpretation of Ephesians 6:1–3 offers one example. "If our children disobey this command of the Lord, they could not only be cut off from all God has for them; but their lives could be cut short as well...The fact that we can affect the length and quality of our children's lives is reason enough to pray, instruct, and discipline them."[28] She goes on to say that children not taught to obey their parents become rebellious, and, "Rebellion is actually pride put into action...The Bible says 'rebellion is as the sin of witchcraft' (1 Sam. 15:23) because its ultimate end is opposition to God."[29] Parents can prevent a child from falling into opposition to God. To do so they must use parental restraint of childhood's rebellious tendencies. They accomplish this through discipline and enforcement of a divinely established structure of authority (the patriarchal family).

Dobson speaks in a similar way but uses the more neutral-sounding language of psychology. He places at parents' feet the responsibility for preventing everything from low grades and drug abuse to homosexuality, as he writes "prehomosexual [sic] boys are sometimes the victims of their parents' unhappy marriages."[30] The solution to that problem in Dobson's view, of course, is a "properly ordered" marriage in which men are providers, leaders, protectors, and spiritual directors of the home, and women play a supporting, nurturing role.[31] Dobson is highly critical of "secular and liberal parenting experts" who assert the basic goodness of the child:

> I wish that Gordon's[32] assessment of human nature were accurate. But again, it contradicts Scriptural understandings. Jeremiah wrote, "The heart is deceitful above all things, and desperately wicked: who can know it? (Jer. 17:9 KJV)...greed, lust, and selfishness have characterized us all. Is this nature also evident in children? King David thought so, for he confessed, "in sin did my mother conceive me" (Ps. 51:5 KJV)...My entire book, you see, is a product of the biblical orientation to human nature. We are not typically kind and loving and generous and yielded to God. Our tendency is toward selfishness and

stubbornness and sin. We are all, in effect, "strong-willed children" as we stand before God.[33]

According to Dobson and others, part of the work of parents is "training" children to submit to the will of God. Such submission is necessarily contrary to the child's own human will, but parents have a responsibility to effect such training as part of ensuring the salvation of their children.[34]

As J. Richard Fugate explains his "system of child training,"

This system is divided into two distinct phases, controlling and teaching. The control phase is the establishment of the parents' right of rulership over the will of the child. When parents control their children, they have laid the necessary foundation for the fulfillment of the Biblical commandment for children to obey their parents. The teaching phase can be accomplished by parents who have first trained their child to obey...Col. 3:20a, 'Children, obey your parents in all things.'"[35]

At the same time that the Religious Right emphasizes childhood's special captivity to sin, some of their discourse on childhood retains a small place for the language of innocence and wonder. It tends to appear in relation to claims for the divine mandating of paternal responsibilities to protect children from the evils of secular culture. Dobson, for example, warns parents–especially fathers–that they bear the responsibility of protecting their children from the violence of the media and culture and especially from the supposed dangers of homosexuality, "of particular danger to your wide-eyed boys who have no idea what demoralization is planned for them."[36] The perspective on children Dobson and others put forth is one of innocence in relation to the divinely ordained role of fathers to protect their children, but sinfulness in relation to their own essential natures.

Critiquing the Religious Right

We can find much to quarrel with in these perspectives, not the least of which is their interpretation of Christian faith as properly promoting (rather than resisting and critiquing) unjust patriarchal hierarchies. These interpretations are grounded in a doctrinal view of God that ignores any contrary understandings of God from the tradition and scripture except this hierarchical rulership model. These conservative Christian theologies' "pro-family" stance elevates as sacred (and, more important to them, as "biblical") a particular form of family life that in most estimations is a relatively recent historical occurrence,[37] and which is a form strongly associated with women's occupation of circumscribed and subordinated roles. Stripped to its most basic theological points, the theological anthropology on which the Religious Right's view of childhood depends is an idea of all persons as inherently sinful and evil. But in this hierarchical understanding, children's dependency on adults for correction and restraint positions them in an especially problematic relationship with evil. Children's "willfulness" and tendency toward rebellion requires adult intervention. Apart from this intervention, parenting literature portrays children as destined for a life of "sexual promiscuity and drug abuse and academic difficulties." This is destined to happen unless parents, acting as God's agents, fulfill their Christian responsibility to train children into obedient submission.[38] Larry Christenson puts it most explicitly: "The Bible does not look upon a child as basically good! 'Behold, I was brought forth in iniquity, and in sin did my mother conceive me' (Ps. 51:5). The Bible does not view a child as one who essentially wants to do the wise and right thing."[39]

In drawing such an extreme picture of children as fundamentally (i.e., by nature) existing in opposition to God, popular Christian parenting manuals reproduce a culture of ambivalence toward children. In this culture children are desirable because God ordains and blesses family life, yet are simultaneously positioned as little devils, residing close to evil and against God, by virtue of their willfulness and rebelliousness. Their view results from an easy slide from the classic Christian theological idea of a sinful person as a self who is turned away from God or "misses the mark" to conservative Christianity's portrayal of a child whose behaviors bother adults as a sinful child. This understanding can quickly invite a too-narrow view of sin in terms of a child's individual behavior only and not as a feature of the human condition with individual and social-systemic dimensions.

Responding to Conservative Christian Parenting Writers from within Reformed Theology

Numerous outsiders to Christian theology critique and dismiss the perspectives on children and parenting found in the literature of the conservative Christian parenting movement. Their dismissals often constitute a full-scale dismissal of Christianity as a whole, as they equate the perspectives expressed by Dobson and others of the Religious Right with some "essence" of Christian theology they would reject. Some feminist theologians' critiques can sound similar to these anti-Christian perspectives, when they either engage a post-Christian theological vocabulary or focus on critiquing the tradition while offering little or no retrieval or constructive work within that tradition through which to foster an alternative Christian theological perspective on childhood.

Since I am not willing to identify the views of the conservative Christian parenting movement with the Christian faith I profess, it is important for me and other critics of that movement to make clear responses to those perspectives from within the language and thought-world of Christian theology. We must not (through our abdication of the argument) allow simplistic equations of Christian faith with the perspectives of the Religious Right in America to be the only voice on this issue. In my search for a "usable past" in Christian theology that can assist in addressing the problems in conservative Christian parenting writers' theological views of childhood, I find help in a figure who will be a surprising resource to some feminist thinkers: twentieth-century Swiss Reformed theologian, Karl Barth.

Karl Barth as a Theological Resource

As I mentioned in the opening chapter of this book, Barth remains a controversial figure among feminist theologians because, as one who was very much a person of his own time and cultural context, he presents a rather uneven track record with regard to women and their issues. He may also puzzle those concerned about a liberatory perspective on childhood because, upon first reading, Barth often appears to agree with and support the claims of evangelical parenting writers concerning the nature of children.

For example, Barth states quite directly, "When the command of God is heard in this sphere [i.e., in the relationship between children and parents], it means that the children are directed to assume a very definite attitude of subordination in relation to their parents."[40] He calls the parents "God's primary and natural representatives for the child"[41] and considers their parenting work to be a mission. Barth says children who resist submission to their parents are "necessarily resisting the grace of God."[42] Respect for parents "consists in the correspondence of their parenthood to the being and action of God."[43] Barth, like the conservative parenting movement writer Larry Christenson, considers parents to be *presbyters* or elders over their children. They are "charged to imitate God's action, and in so far as they do so in all honesty, the children are summoned to honour God by honouring their parents, by being content to accept this action of their parents."[44] When children honor their parents, they honor God. So far, Barth appears to be fully in league with the evangelical parenting manual writers who propose a hierarchy of theologically legitimated domination of children by their parents.

It is important to remember in interpreting Barth, however, that for him every human institution and invention is relativized by the sovereignty of God and God's revelation of grace through Jesus Christ. Generally, Barth sets out a particular claim, such as the above claim of parental authority over children grounded in the parents' representation of God to the child, after which he sets out the limitations and relativity of that claim. The limit statements are, in a sense, the "punch line" for Barth, the place where he stakes his theological claim. In this case, Barth goes on to note that human fatherhood gets its meaning and value, as well as any entitlement to respect due it, from God: "No human father, but God alone, is properly, truly and primarily Father."[45] *At the same time, Barth stresses, the only reason any of us—adult or child alike—may call God our Father/Parent, is that Jesus Christ is our brother.* That is, Barth has immediately relativized any adult claims to superiority over children based in the correspondence between human and divine parenthood by his reminder that it is only through God's partnership with humanity in Christ, by which Jesus is our brother, that we have a familial relationship with God who adopts us all as children. Parenting is not a higher status in itself then, but only happens as parents understand their children as ones whom Christ "wills to call his little brothers and sisters...And in practice this means that parents are challenged to see their children from the divine standpoint."[46]

It is not only children who are called upon to honor their parents, notes Barth, but also adults who remain the children of their parents as well; and to them the parents are still God's representatives. Of course, in terms of adults, parental honor takes different forms. (Barth makes a parallel argument about adolescents honoring parents.) Such honor is best reflected when we order and live life so as to "heed their counsel in a way which is deeper, finer, and more worthy than anything which has perhaps preceded."[47] Barth thereby recognizes that developmental change across the human lifespan reshapes what honoring one's parents means, but reaffirms that this command applies not merely to young children but to all ages of persons.[48] This represents an important departure from the theological position of evangelical and fundamentalist parenting manuals that only apply the command to honor parents to the young.

Parental authority, so heavily stressed by the Religious Right, likewise encounters its limit within Barth's theology, as the "sonship" or childhood of humanity that is revealed in Christ means that "parental authority can no longer in practice remain unchallenged." Barth explains that children's relationship to God is not merely mediated through the parents but involves the child's "free and individual decision." He cites as scriptural example for this the story of Jesus as a twelve-year-old child, going to the temple without his parents' knowledge and permission (Lk. 2:41–51). Barth queries,

> Is it possible to honour one's father and mother apart from and even against their will and knowledge? The answer of the child is amazing for it is undoubtedly an affirmative to this question: Yes the divine command first heard through the mediation of parental authority can have shape and force apart from and in contradiction to parental commands, and when this is so it is not

only permitted but required that man [sic] should obey it in this new form and force, and therefore honour father and mother without their knowledge and will.[49]

For Barth, the possibility of a child's direct encounter with divine command supersedes its mediation from parents to children. Human parental authority, while real and grounded for Barth in divine authority, is not absolute. To make it so, as evangelical parenting manuals often do, is to usurp for humans what rightly inheres only to God. As if anticipating the writings of Dobson and others, Barth wrote, "We have said that children must honor their parents as the natural and therefore the closest representatives of God. I should consider it unreasonable and dangerous to invert this proposition and to say that parents should feel and act toward their children as God's representatives."[50]

THEOLOGICAL RELIEF FOR PARENTS

It is a relief to think that my children's moral and spiritual lives do not totally depend upon my ability to adequately "represent God" to them. There are, after all, those days when I lose my temper and speak in anger or impatience words that hurt. Some times I seriously misunderstand the intentions of my sons' constant bids for my attention and react with irritation instead of careful listening and care. At times I am just plain wrong or self-absorbed or otherwise inadequate to the tasks of parenting. If my children's knowledge of the loving parenthood of God completely depended upon their experience of it through their relationship with me, we would all be lost. What Barth does is to flip on its head the Religious Right's claim that children should see their parents as representations of God. Barth asserts, instead, that parents should see their children as God sees all of God's children, namely as those taken into the family of God through our shared sibling status with Christ.

The role of parents as presbyters to their children is similarly relativized by the fact that "God alone is true Wisdom, and therefore the true Teacher, Guide and Educator."[51] Accordingly Barth qualifies his call for the subordination of children in terms of its basis in the responsibility parents have to their children. This responsibility is not primarily based upon the physical fact of procreation, but upon the parents' position in God's history. Parents, having been around longer and possessing the knowledge passed on by their parents, have responsibility to their children on the basis of their greater knowledge and experience.

Barth later extends this claim that places parents in the role of presbyters, or elders, in relation to their children. Barth contends that all Christians, whether married or single, with or without children, are called to be elders in this sense. "From a heavenly standpoint, they are indeed only older children,"[52] and therefore parents should look upon their children the way God looks upon them. Accordingly, the subjugation of children is relativized. It should not be in the manner of property, subjects, or servants, but of "apprentices, who are entrusted and subordinated to them in order that they might lead them into the way of life."[53] Parenting confers both honor and duty upon fathers and mothers. "Broadly speaking, the main essential in the parent-child relationship is that the parents are summoned to regard their children from the angle of the divine will, and to deal with them, to live for them and with them, accordingly."[54]

PARENTAL PERFECTION NOT EXPECTED

Such a high view of parenting might seem to imply an expectation of parental perfection by Barth. To the contrary, however, he limits the claim that parents must act as elders to their children. This limit comes from a recognition that adults may not always act in ways that make plain their mission to represent God, or may live in ways that fail to "elicit and justify the respect which the child owes to them."[55] In fact, Barth asks, Are there any parents who get it right all the time, amidst the vagaries and difficulties of life with their children? The answer is, No! On this point, Barth is quite realistic about the difficulties and foibles of parenting: "There are weak, foolish, self-seeking, flippant and tyrannical parents. Indeed, even the best parents have their limitations and failings."[56]

Like conservative religious parenting manuals, Barth does assert that the command to honor parents does not depend on the adequacy of parenting any more than it depends ultimately upon the works of a child's obedience. At the same time, he emphasizes that the fulfillment of "the Law" and human sanctification are found not in human works but in Christ. Barth thus levies a stinging critique against conservative Christian parenting writers who put parents in a position of ultimate control over the fate of their children. In fact, the task of human parents is limited to "offering children opportunities. [Parents] cannot even make their child healthy in body and soul, let alone happy or successful, or one who seeks and hears and pleases God, i.e., a Christian."[57] Contrary to the Religious Right's assertion that parents bear responsibility for their children's salvation, Barth holds that like grace, faith comes from God and not from parental interventions.[58]

Such concerns about a child's salvation may seem a bit cosmic and abstract in relation to the stresses and strains of everyday parenting. In fact, they show up in the anxieties parents have about their children's participation in the church or about behavior that falls within or outside the boundaries of what a particular church deems acceptably compatible with norms of Christian faith. For instance, in one of the churches in the Children in Congregations Project, parents of teenaged children described, in informal conversations, the pressures they feel to "have successful children." Said one father bluntly,

If your son is wild, it reflects poorly on you as a parent, like you aren't raising them properly. But the problem is that I realized a long time ago, like maybe when he was a toddler, that my ability to control this human being who is my son is extremely limited. I can guide; I can do my best, but at some point, I don't have much say in the decisions he makes or what happens with his life.

Another parent confessed that one of her greatest fears is that, after a lifelong involvement in the church, her college-bound daughter will not profess a Christian faith identity: "I will have failed totally as a parent and a Christian if my own children don't even belong to the church anymore." In response to such wrenching concerns, Barth makes clear that faith is a gift from God that is not under the control of parents to effect in their children and that parenting happens through the lives of human beings whose primary source of being "one-up" on their children is their greater life-experience and not their moral superiority or God-likeness.

SEPARATING HUMAN HARMONY AND THE KINGDOM

Conservative parenting literature that depends on a theological anthropology of human harmony resulting from living in a natural and divinely established political order of the family, also finds strong condemnation in Barth. He distinguishes between relationships in *human history* and the establishment of the *basileia* of God. Barth is quite clear in his refusal to interpret the New Testament epistles' household tables, texts about Jesus' relationship with his family (e.g., Lk. 14:26), and other texts calling for the subordination of children, as divine establishment of a natural order of human relations that will issue in harmony: "It is really not true that Jesus has come to bring peace on earth, i.e., to secure for human history and human relationships a harmonious continuation with the goal of a state of perfection. What is true is merely that in coming he has not destroyed this peace, nor prevented the continuation of human history and relationships."[59] This peace is a provisional peace, Barth asserts. He insists that the reign of Christ is not

> limited to a single form and shape, namely, to that in which we are bidden and enabled to live soberly, righteously, and godly in this present world. If such were the case, the result would be a domesticated churchmanship and Christianity and humanity which–far from knowing the reality of the peace which we Christians may have here and now–might be so comfortably settled in the present world and so busily and pleasantly occupied with its maintenance and amelioration that it could very well dispense with the kingdom and *eschaton,* honestly regarding it as no more than a theory.[60]

Such a statement evidences strong resistance to any tendencies to equate the reign of God with peaceful and harmonious human relations in the present, including those promoted by the Religious Right as evidence of a "natural" harmony between human living and the will of God for families.

The equation of godliness and harmony bring an unnecessary negative pressure onto families, especially those in cultural or socioeconomic contexts in which other norms prevail. For example, when Pastor Carol describes Jo-Jo and his family, I get the picture of a family that is a lot like the family of my childhood in some ways, although my family is European American and Jo-Jo's is a mixed race family of Mexican and African American heritage. As several recent studies of children, race, and class show, socioeconomic class may create more commonalities at times than race.[61] A fair amount of shouting, sometimes punctuated by unprintable expletives, is common to interpersonal interaction among Jo-Jo's family members. One neighbor told Pastor Carol, "They're loud, and sometimes they sound mean, but they're just being folks." The pastor speculates that one reason the family stays away from the church is their sense that they would not be judged a "Christian family" on the basis of standards of harmony that constitute the cultural measuring stick of such things among the more middle-class majority of the congregation.

Jo-Jo's family deals with real and sometimes serious financial insecurities, such as the lack of health insurance. The absence of overt expressions of harmony in their situation reflect, among other things, the nonharmonious circumstances of their lives—which are stress-filled and difficult—rather than necessarily signaling a lack of attunement with God. Mistaking social norms of harmony for religious norms of faithfulness is bound to leave many a family feeling religiously inadequate and incapable of belonging except as imposters. Like families in the Bible, real families of today sometimes shout, argue, and have conflicts. I draw the line at the point of physical violence and certainly recognize that verbal conflict that is destructive and dysfunctional can be a harmful form of violence in family life. Still, I think it is important to recognize the cultural situatedness of family styles and norms and to avoid judging as unfaithful that which may be the most honest and faithful response possible in a given situation. Barth obviously included experiences of dissonance within families alongside Christians' struggles with the ways of the world as an important part of his perspective on family life. He refused to associate harmony with godliness any more than he would automatically associate a state of comfort and ease with the practice of Christian faith.

Barth's most direct opposition to conservative religion's idealizing of the nuclear family occurs as he once again describes the limits of parental authority in terms of all true authority being God's:

It is said that parents must exercise authority over their children. This statement is true enough in itself. But it must not be taken to mean that in their dealings with them they will want to build up a kind of domestic hierarchy, dangling before them a traditional or invented picture of superiority and inferiority. For sooner or later children will always revolt either mildly or violently against this type of procedure...[T]rue parental authority is a wholly unspectacular, unintentional and hence unobtrusive manner of life and conduct...[that] cannot be exercised but only attested, namely, by those who themselves know and respect its divine basis, because ultimately only God Himself is and has authority.[62]

In other words, Barth insists at all points that any discussion of authority must have as its ultimate limit-condition the relativizing of human forms of authority by God.

Ultimately for Barth, the crux of every theological argument about children and their parents rests on two basic tenets:

1. a reference to the shared status of young and old before God
2. the meaning of parenting as that of viewing one's children from the perspective from which God sees them

In this vein, parenting constitutes not a status, but a form of service, comparable to other kinds of vocations to which Christians are called: "[E]verything depends on whether parents view their children from the divine angle and therefore as the children of God, and can thus regard their service to them as a direction toward God."[63]

What Barth helps us to recognize about conservative Christian parenting theology is its failure to grasp the "limit situations" within the Christian tradition that place boundaries upon, or sometimes constitute reversals of, its claims. Conservative Christian parenting theology is problematic not merely for its narrow and literal interpretation of scripture, but also for the ways it fails to engage the wider scope of Christian theology in relation to any singular claim it makes. Theologically, these conservative Christian parenting programs are extremely problematic in the ways they understand human personhood and childhood in relation to God.

The Popularity of Conservative Christian Parenting Programs

But if they are so problematic, then why are these conservative Christian parenting programs so popular? One reason that resources such as Focus on the Family and Character First! are so popular is that they provide parents and others caring for children with concrete and practical suggestions for life with children. Examples include how and why to pray with a three-year-old; how to teach a child respectful behaviors and good manners; or ways to teach children the spiritual significance of Christmas amidst a materialistic holiday culture, or the practice of certain virtues and values important in American civil society.[64] Furthermore, these programs and writers seem to recognize that life with children is difficult for adults, even and especially when they care deeply for children.

The Critical Academic Lack

Somewhat strangely, this notion remains largely absent from the critical academic perspectives surveyed above. Such perspectives often seem to imply, with their assertions of children as innocent victims, that exasperation with a child necessarily comes from some failing in the adult's ability to understand the child's true self and never from any co-occurring problem or failing on the part of the child. When my child screams, "Shut up!" along with some expletive, shoves his sister, and throws a plate to the floor and breaks it before he stomps out of the room, it may well be that I have failed to understand a true and valid need of his. This does not, however, rule out the possibility that he also "needs" adult direction and aid to change what is an inappropriately aggressive way to express himself. Because Dobson and his colleagues from the Religious Right acknowledge such difficulties by writing about them, their work is immensely popular with adults who deal with children in the real world.

The efforts of religious conservatives such as Dobson and others to address issues of childhood and parenting from within their perspective of the Christian faith has developed into a popular movement and a multi-billion dollar industry. Interestingly, though, some of the literature, if not the theology supporting it, now finds its way onto the shelves of mainline church libraries and in mainline and theologically liberal parents' homes. Bendroth contends that this crossover happened as a result of the vacuum left by mainline theology's inability to say anything directly about sex and theology. In this vacuum, she says, even the more rule-oriented take on sex and family life became a welcome alternative to "the randomness of mainline parenting."[65] Lots of parents can relate to that situation. We find ourselves caught in the frightening space of being responsible for the lives of children who come without operating instructions; sometimes it is very appealing to think that someone out there knows exactly what to do. Tapping into mainline nostalgia for its heyday in the 1950s when the general population's surge of two-parent households with children filled its Christian education classrooms and sanctuaries, the evangelical parenting movement crosses the boundaries between evangelical and mainline faith communities specifically around their shared concerns about parenting and children.

I am convinced I know part of the reason for the popularity of the evangelical Christian parenting movement in the United States, including its crossover into nonevangelical mainline Protestant congregations and families. Such popularity comes because these evangelicals have demonstrated the ability to bring a kind of theological thinking to bear on such practical and mundane concerns as a two year old throwing a no-holes-barred, all-out tantrum in a crowded grocery story. People overstressed by the demands of parenting, work, and negotiating the complexities of postmodern cultural life are hungry for help in making the connections between everyday life and the religious worldviews by which they make sense of and cope with their lives.

Many mainline families might be more at home with the more egalitarian perspectives on marriage and family life and the more theologically optimistic view of childhood issuing from the feminist strand of the religious conversation on children in the United States. And yet, at the same time, adults in mainline and progressive Christian communities are left with a void. This results from the absence of a clear-cut constructive framework from feminist critiques. These critiques stress the abusive potential in Christian theology. They overly emphasize critique of religion and of religious communities with little regard for their role providing significant social support for families. They lack a clear embrace of Christian faith, and they fail to acknowledge the less-than-innocent realities of everyday life with children. Conservative parenting programs step in to fill the void, however inadequately.

The Evangelical Marketing Success

A second reason for the success of the evangelical parenting movement lies in its use of language and distribution methods familiar to a public schooled in consumer processes. The evangelicals make good use of contemporary media that render the movement widely and easily accessible in popular mass-market bookstores and over the Internet. An important aspect of this accessibility is the ability to render complex theological concepts into everyday language at a "common-public" reading level (variously reckoned at a fifth-to--sixth-grade level). This capacity parallels what many mainline congregations unreflectively understand themselves to be doing in religious education with children and children's sermons: taking complex ideas and simplifying them so that anyone can understand them. Mainline Protestant adults who might not be so inclined to buy into more conservative Christian theology and piety as a whole nevertheless find elements of such a popularly rendered theology useful when it comes to them in the form of parenting help.

A consumerist culture that encourages people to pick and choose between available options habituates people to isolate various theological beliefs from one another and choose among them without consideration for how these various components contribute to a larger framework or worldview. I am not suggesting here that any of us should take an "all or nothing" approach to Christian theology. I am simply pointing out what occurs when an adult accepts as valid and useful the idea from conservative Christian parenting theology that human relationships with other less powerful humans (such as children) are best modeled on the view of a kingly God relating to subordinate human subjects. When a mainline Protestant accepts that view, the rest of one's beliefs and practices will not remain unchanged and unaffected.

Consumer culture habituates persons to believe that the choices they make are independent and autonomous acts of consumption.[66] Applied to religious belief, such processes invite religious consumers to take in the stories of Jesus with children detached from their wider context in an anti-imperial counter-narrative. Or these processes encourage us to read the New Testament household tables and various other texts concerning the obedience and subordination of women and children as independent, transhistorical, and acontextual claims. We are somehow to separate these "biblical" claims from other scriptural claims focused upon Christ's inauguration of a radically egalitarian community in which the gifts of each one are used for the common good and status distinctions are abolished (cf. Gal. 3:28; 1 Cor. 12).

Shared Theological Perspectives

Third, some theological perspectives on which these parenting programs depend have until quite recently shared a firmly established and welcome home in mainline Protestantism's embrace of neoorthodoxy in the mid-twentieth century. This would include a high view of scripture and revelation or the importance and centrality given to Jesus Christ among the persons of the Trinity, and an emphasis on the "otherness" of God in relation to humanity. Viewpoints stressing this set of theological interests, such as those posed by Dobson and other parenting experts from the Religious Right, therefore may not seem entirely strange to many mainliners, particularly in their more moderate evangelical expressions.[67] There exists some level of theological resonance between these differently oriented groups of Christian believers. This theological resonance operates alongside another point of resonance, namely a shared concern for how to relate Christian faith to everyday life with children. Such resonance contributes to a situation in which mainline faith communities may adopt theological perspectives and religious practices in relation to children that do not particularly fit with the rest of their theology and mission.

Class and Cultural Differences

Last, the disciplinary practices and rationales given in conservative Christian parenting manuals may appeal to those persons in mainline Christian communities who do not share the largely European American race and middle- or upper-middle-class perspectives reflected in much of the feminist theological work on childhood. Sociologists and clinicians concerned with offering "culturally competent care" give increasing attention to the different norms concerning child rearing and discipline among lower- and working-class families and within some communities of color, in comparison to middle-class Anglo norms. Recent studies, for example, suggest that some differences in the disciplinary approaches parents take with their children have been judged against middle-class Anglo standards as harsh, but would not be deemed so within the standards of some other communities. This is an extremely complex issue. Some child protection experts would argue for a firm standard for judging the mistreatment of a child that applies across all boundaries. Arguing that "a hurt child is a hurt child," some claim that racial-ethnic and class status cannot be used as a means of differentiating standards of treatment of children. In fact, some childcare experts from within communities of color label such efforts to factor in a community's different standards for discipline as a way of pathologizing their families.

At the same time, though, the *meanings* given to a particular disciplinary practice do vary across groups and communities. Norms emerging from middle-class Anglo cultural contexts in which individualism holds pride of place may give more room for a child to act in ways expressing her individuality with less attention to how those behaviors impact others. Among middle-class Anglo parents and their children, the skills of negotiating a racist or classist society "from below" or from the margins of society do not have to figure into disciplinary practices in the same ways they must among people of color or working- and lower-class communities. This allows for the kind of child-centered approaches informing much of the feminist theological work on child abuse.[68]

Communities of color often face challenges of socializing children into resiliency in the face of racist and classist society. Thus parents from these communities often hold different expectations about discipline and authority relationships between children and adults within the community in relation to the necessity to teach survival skills needed by children in their relationships with persons and systems outside the community. For example, sociologist Annette Lareau conducted an ethnographic study of how class and race impact childrearing practices. She reports on the frustrations of working-class and poor families when standards of behavior they considered appropriate (such as support for a son's engaging in a fistfight when insulted, or the use of physical punishment as a form of discipline with children) were denigrated.[69] The conservative Christian parenting movement, therefore, may well appeal to persons in mainline churches who do not relate to the middle-class and Anglo behavioral norms implicit in some academic theological notions of childhood and childrearing.

In sum, mainline Christian parents who are not at all convinced by fundamentalist and evangelical *religious* tenets may nevertheless find elements of these parenting programs attractive. This attraction comes as these mainline parents try to understand why their children behave in particularly problematic ways, or as they try to deal with the very real difficulties and struggles with children that are a normal but unpleasant aspect of parenting. At the same time, such parents undoubtedly would find it difficult to fully embrace a concept of their child as basically evil. Just as was the case with parents faced with academic feminism's theological assertions of childhood innocence, many mainline parents would certainly hold this evangelical view of childhood with considerable disease, if not outright ambivalence. The contemporary U.S. religious conversation concerning children, dominated by the polarized voices of academic feminism and the popular conservative Christian parenting movement, offers perspectives on childhood that seem quite difficult for individuals and congregations in mainline American Protestant contexts to fully embrace. This highly polarized conversation has the effect of recreating market culture ambivalence toward children, with its dualistic positioning of children as either innocents or devils.

Ambivalence Revisited

It is not my intention to force a false connection between feminist and other scholars in the academy concerned with theology and childhood and the writers of popular Christian parenting manuals, by naming them both as parties to the recreation of the wider consumer culture's ambivalence toward children. Obviously, these two groups have different agendas and engage different audiences. Nor do I mean to imply that only two parties are participating in the religious discourse about children in America. What I can assert, though, is that these two voices function as two of the more dominant voices in that conversation and that they inadvertently depend upon each other for their own positions. Both voices speak of the need to protect children—but have a vastly different perspective concerning from what children need protection. Pro-feminist academic critiques locate the danger in "poisonous pedagogy" of parental self-assertion at the expense of the needs of innocent children and in conservative religion's capacity to legitimate abuse. Conservative Christian critiques locate the dangers in liberal, postmodern culture's embrace of relativism including nontraditional family forms, feminism, and homosexuality, all of which fail to understand that a child's nature is not oriented toward the good, but rather toward defiance and rebellion associated with the powers of evil.

These two voices obviously have differing and sometimes even opposing theological interpretations of Christian faith and very different constructions of childhood, such that they easily constitute polarized perspectives. In a sense, they map the extremes in the religious conversations about childhood, each painting a particular "worst case scenario." To drive home their points, the two voices neglect the possibility that parents, culture, and theology have mixed capacities for acting in both constructive and destructive ways in relation to children. For instance, the feminist and feminist-influenced theologians I survey above are interested in critiquing religion while affirming children and, above all, honoring their needs. These academicians, however, almost never name any way for parents and communities to *appropriately* educate or shape children in their ways of dealing with and expressing their needs.[70] These thinkers seem to deny the possibility that there might be constructive, nonoppressive ways for adults to provide appropriate boundaries and limits that help children grow and address their needs.

Similarly, these theologians offer strong critiques of the abuses of religious communities–their oppressive positioning of women, the scandal of clergy sex abuse, and the various ways churches harmfully marginalize children. Yet some of these academic perspectives neglect the important function of Christian churches as institutions mediating social capital for families amid their decline in the society at large.[71] Congregations are not dichotomously problematic *or* wonderful; they are sites of both liberatory and oppressive dynamics for children and their families. Clearly, there is no place for clergy sex abuse, and positive elements in a congregation cannot offset this horrendous exploitation of children and misuse of power. In terms of the many other ways congregations may act to marginalize or exclude children, however, it is important to keep in mind a sense of balance. Within wider societal contexts of declining social capital, the relative importance of finding some religious-social supports for families may outweigh these more negative elements.[72]

In contrast, the other main voice in the contemporary discussions of childhood, popular religious parenting education, takes a largely negative view of children's needs as that which parents help constrain to make an otherwise bad child good. Religion provides the necessary support for this parental role. In the interests of affirming religion as the way to help children, parents and children are criticized as inadequate and faulty by nature, but never religion (or at least not "true"–conservative–Christian religion).

Neither of these voices addresses the possibility that for children to thrive, *both* deep respect for their needs *and* education by communities and parents are necessary. There is almost a sense in which children as children become incidental to the conversation, functioning instead as examples or props to make other, deeper points that go "beyond" the import of children. It would not be too great of a stretch, I think, to suggest that the religious conversation on childhood in the United States, polarized between these two major voices, inadvertently commodifies children. Children seem to operate within the discourse as objects for ideological battling, valued more for their "exchange value" in the argument than for themselves. Please note: I am *not* saying here that feminist theologians (a group in which I am included) or Christian parenting writers from the Religious Right are intentionally "using" children as mere commodities without any regard for the actual lives of children in the world.[73] I am saying that within the regime of consumerist culture in which discourse and practices with children are situated in North American, a conversation on children that both parties intend to be empowering and constructive for children inadvertently commodifies them. The conversation inadvertently transforms the children's role to that of ideological symbols for larger ideas that ultimately may have little to do with children and their welfare.

Like the constructions of childhood within market capitalism, children and childhood in contemporary religious discourse remain constructed around a lack–in their innocence and vulnerability children lack the capacity to defend themselves from powerful impositions of abusive theologies, or in their willful sinfulness they lack the capacity to act morally. A child is one defined in an over-determined way by the need for protection or the need for correction. As marketing creates desires in children and their caregivers for products that the market can then supply at a price, so the religious discourse on childhood in America involves a similar strange match between the problem and its solutions. This match then creates a multi-million-dollar industry in religious parenting literature and programs and contributes to an atmosphere of anxiety about the possibilities of nonpoisonous, liberatory pedagogies at home and church.

In the meantime, mainline Christian faith communities sit in the difficult position of waffling between the two available but polarized concepts of children as demons or angels, unable to adopt either one wholeheartedly, holding each ambivalently and temporarily. These congregations are filled with parents who would not subscribe to Dobson and company's overt ideology of child-control, but at the same time deal with the very real difficulties of how to help children develop appropriate limits and discipline. They know their children are not evil through and through. And yet they also would reject assertions that these same children are wholly innocent, just as they would not recognize themselves in reports of Christians who use their theology to legitimate child abuse. They are simply ordinary folks who come together week after week to practice a faith-oriented way of life amidst and through the joys and difficulties of family relationships variously configured in relation to religion.

Christian Educational Practices with Children: Equating Faith with Good Behavior

Mainline Protestant congregations get caught in the middle of these ambivalent portrayals of childhood. Many of the persons in these congregations are concerned about the care and nurture of children. They stand ready to appropriately critique elements of their faith group's theology that pose problems in relation to children and abuse. Problematically, however, mainline Christians have discovered that there is little material in critique alone for building a coherent and vital ministry to nurture their children into the practices of faith. What should they do after the critique? They look for better ways to nurture children in a faith that supports children and contributes to their thriving. Lacking alternative visions for what faithful education with children might look like, most mainline congregations turn to methods and practices into which they have been apprenticed by a lifetime of participation in consumer culture. They buy a curriculum for a program and offer it to children during a time when the rest of the congregation is otherwise engaged, usually in worship.

Curriculum Problems

Increasingly, these curricula generally are chosen from a large selection of available products on the basis of two main criteria: their ease of use for teachers and their appeal to media-savvy, entertainment-oriented generations of children. Many of these curricula, needing to cast the broadest possible theological net to be marketable, offer a theology that reduces Christianity to the "lowest common denominator" of moralisms and simple platitudes. Organized around the use of religion by families to socialize children into "good values" and good behavior, such educational processes over-identify children's faith in terms of the cult of the nice, happy, and cooperative child. These modes of religious education frequently include children's sermons developed around some moral lesson that is then reinforced in the Sunday school curriculum of the day.

We can put these congregational realities into the earlier social-psychological language of unresolved ambivalence, leading to neurosis that comes to be expressed in dysfunctional symptoms. I am saying that the ambivalence toward children being lived out in mainline congregations today evidences itself in a variety of distorted ecclesial practices. Not the least of these practices is that of *educating children into a kind of theology that most of their membership would not embrace for the adults in the congregation*: namely, a theology centered around simple moralisms and an ecclesiology that segregates persons based on age.

For example, a United Methodist congregation includes in its mission statement that "we endeavor to be a place of welcome and faith-learning for people of all ages, especially children." A theologically moderate to liberal congregation, this church preaches engagement with the world, resistance to structural forms of sin, and a meaning to the life of faith that goes beyond one's individual state of salvation. But this summer, it used a packaged curriculum for its vacation Bible school from a nondenominational publisher whose materials cross over into mainline congregational use.

The motto of this material is "The *Easy* VBS,"[74] which children's ministry planners at this congregation admit was the primary guiding force in their decision to use this material. The curriculum is organized around an excitement-adventure theme, with a particular point emphasized each day through a Bible verse and activities during VBS and at home. The daily "points" this year were: Jesus brings us hope; Jesus follows God's Word; Jesus gives us courage; Jesus saves us; Jesus gives us a reason to celebrate. The last of these concerns John 14:2 and the idea that Jesus prepares an eternal home in heaven for those who believe in him. Publicity materials about this curriculum call it easy and fun for everyone because it "requires fewer teachers...It's flexible... Minimum Prep Time!...Use your gifts!" The orientation behind this material, found in goal statements, the company's statement of faith, and interspersed throughout the material, is to bring children to a personal "relationship with Jesus."

Connecting Curriculum and Mission

I have no argument with teaching oriented toward assisting children (or adults for that matter) with making personal appropriations of biblical and theological concepts, although my hopes would be to broaden these beyond individual personalism to community engagement and social perspectives. The real problem with this vacation Bible school material in its use by this particular congregation is that there is little or nothing in the teaching and learning offered to children that matches the theological perspectives of that church at large. If the same kind of theological material oriented toward personal salvation and moralisms were offered to adults, it would be soundly rejected. Little in this material connects to the primary practices of faith into which this congregation seeks to invite and shape its members, such as service to persons in need and collective efforts to achieve structural change in systems that cause harm.

This material, instead, is directed toward an individual's personal sense of salvation and individual relationship with Jesus. Congregations who use such curriculum but seek to live out a theological identity oriented around a more socially engaged witness to the faith are educating children into a different theology and worldview than those around which the churches base their adult proclamation and ministries. Given the structural separation between children's educational ministries and the rest of congregational life in most mainline churches, such a huge discrepancy may well go unnoticed by almost everyone, including the pastor(s).

In short, mainline Protestant congregations suffer from a kind of "cultural neurosis." This neurosis has two causal factors–the shaping power of consumerist culture upon congregational practices, and the religious recreation of the wider culture's ambivalence toward children. The primary symptoms of this neurosis in relation to children include (1) a market-oriented ecclesiology and (2) an over-determination of childhood and children's faith in terms of their behavior in relation to adults.

The market-oriented ecclesiology seeks to satisfy the needs of individual niche groups. But the practical result of such efforts separates children and adults into what becomes in effect separate experiences of church. Determining faith in terms of behaviors in relation to adults leads to depoliticized and atheological ecclesial practices. These focus on religion as the means to socialize children into "good" (middle-class Anglo) behavior. I will explore each of these ecclesial practices with children in greater detail in the next two chapters, which focus on liturgical and educational practices in a feminist practical theology of childhood. The key point for now is to note the convergence between religious discourse and ecclesial practices with children in the United States, both of which fall captive to the commodifying, reductionistic processes of consumerism.

More Resources from Christian Tradition for a Feminist Practical Theology of Childhood

Ways are available to think about the religious meanings of childhood without slipping into the trap of inadvertently commodifying children and without limiting the conversation to the moral status of children. Although many theologians across the history of Christian thought offer resources for constructing a liberatory theology of childhood, one whose work I find particularly insightful is the twentieth-century Roman Catholic German theologian Karl Rahner. As the primary theological voice of Vatican II, Rahner's influence in Catholic Church circles is vast. Rahner has much to offer to Protestant Christians as well.

Karl Rahner's Recovery of Thomas Aquinas

As a theologian intent on recovering the insights of Thomas Aquinas from their neo-scholastic distortions, Rahner's theology includes a strong sense of the mystery of God and of all of human existence that Protestant theologians do not often evoke in their work. In Rahner's thought human capacities for self-transcendence make possible the experience of God who *is* transcendence itself. This ability to "be in touch" with the Divine through the human capacity for self-transcendence is basic to human nature. Thus Rahner's theological anthropology is one that affirms that all human beings—including children—have the capacity in human freedom to experience the divine self-communication.

While Rahner did not write extensively on children and childhood, he did write *particularly* on them.[75] That is, unlike so many theologians of his time and previous eras who only mention children as case examples to discuss other theological points, Rahner wrote an essay, included in volume 8 of his massive, twenty-three–volume corpus *Theological Investigations,* entitled "Ideas for a Theology of Childhood." In his essay, Rahner relocates the discussion of childhood. Other theologians generally address the topic exclusively within discussions of infant baptism and questions of the moral status of children before baptism. Rahner's concern is for the nature of childhood as such.

Childhood as Eschatological Future

Rahner's essay has three sections. The first, on "The Unsurpassable Value of Childhood," critiques the tendency of humans to view life as a progression of phases, "each of which as it is exhausted leads on to the next, the very meaning of which is to disappear into the next, to be a preparation for it, to 'exist' for the further stages beyond itself."[76] Christians are especially guilty of emphasizing the subordinate character of childhood as preparation for the *real* life of adulthood, he says.

Rahner's contrasting view of childhood is grounded in his understanding of eternity as a gathering up of all time, not simply the infinite linear extension of more time onto the time of human life. We go forward to meet our childhoods in the future because they are part of that eternity. "Childhood endures as that which is given and abiding, the time that has been accepted and lived through freely. Childhood does not constitute past time."[77] Childhood has enduring validity in God's sight: "childhood itself has a direct relationship with God...It must be the case that childhood is valuable in itself, that it is to be discovered anew in the ineffable future which is coming to meet us."[78] Childhood, then, is not limited to a stage to be put behind us as quickly as possible. It is enduring. It is a part of our eschatological future.

Children in Sin and in Grace

Rahner's second section, "The Christian Awareness of Childhood," puts forth his theological anthropology in terms of a Christian understanding of the nature of childhood. A child is from the beginning "the partner of God...a man [sic] right from the start."[79] For Rahner a child's life is not only a personal beginning but also happens within a larger preexisting context of human history. This history includes a history of guilt. By virtue of participation in the larger whole of humanity, the individual born also participates in that guilt. However, children can also count on God's grace: "Christianity knows that the child and his origins are indeed encompassed by the love of God through the pledge of that grace which, in God's will to save all [hu]mankind, comes in all cases and to every man from God in Christ Jesus."[80] Rahner worked in a context that included his efforts to throw off a long but pernicious theological argument about the moral status of children (their salvation) before baptism. The argument resulted in the tradition's construction of the idea of *limbo* as an in-between place where unbaptized children's souls dwelled. In this context the importance of Rahner's point here becomes especially prime. Children are always already in the grace of God because of Christ.

At the same time, Rahner's insistence that to such graced children the human existential status of being in sin nevertheless applies constitutes a bold refusal to romanticize childhood morality. Rahner thus offers an important corrective to idealized perspectives of childhood that focus only upon childhood as an innocent state a person loses in the progress of years.

> Christianity cannot on this account regard the origins of childhood as a sort of innocent arcadia, as a pure source which only becomes muddled at a later stage and *within* the sphere of human care...It cannot view childhood as though prior to this stage it was simply the same as when it came from God as its eternal source...No, Christianity views even childhood as already and inevitably the origin precisely of that man to whom guilt, death, suffering and all the forces of bitterness in human life belong as conditions of his very existence.[81]

For Rahner, then, the moral life of children is one of "existential guilt" blanketed on all sides by the grace of God. His perspective constitutes an important way of holding in check the modernist propensity to treat children as if they are not subject to the state of being which Christians theologically affirm all participate in as a part of being human, the state of sin. Yet Rahner is not inclined to conflate sin with wrong behavior of individuals nor to over-determine childhood in terms of sin. It is, theologically speaking, an existential status of human personhood. Therefore all who are fully human, including children, participate in it.

Applying Rahner's Thought

Remember Megan, whose story we mentioned at the opening of the previous chapter? She fantasizes about the accumulation of dolls even as her mother participates in their congregation's efforts to address the ethics of U.S. consumerist practices and their impact on other people's children. For this family Rahner's notion of children as "already and inevitably" participating in the state of human sin speaks with far greater theological credibility and integrity than do notions of childhood as an "arcade of innocence." This is true in spite of the fact than a particular individual child may appear just short of angelic.

Megan means no harm to the children in Thailand who labor in unsafe conditions to produce the dolls she covets. She may not even know or think about anyone being harmed by her desires to play with these dolls. Nor is she individually "responsible" per se for the consumptive and acquisitive desires that her society's market forces kindle in her. At the same time, Rahner's refusal to excuse children from their ownership of and participation in sin as a human condition means that children like Megan (and children of God like Megan's mother and like me) in fact *are* responsible. Megan and those who bear the role of parents, presbyters, and companions in the Christian life with Megan are responsible. This statement involves a paradox and tension not easily resolved. Its ambiguity is therefore much more difficult to live with than conservative parenting programs in which sin much more simply and directly equates with an individual child's behaviors and intentions.

What then is childhood in Rahner's theological framework? Childhood is the state in which one fully realizes one's own dependency upon others, one's neediness and vulnerability. It is the knowledge of those who, in relation to God, "*know* that they have nothing of themselves on which to base any claim to his help, and yet who trust that his kindness and protection will be extended to them and so will bestow what they need upon them."[82] It is as if, for Rahner, children function as a metaphor for humanity before God, and in their neediness actually evoke the providential care of the Divine.

These qualities with which Rahner associates childhood are qualities that allow persons to willingly hand themselves over into the mystery that is God. Childhood itself is a mystery, asserts Rahner. But childhood is first and foremost to him a state of openness: "Childhood is openness. Human childhood is infinite openness. The mature childhood of the adult is the attitude in which we bravely and trustfully maintain an infinite openness in all circumstances and despite the experiences of life which seem to invite us to close ourselves."[83] For those who live into mystery,

> life becomes for us a state in which our original childhood is preserved forever; a state in which we are open to expect the unexpected, to commit ourselves to the incalculable, a state which endows us with the power still to be able to play, to recognize that the powers presiding over existence are greater than our own designs, and to submit ourselves to their control as our deepest good.[84]

In that sense Jesus Christ is good news for children like Megan and others who are responsible for the way our lives, choices, and practices impact the life of the world. Responsible yet forgiven, children and those who walk with them in faith are empowered to work for transformation, as they are open to God's care.

The Childhood of God

Living in such a spirit of infinite openness brings one into the "childhood of God." Rahner explores this topic in the third section of his essay. He entitles this section "The Fullness of Childhood Consists in Being Children of God." He insists that human and divine concepts of childhood should be considered together because of their ability to mutually illumine each other. Therefore, he looks at the relationship between human childhood experiences, particularly with parents, and the image of God. The experience of secure childhood relationships can have a decisive influence for "that attitude of committing oneself to trust" which unites persons to God as parent [he says father]. And yet, Rahner cautions against making too close a correspondence between God and the experience of human parents, which paints God as the mere projection of a parental image onto "the dimension of the infinite." Still, Rahner writes of the importance of the relationship between children and their parents for their knowledge of God. "We 'transfer' the experience of a child-parent relationship in the earthly and human sense to a relationship with God, and then speak in a 'transferred' or metaphorical sense of God as Father."[85] Yet Rahner, in a move similar to that of Barth (discussed earlier), and in stark contrast to evangelical Protestant parenting theology of our time, refuses to stop the analogy with the comparison between earthly parental fathers and God as metaphorical Father.

Rahner goes further than did Barth, however, in extending the theological argument about how parenthood garners its significance in relation to God. Rahner insists that if all fatherhood derives its meaning from God, so too "all childhood in heaven and on earth derives its name and its origin from that one childhood in which the Logos itself receives its own nature...Childhood is only truly understood, only realizes the ultimate depths of its own nature, when it is seen as based upon the foundation of childhood of God."[86] Not only does parenthood derive its status and meaning from analogy with God, but so also does childhood derive its significance from the childhood of God.

Recall for a moment the discussion from chapter one about how a particular idea within Christianity relates to a particular practice. There I engaged theologian Kathryn Tanner's framework for thinking about factors that might cause an idea to issue in different practices. Tanner identified as one important factor in the relationship between belief and action the scope of the belief, or to whom it is applied. The Christian theological assertion that human parenthood derives its meaning from the parental character of God in relation to humanity is a claim shared by feminist theologians, James Dobson and other conservative Christian parenting writers, Karl Barth, and Karl Rahner.

For many conservative Christian parenting writers, grounding the meaning of parenting in the Divine is applied to the relationship of fathers to children, and from the perspective of the fathers. Barth invites us to apply this Christian belief to persons of all ages, and then to view it primarily from the position of childhood in relation to God. For Barth this childhood is shared by all, such that the point becomes for parents to see their children as God sees God's children (and, by definition, their children). Rahner extends the scope even further. Not just parenthood derives its meaning from God's parental being, but also childhood, since God in Christ also has a childhood. In Tanner's terms, what Barth and Rahner have done is to extend those to whom the idea or doctrine applies. The effect of this extension in practical theological terms is to move it from privileging fathers and subordinating children, to leveling the terms so that children and parents are in the same theological boat, so to speak. Practices authorizing the oppressive domination of children by their parents or other adults are ruled out by virtue of the equal status of older and younger human beings as alike in being the children of God. Rahner elevates the status of childhood by claiming that it finds its full meaning in the childhood of God.

When writing about childhood, Rahner (like Barth) does use some problematic language. For example, he writes about childhood "entailing *an orientation to God*" (italics in original) that he further defines in language of control and submission: "Childhood as an inherent factor in our lives must take the form of trust, of openness, of expectation, of readiness to be controlled by another"[87] Rahner lacks sensitivity to the particular problems a practice of openness framed as "readiness to be controlled by another" poses for women. Far too often women are socialized into, or forced into, experiences of being controlled. Rahner's thought, likewise, poses problems for children in situations of victimization where control by another who is not benign leads to harm. Obviously this is not a liberatory way to speak about childhood today.

What is significant about this usage, however, is that Rahner speaks here *not* of children being under the submissive control of adults who act as stand-ins for God, as the evangelical parenting literature so often describes. Instead, Rahner is talking about *adults* in relation to God. Here he refers to childhood as a state of being that is "an inherent factor in our lives"; that is to say, "in the lives of we adults," who manifest it when we embody "infinite openness" in our lives, a capacity made possible by God's "self-bestowal" in Christ. Radical openness is the contribution made by childhood as it inheres eternally in the religious life of adults. Children's social positioning thus makes them a model for a kind of faithful posture Rahner advocates for adults, that of "infinite openness" to God.

Overall, then, Rahner offers a strikingly positive view of childhood. He is assisted by the fact that he writes specifically about children, as opposed to other theologians whose thoughts on childhood are generally imbedded in discussions about human depravity, election, or sacraments. His concern to view childhood as valuable in itself, instead of as a preparation for adulthood, upholds children as having integrity and worth–and faith–appropriate to their time of life. His discussion on the problem of "original sin" and childhood displays a certain realism that avoids the idealization of childhood innocence. Yet he does not, it seems to me, become mired in a need to assert human sinfulness at all costs, with grace as a mere footnote to protect the greatness of God by way of contrast with human weakness. Accordingly, his perspectives become a helpful resource from Christian tradition toward a liberatory theology of childhood.

More Clues toward a Critical Feminist Practical Theology of Childhood

To stay focused on the moral status of children alone–the degree of innocence or evil attributed to children–is not helpful for me. It keeps the theological spotlight focused upon a narrow notion of moral status rendered in terms of behavior, or on an equally narrow question about the "salvation" of children. Instead, and in the interest of moving beyond the church's current state of religious ambivalence toward children, I want to focus on features of a liberatory practical theology of childhood in the context of the North American market regime within which the church finds itself today. I want to imagine a theology that can fund good ecclesial practices with children and in turn be funded by children's practices, toward the continual renewal of both. Amidst intense cultural and religious ambivalence about children, multiple resources exist within

Christian scripture and tradition for a practical theology of childhood that supports children's thriving, some of which I explore in this and previous chapters. Such a theology must be grounded in the real struggles and blessings children experience together with their parents/caregivers.

As a starting point, such a theology must begin by replacing ambivalence, in which no available image of childhood can be fully embraced, with the acknowledgement of *ambiguity*, a sense that children exist as the same strange mixtures of moral capacities as the rest of humanity. I am using the term *ambivalence* to denote a problematic inability to embrace children in their wholeness and complexity, while engaging the term *ambiguous* in a positive sense to refer to that quality of complexity.

Neither Angels nor Devils

The first clue that comes from exploring religious discourse on children in North America today points to this reality. Children are not angels or devils, but as full human beings manifest all the "gray areas" and ambiguities of adult human beings, who are complex and multifaceted. Parenting is a similarly ambiguous vocation, fraught with pitfalls and mistakes alongside multiple possibilities for providing appropriate, just, and loving forms of nurture. Such perspectives on childhood and parenting would seem to parallel those in Christian tradition for understanding human persons as " *simil justis et pecator*" (or, "at the same time a sinner and one who is justified") and offer resources for understanding children as complex moral beings for whom categories of grace, sin, sanctification, and redemption (and more!) have an appropriate use. In these more complete and complex notions of human personhood, children are not reducible to their behaviors in relation to adults, any more than Christian identity can be reduced to arguably middle-class, Anglo behavioral norms of cooperation and the bearing of an outwardly happy and contented countenance.

Childhood's Eternal Significance

A second clue can be found in the juxtaposition between the ambivalence toward children and Karl Rahner's affirmation that human childhood draws its meaning and fullness from the childhood of God in Christ. As I have described it, the kind of ambivalence toward children found in contemporary North American religious discourse easily issues, in the hands of a society driven by market utilitarian and individualist interests, in ecclesial practices that separate children from adults. In so doing the church abdicates responsibility for a coherent education in Christian beliefs and practices that forms children into a Christian identity shared by the larger community of faith.

Rahner's invitation to see childhood less in temporal terms than in eternal and eschatological ones indicates that childhood is not merely important for children such that it may legitimately be separated off from adulthood or treated as an alien culture best avoided. As Rahner suggests, childhood also has import for adults. Childhood is of eternal significance because it stands as an aspect of the being of God that matters for who God is. Such an unambivalent notion of childhood's theological significance invites similarly unambivalent ecclesial practices. In these practices children and adults worship together. Children are formed in faith by a Christian education that invites and equips them to share in the beliefs and practices of the community of faith in which they participate, rather than constituting them as a separate culture and community from that of the adults.

Seeing Children as God Does

Third, Barth's call to view children from a "God-ward" direction surely is worthy of retrieval in a feminist practical theology concerned with liberating children from subordinated positions in patriarchal family structures while insisting on their need for good care and relational nurture in families. Together with Barth's insistence that parenting is (along with other Christian vocations) a form of service, rather than a position of status, the idea of seeing children "from the divine standpoint" undermines any rationalizations of parenting as a claim to higher status divinely authorized. The divine viewpoint forbids cementing a single form of family life in which parents wield authoritarian control over children as property. Seeing children from a God-ward direction suggests seeing them as beloved ones, those called into relationship with God as "little brothers and sisters" by Christ through whom God embodies the divine partnership with humanity.

These clues, along with the others from previous chapters, begin to piece together what a feminist practical theology of childhood might look like. The following two chapters are efforts to construct that theology in two areas of ecclesial practice with children—education and liturgy.

SOURCES CITED

Adams, Carol J., and Marie M. Fortune, eds. *Violence against Women and Children: A Christian Theological Sourcebook.* New York: Continuum, 1998.

Ammerman, Nancy Tatom. *Bible Believers: Fundamentalists in the Modern World.* New Brunswick, N.J.: Rutgers University Press, 1987.

_____. *Baptist Battles: Social Change and Religious Conflict in the Southern Baptist Convention.* New Brunswick, N.J.: Rutgers University Press, 1990.

Ammerman, Nancy Tatom, and Wade Clark Roof. "Introduction: Old Patterns, New Trends, Fragile Experiments." In *Work, Family, and Religion in Contemporary Society*, ed. Nancy Tatom Ammerman and Wade Clark Roof, 1–20. New York: Routledge, 1995.

Aries, Philippe. *Centuries of Childhood: A Social History of the Family.* Trans. Robert Baldick. New York: Vintage Books, 1962.

Balmer, Randall Herbert. *Encyclopedia of Evangelicalism.* Louisville: Westminster John Knox Press, 2002.

Barth, Karl. *Church Dogmatics. Vol. III, Part 4,* ed. G.W. Bromiley and T.F. Torrance. Edinburgh: T. & T. Clark, 1961.

_____. *The Christian Life: Church Dogmatics IV, 4 Lecture Fragments.* Translated by Geoffrey W. Bromiley. Grand Rapids, Mich.: Eerdmans, 1981.

Bendroth, Margaret Lamberts. *Growing Up Protestant: Parents, Children, and Mainline Churches.* New Brunswick, N.J.: Rutgers University Press, 2002.

Brock, Rita Nakashima. *Journeys by Heart: A Christology of Erotic Power.* New York: Crossroads, 1991.

_____. "Ending Innocence and Nurturing Willfulness." In *Violence against Women and Children: A Christian Theological Sourcebook,* ed. Carol J. Adams and Marie M. Fortune, 71–84. New York: Continuum, 1998.

Brock, Rita Nakashima, and Rebecca Ann Parker. *Proverbs of Ashes: Violence, Redemptive Suffering, and the Search for What Saves Us.* Boston: Beacon, 2001.

Brown, Joanne Carlson, and Carole R. Bohn, eds. *Christianity, Patriarchy, and Abuse: A Feminist Critique.* New York: Pilgrim, 1989.

Brown, Joanne Carlson, and Rebecca Parker. "For God So Loved the World?" In *Christianity, Patriarchy, and Abuse: A Feminist Critique*, ed. Joanne Carlson Brown and Carole R. Bohn. Cleveland: Pilgrim Press, 1989.

Bussert, Joy M. K. *Battered Women: From a Theology of Suffering to an Ethic of Empowerment.* New York: Division for Mission in America, Lutheran Church in America, 1986.

Capps, Donald. "Religion and Child Abuse: Perfect Together." *Journal for the Scientific Study of Religion* 31, no. 1 (1992): 1–14.

_____. *The Child's Song: The Religious Abuse of Children.* Louisville: Westminster John Knox Press, 1995.

Carr, Louise. "Feminist Theological Approaches to (the) Sexual Abuse of Children." *Feminist Theology: The Journal of the Britain and Ireland School of Feminist Theology* no. 12, May (1996): 21–42.

Character Training Institute. Character-Based Correction. Character First!, 08/30/2004. Accessed 11/12/2004, www.characterfirst.com/business/gettingstarted.

Christenson, Larry. *The Christian Family*. Minneapolis: Bethany House Publishers, 1970.

Coontz, Stephanie. *The Way We Never Were: American Families and the Nostalgia Trap*. New York: Basic Books, 1992.

Couture, Pamela D. *Blessed Are the Poor? Women's Poverty, Family Policy, and Practical Theology*. Nashville: Abingdon Press, 1991.

_____. *Seeing Children, Seeing God: A Practical Theology of Children and Poverty*. Nashville: Abingdon Press, 2000.

DeMause, Lloyd, ed. *The History of Childhood*. London: Souvenir Press, 1976.

Dobson, James. *The Strong-Willed Child: Birth through Adolescence*. Wheaton, Ill.: Tyndale House, 1978.

_____. *James Dobson On Parenting: The Strong-Willed Child and Parenting Isn't for Cowards*. Nashville: World Publishing, 1997.

_____. *Bringing up Boys: Practical Advice and Encouragement for Those Shaping the Next Generation of Men*. Wheaton, Ill.: Tyndale House, 2001.

Engel, Mary Potter. "Evil, Sin, and Violation of the Vulnerable." In *Lift Every Voice: Constructing Christian Theologies from the Underside*, ed. Susan Brooks Thistlethwaite and Mary Potter Engel, 152–64. San Francisco: Harper and Row, 1989.

Focus on the Family. "Calling Godly Parents." Focus on the Family, 2004. Accessed Web page 5/21/2004, www.focusonyourchild.com/faith/art1/a0000479.html.

Fortune, Marie M. *Violence in the Family: A Workshop Curriculum for Clergy and Other Helpers*. Cleveland: Pilgrim Press, 1991.

Fugate, J. Richard. *What the Bible Says About...Child Training*. Garland, Tex.: Aletheia Publishers, 1980.

_____. *What the Bible Says About...Child Training*. 2d edition. Foundations for Biblical Research, 2000. Accessed 05/15/2004, www.rfugate.org.

Gordon, Thomas. P.E.T., Parent Effectiveness Training: The Tested New Way to Raise Responsible Children. New York: P.H. Wyden, 1970.

_____. Parent Effectiveness Training: the No-Lose Program for Raising Responsible Children. New York: P. H. Wyden, 1970.

_____. Teaching Children Self-Discipline–at Home and at School: New Ways for Parents and Teachers to Build Self-Control, Self-Esteem, and Self-Reliance. New York: Times Books, 1989.

Greven, Philip. *Spare the Child: The Religious Roots of Punishment and the Psychological Impact of Physical Abuse*. New York: Alfred A. Knopf, 1991.

Group Publishing. "Lava Lava Island Vacation Bible School." Loveland, Colo.: Group, 2003.

Gudorf, Christine. *Victimization: Examining Christian Complicity.* Philadelphia: Trinity Press International, 1992.

Haight, Wendy L. *African-American Children at Church: A Sociocultural Perspective.* Cambridge: Cambridge University Press, 2002.

Horvat, Erin McNamara et al. "From Social Ties to Social Capital: Class Differences in the Relations between Schools and Parent Networks." *American Educational Research Journal* 40, no. 2 (2003): 319–51.

Hunt, Mary. "Change or Be Changed: Roman Catholicism and Violence." *Feminist Theology: The Journal of the Britain and Ireland School of Feminist Theology* no. 12 (May 1996): 43–60.

Isherwood, Lisa. "Editorial." *Feminist Theology: The Journal of the Britain and Ireland School of Feminist Theology* no. 12 (May 1996): 5–9.

Lareau, Annette. *Unequal Childhoods: Class, Race, and Family Life.* Berkeley, Calif.: University of California Press, 2003.

Miller, Vincent J. *Consuming Religion: Christian Faith and Practice in a Consumer Culture.* New York and London: Continuum, 2004.

Miller-McLemore, Bonnie J. *Let the Little Children Come: Reimagining Childhood from a Christian Perspective.* San Francisco: Jossey-Bass, 2003.

Nelson, Janet L. "Introduction." In *The Church and Childhood: Papers Read at the 1993 Summer Meeting of the Ecclesiastical History Society*, ed. Diana Wood. London: Blackwell, 1994.

Ng, David, and Virginia Thomas. *Children in the Worshiping Community.* Atlanta: John Knox Press, 1981.

Okin, Susan Moller. *Justice, Gender and the Family.* New York: Basic Books, 1989.

Omartian, Stormie. *The Power of a Praying Parent.* Eugene, Oreg.: Harvest House, 1995.

Pattison, Stephen. "'Suffer Little Children': The Challenge of Child Abuse and Neglect to Theology." *Theology and Sexuality: The Journal of the Institute for the Study of Christianity and Sexuality.* September 1998, no. 9 (1998): 36–58.

Pellauer, Mary D. et al., eds. *Sexual Assault and Abuse: A Handbook for Clergy and Religious Professionals.* San Francisco: Harper and Row, 1987.

Putnam, Robert D. *Bowling Alone: The Collapse and Revival of American Community.* New York: Simon and Schuster, 2000.

Rahner, Karl. "Ideas for a Theology of Childhood." In *Theological Investigations*, 8, 33–50. London: Darton, Longman and Todd, 1971.

Redmond, Sheila A. "Christian 'Virtues' and Recovery from Child Sexual Abuse." In *Christianity, Patriarchy, and Abuse: A Feminist Critique*, ed. Joanne Carlson Brown and Carole R. Bohn. Cleveland: Pilgrim Press, 1989.

Reid, Kathryn Gering. *Preventing Child Sexual Abuse: A Curriculum for Children Ages Nine through Twelve.* Cleveland: Pilgrim Press, 1989.

Thorne, Barrie, and Marilyn Yalom, eds. *Rethinking the Family: Some Feminist Questions.* New York: Longman, 1982.

CHAPTER FIVE

Educating Children in Congregations

One afternoon in the weekday afterschool children's program of a church in San Francisco, as we were settling in and enjoying a snack I asked some children to tell me something important to them from their earlier day at school. Amidst various responses involving bathroom humor and assertions of the central place of soccer in human life, one kindergarten-aged girl named Amy responded, "We had communion."

Since I knew that this child attended a public school, I found this reply both curious and interesting. When asked to say more, she offered, "In my class we baked bread together. Then we talked about being thankful to the farmers who grew the wheat and for the sun and rain. Then we ate some. The other class next door didn't have any, so we shared some with them—and I made up with my friend in that class 'cause we had a fight that morning. Then we all went out to play."

Communion indeed! Of course there was no eucharistic celebration per se in this young child's public school classroom, where legal sanctions about the separation of church and state prevail. She communicated in her comments, however, that her identity and imagination have been formed by the actions of the eucharistic meal. She sees and understands the world in terms of this Christian practice–taking bread, giving thanks, breaking and eating, sharing with others in a spirit of reconciliation, going out into the world to live having been fed. The stories and practices of Christian community populate her imagination and frame her way of making sense of everyday life. In short, this child is "learning" Christian faith by being formed in an identity through which she construes and negotiates meaning religiously.

Learning as Identity Formation

In many of its contemporary forms, Christian education bears little relationship to this picture of learning as identity formation. Instead, much of what passes for education in the church remains based on an understanding of learning as the process by which an individual mind accumulates and integrates information such that teaching is the provision of information at the developmentally appropriate time for the mind to internalize it. In previous chapters I refer to education in faith as the construction of an alternative identity, particularly in relation to the dominant identity of a child as a good consumer provided by the reigning culture of consumerism. Additionally, I briefly commented on the captivity of education in congregations to the regime of consumerism. One key aspect of that captivity concerns the reduction of Christian education to instructional downloading of moralistic sound bites delivered to children through entertainment-oriented styles of teaching in a context sequestered from the practices of the wider community of faith.

In this chapter I will elaborate briefly upon this critique of Christian education of children in mainline churches of the United States today in terms specific to Christian education's history and to the learning theories utilized by churches concerned with children's faith education. Then I will pose an alternative notion of education, learning, and church more congruent with the feminist practical theology of childhood unfolding so far in this work. This idea will see Christian education as formation into an alternative identity. This identity is learned through participation in the church as a "community of practice" that seeks to walk in the ways of Jesus and organizes its life and practices around the central symbol of the kin-dom of God, with its reordering of power and its transforming commitment to an alternative way of life.

What Counts as Knowledge

In spite of their positive intentions to foster children's learning in faith, many people of good will who are concerned with the education of children in the church give little reflective consideration to the question how children learn. They understand their task as that of instilling knowledge about the faith into the minds–and perhaps also the hearts–of children. Learning, in this framework, amounts to "an unproblematic process of absorbing the given."[1]

Methods and Theories of Learning

Many creative methods are available for accomplishing the instillation of knowledge, and congregations across the United States today engage in various models and methods to convey to children the perceived object of education, namely the imparted knowledge of God and of the Christian faith conceived in object-like fashion. These methods cover the gamut:

- the currently popular rotation method of education, in which children engage the same text or story from the Bible through four or more different media (e.g., videos, creative arts, drama, computer lab)
- denominational curricular methods organized around official catechisms or doctrinal priorities
- activity- and experience-based approaches with minimal attention to theological content
- exclusively "didactic" approaches focused entirely around content-as-information delivery
- "discovery" learning approaches such as those based in Montessori educational theory (e.g., Godly Play, Catechesis of the Good Shepherd);
- lectionary-based models that shape various learning activities around parallel engagement between the texts used in children's education with those used elsewhere in the church

Each of these methods of teaching has its merits. Still, all issue from a similar implicit theory that sees learning as an activity that takes place within the individual mind of a child. In this theory leaning is facilitated by some combination of input from a teacher and the teacher's arrangement of a learning environment that will cooperate with that individual child's internal cognitive processes.

Two basic notions of how children learn are embedded within this theory. In the first, learning consists in the acquisition of knowledge as data, and the kind of knowing educational theorists term "procedural knowing"—or knowing *how*—is simply assumed to follow from knowing *about*. A second theory of learning often implicit in congregational education of children is essentially a socialization theory. In this framework, children are imitators of adult behavior. Learning consists in the acquisition of knowledge understood as simple habit or knowing how, which takes place as children have multiple opportunities to practice what they imitate in the actions of adults, without the need of any conceptual reflection on these actions.[2] Educational methods deemed "experiential learning" and "discovery learning" often fall under this implicit theory of learning as a process of socialization, as do the perspectives of some proponents of practice-based learning, who claim that practice alone apart from any conceptual reflection creates an adequate framework for children's learning.

Such theories concerned with how children learn rarely are articulated explicitly in educational curricula designed for use in churches, however. One major reason behind this gap in explicit theories concerning children's learning in church education lies in the taken-for-granted achievement of facticity enjoyed by Piagetian perspectives of learning. These perspectives in their various popularized forms hold that learning takes place through the individual's development of increasingly complex mental structures for increasingly complex acts of internalization, whether such internalization takes place through vehicles of didactic or experiential modes of transmission. If children learn by internalizing, then educational efforts logically orient around giving them "material" to internalize. With this as a taken-for-granted idea about the nature of knowledge, far too often in churches the question of how children learn remains unasked–and therefore unanswered and unexamined, even in the very teaching material intended to help them do so.

The Rotation Model as Example

The rotation model of Christian education provides a clear example of how Christian education so often operates with an assumed theory of children's learning. In this method, as mentioned above, children rotate through a series of "workshops"–carefully designed classroom experiences, each using a different focal medium for teaching–over the course of four to six weeks. Teachers prepare one session and offer it to a different group of children each week. During the weeks of a given rotation period, children hear and interact with the same story from scripture through the lens of a different kind of activity or instructional process each week.

In examining this theory we must see first that the theory of learning being employed in this practice of children's education is the idea that repetition of exposure to "content" increases learning. All the workshops addressed the same particular story from scripture or the same theme. The theory assumes that children will be more likely to recall a story they encounter multiple times. Learning thus means the ability to recall, which represents the internalization of the story or theme.

Second, the method takes seriously Howard Gardner's theory of multiple intelligences.[3] By intentionally engaging a variety of "intelligences" or ways of learning among children, this method acknowledges that different children have different preferences and "best means" for learning. Some learn best through artistic creation; others through the visual and aural stimulation of film; and some through independent contemplation, etc. Gardner's theory is not a theory of learning per se. It does not offer an explanation for how children learn. Rather Gardner's theory of multiple intelligences provides a framework for recognizing that children and adults alike exhibit diverse kinds of knowing that contribute to different learning styles and to different abilities among people.

Churches employ the rotation method of Christian education in different ways depending on the resources of the congregation and the skills and inclinations of its educators. Sometimes the various "workshops" in which children participate constitute elaborate imaginal worlds in which stories from scripture come to life through drama and props. In these cases children enjoy participating from within the drama as part of the story. In other places, the workshops constitute little more than a menu of varied activities organized around a particular scripture text or theme.

Many congregations using this educational method report that it revitalized their Sunday school program with increased attendance by children, and solved their teacher recruitment problem through its requirements of shorter term commitments by teachers who can operate within a workshop modality that engages their particular gifts and interests. Thus, for instance, a person with computer skills need not teach a workshop focused around a craft, but can simply prepare for and repeat the same computer-based class session for the duration of the rotation. Children report interest in and motivation to participate in such Sunday school experiences because they enjoy the variety. As five-year-old Dana commented to me when I visited her Sunday school and followed her group of kindergarten-to-first-graders through a complete four-week rotation, "It's not boring like regular Sunday school. We have fun." Dana's older church friends in the fifth and sixth grade group told me that they preferred the computer and video sessions, "but the other ones can be okay too. At least every week it changes."

Christian educators are all too glad to have engaged and interested children in Sunday schools. And yet we can recognize that the rotation method of education, for all its positive dimensions, also displays several problematic features of Christian education's colonization by consumer culture. It constantly shifts between ever new forms of activity to address children who themselves are constructed in terms of a ceaseless hunger for novelty. It shifts between entertainment and education in the production of "spectacle-like" experiences consumed by children. It diminishes the commitment in terms of duration and quality of social relations between children and adults. This is true because most adults involved in teaching only need to commit to do so for the duration of one rotation cycle, rather than for a full year of teaching, as is the case in traditional Sunday school classes. What makes this method "work" in so many congregations using it, in part, is its good fit with these and other cultural forms and practices of consumerism.

Defining Learning and Knowledge

Still the question remains: how does learning happen for the children who participate? What is meant by saying that this or any other method of educating children for faith "works"? Is it simply a matter of exposing children to a Bible story and reinforcing the story frequently enough and through multiple media of sufficient interest to children that they can recall the story and thus are considered to "know" it? Is knowledge something that children acquire from adults who teach? What do "learning" and "knowing" mean in relation to children and Christian faith?

I intend to suggest with these questions that the use of the rotation model or any other curricular method in Christian education neither guarantees nor prohibits learning among children. These methods of education may well teach children, and children may well learn something. But unless we clarify what counts as knowledge, identify what we mean to accomplish with our Christian educational efforts, and think through an understanding of how children learn, the likelihood of a match between educational processes and learning among children seems rather slim.

Educators in the church continue to attempt to locate the problems of Christian education in given curricular resources. Year after year they replace one resource or model for education with another without exploring the nature and purpose of Christian education in their community of faith and its perspective on children's learning. By so doing, they do much for the bottom lines of companies producing church curricula, but little for the education of children.

Learning: Making Meaning and Forming Identities

What kind of Christian education can welcome children into the church and contribute to their flourishing? I differ from educators who equate learning with the ability of an individual's memory to store and recall information. I use the term *learning* to refer to the process of meaning-making, or how persons–including children–make sense of their worlds in increasingly more adequate and complex ways over time. This activity of meaning-making is central in situating a person's identity. Granted, remembering is an important part of meaning-making, as memory constitutes part of the cognitive tool kit through which human beings strive to make sense of reality. Memory gives access to story, symbol, emotional associations, and desires. However, with children, learning too often gets reduced to remembering, as children's responses to questions such as, "Do you remember the story of Jacob and Esau?" signal whether or not they have "learned" that story—that is, whether or not they can recall its details. How they make sense of the story and how they engage the story to make sense of their own worlds are not taken into consideration. Paulo Freire rightly termed this notion of learning a "banking" model of education. It treats learners as empty receptacles waiting to be filled with informational knowledge that could then be withdrawn at another time like a bank deposit.[4] Freire's choice of metaphors is not without a certain irony in the context of my larger discussion of consumerism's effects upon Christian education.

Freire understood that knowledge and learning are never neutral. Education involves power relations

- between teachers and learners
- concerning what counts as knowledge
- over who gets to define the curriculum
- in terms of the purposes to which education relates

With Freire and others concerned about the politics of knowing,[5] we can assert that learning is much more than "cognitive recall." Learning *is* transformation. It concerns understanding and identity, because to learn is to be changed, to take on a new identity, to engage in a process of becoming. Identity, though personal, never takes shape independently of the social and cultural context that provides the resources and materials for its construction. Insofar as learning refers to the processes by which persons change, become different, or undergo transformation, learning centrally concerns identity. Learning, then, is shaped by the particular ways of making sense or making meaning that children experience in their social and cultural contexts. To learn is to be formed in an identity. For children in congregations, learning is a process of Christian identity formation that takes place through participation in the congregation as a community of practice, which gives shape to particular ways of making meaning.

How Do Church Children Learn?

How do children learn, then, in a church understood as a community of practice? More specifically, what does it mean to learn in a community whose practices take shape in relation to Jesus' call into the kin-dom of God as an alternative ordering of power, participation, and action in the world? Such a process of learning means being formed in a counterculture, gaining an anti-imperial identity in which practices of love, justice, hospitality, and compassion replace practices of oppression, excessive accumulation at the expense of others, and abuses of power.

Education into this Christian identity is hardly politically neutral, as Freire understood well. For in this kind of education, children learn not simply in order to "have information" in their heads. In this kind of education children learn to constitute (and "be constituted into") a way of life and an identity as persons participating in the kin-dom of God. How do they learn this identity? Christian education with children is a process of providing opportunities for increasingly full participation in and reflection upon Christian practices, which over time forms them into these peculiar identities as people of faith.[6]

Forming Identity through Participation in Practices

Amy, the young girl whose language of "taking communion" at school I shared to open this chapter, is fortunate to be part of a congregation that plans for children to do more than simply be a part of the various opportunities for classroom education offered within her church. Her church invites Amy and other children to be participants in worship, at congregational meetings, and in fellowship events. Amy did not enter the world knowing how to engage in any of these experiences. She learns the practices of Christian people by participating in them—often in initially more circumscribed ways that open into fuller, more mature and competent engagement in these practices.

Learning Process as Participatory

For example, when Amy was a toddler, her parents gave her coins to put into the offering plate each week. Amy did so with a flourish, clanking her coins against the wooden collection plate with zeal. Her parents report that Amy would become quite upset if for any reason she missed the opportunity to contribute to the weekly offering. Over time, she learned to take the plate into her own hands rather than having adults hold it for her, as well as to pass it along to the next person beside her. This gesture will likely accumulate further significance and meaning in years to come, but for now it signals Amy's inclusion in the congregation as one who "knows how" to be part of its worship life.

Amy gradually developed her motor skills, adding to the competency with which she could participate in this congregational practice. Then, as she gained verbal and cognitive abilities, Amy began to ask simple questions such as, "Who gets the money?" and, "Why do we put money in the offering every week?" At the same time, Amy's imagination became populated with a wide variety of texts and stories from scripture. These included the story of the rich young ruler, the widow's giving of her last coin, the laborers in the vineyard, laws about taking responsibility to care for those who have no means of support, prophetic texts that teach of God's care for the poor and the weak, etc. These stories and the dialogical interpretation of them within the community will come to be part of the framework of understanding and discourse in which Amy's participation in this practice is situated.

Amy's family and other adults in the congregation talked with her about their practices of financial stewardship. They gave her developmentally appropriate opportunities to reflect on her own practice along with that of the congregation. In this process Amy expanded her perspective on this weekly "throwing of coins" from that of an enjoyable shared activity to one that had some particular meanings to her. "The church money helps feed hungry people and make houses for some of them." In the dialogue with others about stewardship practices and her participation in them, Amy certainly received information about this practice and became skilled in its performance. But she did more! She did not merely internalize information about what the weekly offering accomplishes or how to participate appropriately. She extended the range and depth of her understanding and skill in the practice. She could do this because her learning took place as adults, already able and knowledgeable stewards, gradually assisted her. Just telling her about stewardship practices would be insufficient, as would merely expecting her to perform it by rote. Learning is Amy's ever-deepening under-standing of the practice as she is formed into an identity as a Christian steward through increasingly full participation in the church as a community of practice.

Her parents and the pastor of the congregation describe Amy's favorite moment when she was about four years old. She enjoyed standing with the community to sing the Doxology as the offering plates came forward. This provided a further expansion of her engagement in the practice of offering her resources for the work of the church. When Amy began kindergarten, she also set aside a jar for the loose change she would find around her house. Every week she would empty the jar and take the change to church. Thus she participated in the practice of offering financial resources for the ministries of the church. As she continues to grow, Amy will be able to ask even more sophisticated and complex questions of this practice, connecting it with stories from scripture and with her enlarging understanding of the way of life embraced by members of her congregation, a way that includes such practices. And as a part of her growing competency and fullness of participation in stewardship, she will develop her abilities to critique the inadequacies of this and other practices and to transform them, along with other practices that together compose a pattern of Christian life in her community of faith. Already, though, her participation in this practice of stewardship is forming her into an identity of one who offers what she has and contributes responsibly to the work of the community of faith.

Learning Process as Social

Amy's stewardship story illustrates what I am asserting as a theory of how children learn that can fund liberatory practices of education in the church. Children learn by participation in congregations as communities of practice. They learn as they move from initially more limited or peripheral positions of participation to increasingly full levels of participation in community practices. As they do so, they develop increasing degrees of competency and understanding (including critical reflection) in those practices.[7] The learning process is therefore social. It takes place through children's (and other "newcomers'") being apprenticed in those practices by more experienced members of the community who provide the "scaffolding" that allows learners to move from what they can do or understand unassisted and on their own, to newer, more complex, and hopefully more adequate ways of understanding and acting that they can eventually appropriate for themselves. Educational philosopher Jerome Bruner[8] has contributed this concept of learning as a social encounter that takes place when teachers provide cognitive (and emotional and spiritual) "scaffolding." Such scaffolding provides the support necessary to extend the reach of learners beyond that which they can accomplish on their own. This concept is also similar to Russian psychologist Lev Vygotsky's idea of "zones of proximal development." Vygotsky refers to the social space in which learning takes place in interactions between learners and others (including peers), as persons with experience and knowledge assist learners to move beyond where they are already.[9]

Such a mentoring process is not mere imitation or socialization. It also includes the development of critical reflective capacities and opportunities for immersion in the narratives and theoretical perspectives that inform the meanings these practices hold. In effect, learning takes place as children over time come to be "mentored into" an identity as ones who can fully participate in the way of life of the community of practice. This endeavor of meaning-making includes practitioners' critical thought and discourse along with their actions. Its primary and crucial distinction from regnant (and largely implicit) theories of how children in congregations learn is its view of learning as a process of meaning-making and identity formation that happens through participation in a community of practice. This view of learning stands in stark contrast to the more popularly used and implicit theories that understand learning as the individualized activity of taking in, internalizing, and recalling information about a subject matter.

Churches as Communities of Practice

What is a "community of practice"? I borrow this term from Lave and Wenger's studies on learning[10] for various kinds of work through apprenticeship to the group that has the knowledge, experience, and skills to perform that particular work. Here, I use the term "community of practice" in reference to the church to signify the church's existence as a community. By community I mean a group defined by a particular experience of social relations (expressed in the New Testament Greek term *koinonia*) gathered in relation to a peculiar set of practices, activities, and ways of making meaning that persons share and engage in over time and that produce identity both corporate and individual. To call congregations "communities of practice" means that these social groupings exist not simply as ill-defined and unbounded associations of people or as groups tied together by a set of ideas and beliefs only. Congregations constitute communities of practice as groups whose membership is defined by participation in the activities, discourse, and ways of meaning-making shaped in relation to Jesus and his proclamation of the kin-dom of God. Education is the process of being formed into identity as one who holds membership–full participation–in such a community, an identity that cannot be held in isolation from, but only in relation to, the community.[11]

The Dangers of "Community" and "Formation"

Let me begin unraveling these ideas about Christian education and children's learning in congregations by first attending to a couple of objections that often surface in relation to the notion that education centrally concerns the formation of identity, an assertion I have made without comment at various other points in this book thus far. Among Protestants, formation language may resound with Stepford Wives-like associations of imposed identities that violate individual subjectivity and freedom.[12] Such language may be less foreign to Catholic Christians, for whom associations between processes of formation and religious vocation (to the priesthood or in a vowed religious community) are more commonplace. Feminist theorists such as Iris Marion Young[13] discuss the shaping power of groups and communities and point to the possibilities that women's identities may be oppressively subsumed under the homogenizing influences of a community's processes of shaping its members' identities. I share their concern and, from my own critical feminist vantage point, extend it to children by asking about the potentially oppressive aspects of children's education conceived as the formation of identity, aspects that may be peculiar to children. For instance, children bring different cognitive awareness of the dynamics at work in the interplay of individual and communal identities, less ability to "act back" upon the community that shapes them, and/or less freedom to determine their own membership by staying in or leaving the community at will.

Furthermore, to speak of education as formation that happens in congregations seems to assume a rather high view of religious congregations as places "worthy" of forming persons in Christian faith based on how they live and articulate its meanings. Do congregations really look like the sorts of communities of practice I have described, organized around the gospel's counter-narrative to resist imperialism in its various forms and to work toward transformation of life[14] in relation to the kin-dom of God? So many congregations with which I am familiar seem to have more in common with the Rotary Club than with the vision of church I pose here. Where are the congregations positioned to form children in such a way of life? I am inclined to agree with Barth's observation that "In fact, Christians are not particularly faithful people in their relation to God and therefore they are not particularly eminent people, nor do they awaken particular regard in their relation to their contemporaries. If they are children of God, it is certainly not because they have shown themselves to be such."[15]

And what about the possibilities of "negative formation," that is, formation into destructive or negative identities? Acknowledging the fallibility of congregations, an important question occurs. Is it not risky to allow imperfect communities to shape the identities of children? Do we really want children to be formed into the identities and practices of faith communities where racism, sexism, classism, or homophobia (to name just four quick and common examples) constitute a strong aspect of a particular congregation's communal identity? It is a legitimate question; and the answer, of course, is no. The understanding of education as identity formation in Christian faith must have a normative dimension. Certain forms of identity, such as those that are oppressive or destructive, are in fact ruled out by norms from scripture, tradition, and experience that affirm God's love, compassion, and justice, especially for the weak and marginal.[16] Some of the theologically oriented literature concerned with the person-forming power of Christian practices in congregations rightly may be accused of being rather naïve about congregations, lacking a sufficiently critical approach to the negative formation potentials therein. To say that congregations form children and others in particular identities through their participation in community practices does not guarantee that the formation will be positive, negative, or benign. A view of education as identity formation, therefore, must account for the possibility of children being negatively formed into distorted, oppressive, or otherwise problematic identities.

Christian Education as a Compromise Maneuver

It must be said in all honesty that the Christian educational work of identity formation is always a "compromise maneuver" between ideals and actualities. This is especially the case given the provisional and proximal status of congregations as manifestations of the body of Christ in the world. It becomes even more the case given the complicity and embeddedness of all Christians in the very forms of sin against which Christians also struggle. (I refer in particular here to U.S. Christians and their implication in the harms perpetrated by globalized consumer capitalism.) That means that none of us are shaped into Christian identities completely free of distortions and oppressive potential.

For some persons, the inability to find a congregation close to their ideals of church becomes a reason–or an excuse–not to participate and not to involve children in participating in any congregations with enough depth engagement to risk being formed by its practices. The concerns about formation reflected in such objections, I believe, comprise the positive intent behind what I consider the otherwise wrongheaded notion held by some parents. These parents decide that they will not involve their children in any particular faith education because they want their children to be free of any coerced identities and able to choose faith for themselves when they come of age to do so. The positive intent behind such a stance is that it takes seriously the matter of children's (more limited) agency in relation to religious identity. It recognizes the potentially oppressive elements of religious formation in what are inevitably imperfect faith communities. Such concerns also put forward the reality that some people certainly do experience real harm and damage in communities of faith and understandably (in decisions about the faith education of their children) wish to protect their children from similar harm. These notions may also reveal a tendency among adults to view children's faith experiences through the lens of the adults' own remembered childhood experiences in faith communities, with adults seeking to heal their own wounds through "limiting" the religious lives of their children.

I call such notions wrongheaded, however, for two reasons:

1. They assume that in the absence of any process of identity formation in a particular faith group, children will remain "unformed" in their religious identities. Identities are culturally constructed and situated; and children, like adults, are members of more than one community of practice. Every child always exists in multiple and often competing communities exercising formative, shaping influences on the child's identity. As I have suggested throughout this book, the hegemonic identity of consumer that consumer capitalism offers easily steps in to fill any void in the absence of strong alternatives. The choice is not between a particular faith identity and no identity, but between competing identities that are socially mediated within a particular society and culture. In the United States, identities such as that of children as consumers show a great deal in common with religious identities with their claims for ultimacy and their engagement of deep human yearnings and desires.[17] Children will draw resources for forming identities from wherever they may do so, including those of consumer culture if offered no credible alternatives.

2. These wrongheaded notions assume that being formed in a particular faith somehow precludes future negations of that identity or alternative future choice-making of a different faith perspective. This view treats identity as static rather than fluid and dynamic. It also treats faith as a static entity that exists in the same form for persons as children as it will for them in adulthood. Faith development theorists such as James W. Fowler rightly refute either of these notions of faith or identity as static entities.[18] A more cogent viewpoint (which I will expand upon below) asserts the "portability" of knowledge, skills, and practices children learn through formation into identities within a particular faith community, whether they move from one faith community to a different one later in life, or to a more seasoned and mature understanding and practice within the community that shaped them as children. As Wenger asserts, understanding the nature of learning as a process of identity formation allows for the notion of greater flexibility or "portability" because people take their identities with them when they move from one context to another.[19] This suggests that children formed in a particular faith identity will have greater facility at renegotiating that identity later in their lives. That is, children nurtured into a strong sense of identity within the particularity of a faith tradition develop skills and abilities to use religious languages and categories, to make meaning religiously, to engage in practices of commitment-making and decision-making in relation to that which is considered of greatest and most ultimate significance. As they encounter new possibilities, the particularity of childhood faith need not be an impediment. Instead it may be seen as empowering children in a way of making meaning and of knowing.

Summary: Continuing Tensions

We can then summarize our response to these critiques. A certain tension will always mark the relationship between individual and communal identity within the experience of identity formation. Certain groups, including children and women, may be particularly vulnerable to exploitation (given their positions and power relations). The negative aspects of identity formation within communities will always be imperfect. The church faces, therefore, the need for continual critique that "keeps the system open" and mutual, with room for individual persons to reform communal identity and not only to be formed by it. If a particular congregation's practice is not open to transformation and is steeped in problematic understandings of Christian identity, then it probably cannot be, in fact, an adequate and appropriate community of practice within which to nurture children's Christian identity.

Finally, I need to make one more point concerning the theological "adequacy" of congregations as sites for formation of Christian identity. A similar necessary tension exists between utopian imagination that expresses visions of alternative possibilities and futures, and the actual shape of life within systems and organizations as we know and experience them. Feminist theologians, in the constructive work of imagining alternative possibilities to the ones currently available, necessarily engage in utopian-sounding, eschatological yearnings. As Letty Russell suggests about the "liberation church," no one has actually seen one before because it does not exist fully within our flawed experience of church—but we get glimpses of this eschatological ecclesia in our experiences of faith and struggle.[20] Similarly, as I asserted earlier, no one has actually seen a church that fully welcomes children, that completely and without contradiction bears God's hospitality to all God's children, and that constitutes its identity and practices fully in relation to God's reign of abundance and justice. Thus the faith identities in which children (and adults) are formed through participation in any particular church are at best provisional and partial. They stand in need of continual renegotiation and reformulation in light of continual learning and struggle in faith. The vision crafted in theological imagination offers criteria for transforming the church and congregations we know now into those to which God is calling us.

The framework for understanding children's learning in a liberatory theology of childhood holds that the nature and process of children's learning is social. It happens in interaction with others situated in particular communities and cultural contexts of congregations. Just as a necessary and inevitable tension exists between individual and communal practice in congregations, the same tensions exist in learning as meaning-making and identity formation in congregations, a situation that at its best involves individuals and communities in ongoing mutual transformation.

Congregations charged with oversight for educating children often focus more on individual children's cognition and sometimes overlook the serious realities this chapter has exposed. As a social and cultural process, children's learning in the church depends greatly upon three elements:

- the overt and tacit functions or purposes education serves in its given congregational culture
- the role education plays in the lives of those who operate within it—children, parents and other caregivers, teachers, pastors
- the contextual situating of children's learning experiences in relation to the rest of what the congregation does as a community of practice

Alongside these three elements and from the framework of a feminist critical pedagogical inquiry, we also need to consider a fourth element in the form of two questions. Why is children's education situated the way it is within congregational cultures? How does this positioning of education reflect the distribution of power, status, and other forms of cultural capital there?[21]

The Spirit of God and Children's Learning

In what follows I will explore each of these questions and their implications for Christian education with children. I will be operating out of an understanding of learning drawn from educational theorists such as Jerome Bruner, Lev Vygotsky, Jean Lave, and Etienne Wenger. They understand learning as a communally situated activity taking place in the social and cultural spaces between persons in that community, and not merely as the internal activity of an individual child. They contribute to an understanding of children's learning that can fund a church's and theology's efforts to genuinely welcome children and can contribute to their flourishing.

God's Spirit Creating New Identities

At the same time, we need also to consider the work of God's Spirit in the experience of learning for faith. I affirm with other Reformed Christian educators and practical theologians the idea that faith is ultimately a gift from God, graciously given as the Holy Spirit works to offer it to us. Yet I am concerned that this idea not become a way to side-step responsibility for educating children in congregations (i.e., "since it all depends on the Holy Spirit anyway"). Christian education centrally involves taking on a new identity–becoming a new person in Christ, as the apostle Paul put it (2 Cor. 5:17). Since we have our beings–our identities–in and from God, this work of becoming a new person and taking on Christian identity is the very heart of what learning is all about. Such work requires nothing less than the work of God's Spirit to effect the graceful gift of new identities in our lives and in those of our children.

At the same time, I am equally concerned about the way the Holy Spirit as the One who brings about faith in the life of persons (including children) has become a fairly domesticated image in relation to Christian education of children. Water dribbled on the head of a baby with the prayer that God will also baptize this baby with Holy Spirit may invite us to think of this Spirit as a calm and self-contained puff of breeze that blows gently over sleeping babies. We should think of it, rather, as a rushing wind that troubles the waters and stirs up or activates children's lives of faith. Domesticated images of the Holy Spirit contribute little to a liberatory theology of childhood or to a church's ability to fully welcome children, because such tame images encourage adults to associate the work of the Spirit in children's lives with stillness and tranquility. Then when children are active, rambunctious, or even quarrelsome, such ways of being seem far from the work of the kind of Spirit invoked over the waters of baptism. This unexpected work of the Spirit also occurs when children, together with the rest of the church, are called to ministries of activism, constructive conflict with "principalities and powers," or struggle and resistance toward transformation. In addition, many mainline Protestants experience a certain "unreality" about that aspect of the Trinity we call Holy Spirit. We are more accustomed to thinking that much of what happens in our lives is the result of our own labors, our organizing, our planning, our teaching, our efforts. Doubts that anything really happens in baptism other than the baby's head getting wet come easily to a people and culture schooled in slogans like "Just Do It!" and "You Make It Happen!"

The Holy Spirit in Troubling Times

Thus Christian education is too often carried out in the face of domesticated images of a tranquil Spirit and of the surfacing of doubts that this intangible face of God really can be much more than the imaginative naming of a group's "collective effervescence." Christian education in a liberatory theological framework, however, necessarily involves the work–or play, if you will–of the Spirit of God in the forming and reforming of children's identities as people who walk in the way of Jesus. Such work takes place not only in times of deep connectivity between persons in the community who walk together sharing such an identity. In those times persons experience a sense of oneness, harmony, and belonging often explicitly identified with the presence of the Spirit, like the experience in the image of Pentecost when God's Spirit worked to connect persons of different cultures and languages into one community of understanding.

Christian education and life together in Christian communities of practice also involve times of disjuncture between people, experiences of difference, struggles, and negotiations over the nature of the identity being formed and reformed together. In these experiences of difference and contestation, too, God's Spirit labors and plays, as in the image of the Tower of Babel, when God's Spirit worked to bring disjuncture and difference into the midst of people to disrupt their wrongheaded homogeneity.

Christian education depends upon the presence and activity of the Spirit of God. Amidst the hegemonic grasp of globalized consumerism on the identities of children, the possibility of constructing an alternative identity to those posed by such a powerful and destructive imperial regime are slim if they rely on our own efforts alone. This is true because we adults and children alike are thoroughly captivated by that regime. In that sense, I am suggesting that the Holy Spirit works in Christian education as a kind of external critical force of the Divine. The Spirit calls us to identities and practices beyond our own imaginal abilities, claiming us and constituting us as a people who bear a different name and are formed by different practices than those that name children as consumers, captives to this and other death-dealing regimes. Nothing short of God's Spirit, who transcends these powerful forces, can effect transformation in this way.

Many perspectives on the Holy Spirit and Christian education focus rather singularly on the Spirit's gift of faith and transformation of the individual believer through the heart and mind of that individual (as if in a vacuum). In contrast to those perspectives, I see the connections between the work of the Holy Spirit and Christian education as primarily communal ones. The Spirit works in and through the community's practices, its narratives and symbols, its shared story and imagined future, to engender the reign of God. Children learn, inspired by the same Spirit of God, as they participate in the community's practices, come to know its stories and symbols, and become part of its imagined future, engendering the reign of God as they are formed into an identity as people of faith. Certainly in this process, God's Spirit and processes of learning transform individual children. That is unarguable. But the way children "learn to be Christians," through the Spirit's gift of faith and the human processes of learning, takes place in and through a community whose identity is both found and produced in its practices of companioned walking with Christ.

In this theology of childhood and the perspective on Christian education with children with which I am working, then, it is important to retrieve from Christian tradition those images of the Spirit that are active, restless, stirring up, and disturbing. In doing so we must still retain those images portraying the Spirit as a gentle wind and loving advocate. Christian education is, as Carol Lakey Hess writes, education in the Spirit.[22] Faith is a gift of the Spirit. Therefore, in children's learning in relation to faith, the Spirit of God is active. But it seems to me that the particular ways in which God's Spirit is "implicated" in Christian education with children are more unsettling that placid, more restless than comfortable, and more akin to stirring the waters than stilling them.

God's Spirit Present in and through Children

For instance, God's Spirit is present in such communities in and through children whose contributions to the congregation's learning may disturb and unsettle established patterns or ways of knowing and acting. It is also possible to see God's Spirit present and active in the learning processes of children, as the One who invites restless wondering, yearning desires, and encounters with difference that engender new ways of imagining, knowing, and acting in children's lives.

I describe children's learning as both a process of meaning-making and as the formation of an identity within a community of practice. God's

Spirit surely is active in empowering communities of practice to form persons, including children, in identities that constitute powerful alternative identities to those constructed for them by the dominant empire of consumerism, with its demands for full allegiance and its life-destroying regime of consumptive practices. God's Spirit inspires the stories, narratives, and symbols used by children who are part of a community of practices seeking to walk in the way of Jesus and to make sense of their worlds. The same Spirit is at work through these narratives, symbols, and shared practices, infusing the imaginations of children so that they can picture alternative worlds and realities compelling enough that they are willing to struggle for, dream and hope of, labor after, and celebrate such worlds.

The Holy Spirit Engendering Faith in Communities

A thorough treatment of the topic of the Holy Spirit in the Christian education of children is beyond the limits of this chapter. Here, though, I must emphasize that a social and cultural theory of children's learning in the context of Christian education has to include an understanding that the Spirit of God activates children's lives and learning to bring about faith. The Spirit brings faith not merely as an individual phenomenon but as the Spirit of God works in and through communities to engender children's faith. Such learning happens through children's participation with and apprenticeship in the church as a community of practice, whose ways of believing and acting in the world both reflect and produce its alternative identity. The same Spirit is similarly at work to engender the wider community's growth in faith through the participation of its children. Let us now turn, then, to consider the way contemporary practices of Christian education with children position them in relation to participating in the practices of the church.

Education and the Separation of Adults and Children

"And now the children may leave for their Sunday school classes"– these words comprise what is virtually a new liturgical phrase in many mainline Protestant congregations in the United States today. It is spoken in worship week after week to initiate the departure of children from the sanctuary and from the congregation's worship. Increasingly, Sunday school, or church school as it is sometimes called, represents a separate sphere for children within the church, a legitimated means of sequestering children from full participation in the practices of congregations. The Sunday school's firm association with children is solidified enough that, while some congregations include adult classes under the rubric of Sunday school, the terminology of "adult education" is commonly used to depict adult Christian education activities in the church and distinguish it from that of children. Few would contest the claim that Sunday schools are also devalued sites for education. This is evidenced in the fact that the term is virtually synonymous with what is considered overly facile and inadequate, as in the expressions that someone possesses a "Sunday school faith" or "a Sunday school understanding of the Bible."[23]

Sunday schools have not always operated to sequester children from full participation in the church, nor have they always been so devalued. Sunday schools, although often treated as the singular and divinely ordained mode of Christian education possible in congregations, actually are a relatively recent invention. This is particularly true in their current incarnation as the main and sometimes only explicit form of religious education for children in congregations. Sunday schools were initially founded in the 1780s in England as missional efforts to provide literacy education for young urban industrial workers whose labor requirements and poverty did not allow them to attend schools. Sunday school started out quite literally as "schooling on Sundays" in which the Bible and other religious material became the resources for the major agenda of general education. In the United States, Sunday schools became an important part of the "frontier evangelization" movement and a major element of the revivalistic outreach of churches, which would connect the largely unchurched participants in the Sunday school to the congregation's worship services.[24] They were not initially, however, a means for churches to provide for the religious education of their own members.

Initially ecumenically sponsored, over time Sunday schools became more denominationally located, as denominations became more territorial about forming their own Sunday school societies. This issued in the development of denominational curricular materials for use in the Sunday schools. In the United States, "common schools" or public schooling became established[25] and then eventually mandated. Protestant religious education through Bible lessons and moral teachings shaped the curriculum there. Public schools fashioned a supposedly nonsectarian approach to religious education of children, teaching morals and virtues in the weekday school, which were then reinforced by Sunday schools in their denominational specificity. Roman Catholics initiated weekday religious education and Catholic parochial schools to redress the Protestant bias in the public education system. Meanwhile, most efforts to establish Protestant parochial schools for children failed as a result of their redundancy with supposedly secular public schooling.[26]

Over time, Sunday schools took on a more exclusively religious educational purpose, gradually taking their places as the primary vehicle for churches to education their people religiously. When Sunday schools began to be the means of Christian education for a congregation's own children, that education generally took place before or after the Sunday worship service.[27] In other words, the educative aspects of children's participation in the church did not replace children's participation in other aspects of congregational life and practice.

At the same time, however, by focusing the educational aspects of congregations into a separately structured entity within the church, Sunday schools thereby had the effect of gradually removing education from the other activities constituting a practice of faith and congregational life. In so doing, churches treated learning as a separate, rather than a constitutive, aspect of their identity and practice. That is, congregations came to identify their educative practices with the Sunday schools. In so doing they substituted codified knowledge for actual practice with a focus on "instructional structure and pedagogical authority that discouraged negotiations of meaning."[28] They therefore stopped seeing the multiple other aspects of their lives together as mutually reinforcing sites for learning. I will say more about this shortly, in relation to the understanding of learning and education this organizational arrangement produces.

Women, Children, and Education in the Church

Christian education long has been an acceptable and "gender congruent" place for women to exercise their gifts of ministry. From the beginnings of the Sunday school movement in England, women taught. Certainly from the 1800s forward, this resulted from the fluidity of assumed continuities between church and home and between matters concerning the care and nurture of children on the one hand with the lives of women on the other hand. Bendroth and others[29] have documented this continuity well. Women have taught Sunday school even in churches requiring women's subordination and refusing their ordination.

Gendered associations between children's learning and women and between "higher" education and men continue to be reflected in many U.S. Protestant congregations today, where women teach children's Sunday school while adult education is principally the responsibility of men (and particularly of male pastors). Many from the Religious Right insist on the supposedly God-given role of women in educating the children in the church, a role that must necessarily be handed over to men "at the higher levels" of children's and adult education.[30] The separation of children's education into a female-gendered sphere, while not necessarily backed with the ideological perspectives given by conservatives, nevertheless takes shape through the associations among women, church, and children that predominate even within mainline and progressive Christian education efforts. In such efforts parents (especially mothers) are understood to have a higher stake in the church's educational program and thus are recruited to teach in Sunday school.

Even though prior to the 1960s children usually were not separated from participation in the congregations' worship and mission activities, through the gendering of Christian education they nevertheless occupied a separated and devalued space.

When it comes to theology, children, and Christian education, a great irony surfaces even today. Its roots lie in this gendering of educational ministries. Feminist theologians have, for the most part, ignored Christian education altogether, treating it as a kind of "women's ghetto" within the church with which they do not wish to be associated, although many women in Christian education embrace feminist theology as a significant resource in their educational ministries.[31] At the same time, conservative Christian groups, though often limiting women's leadership to the circumscribed and devalued role of work with children as the sole legitimate outlet for their ministry, do affirm the importance of women's contributions to congregations through the ministries of Christian education with children. The irony, of course, comes in the inability of either of these groups concerned with the positioning of women in the church to affirm simultaneously women's leadership in Christian educational ministries (often nonordained) and women's ordained pastoral leadership.

In many church settings, as gender roles and leadership become more fluid and at least some congregations explicitly work to counter sexism by modeling male and female adult involvement in children's nurture, educational work with children today constitutes a far less "gendered" arrangement than it did in the past. At the same time, however, the continuing association among children, nurture, and women in churches often reflects a gendered distribution of power and status in church cultures that marginalizes both women and children. This suggests at least a partial response to the above question about how the positioning of education within its larger context reflects power and status. Education, like the women and children most associated with it, is–in its current configuration, definition, and positioning–a low priority in churches.

Demographics and Developmentalism: Christian Education from the 1950s and Beyond

The 1950s in the United States were years of unprecedented institutional expansion in churches. During the years between 1950 and 1960, the two-parent family with children was the most dominant family form. It became increasingly isolated in single family housing units. This was combined with an increasing sense of the opposition between workplace values of competition and the utilitarian self-interest of individuals with values associated with the church and the home, consisting of harmony, group solidarity, and nurture. This combination made for a continuing affinity between family life and religion that swelled the rolls of churches.[32] In such a context, naturally, Christian education programs also grew in importance and in number of participants. Coinciding with mainline Protestant theology's embrace of the secular social sciences such as psychology and education as disciplines that could contribute to and strengthen religious education, Sunday schools increasingly took the form of age-level segmented classrooms using similarly age-graded denominational curricula.

Elements of Protestant Nurture of Children

This increasingly age-specialized and program-oriented education affirmed several of what Bendroth calls the distinctive elements of mainline Protestant nurture of children:

a. These age-graded classes and curricula honored the integrity of children's faith as valid at whatever age and developmental capacity they might occupy. They showed "respect for the separate world of children"[33] rather than merely treating them as smaller versions of adults.

b. These programs, while tending to put the responsibility for religious education in the hands of professionals (pastors and professional religious educators, and, secondarily, other adults specifically trained by them for the task) generally assumed a reinforcing role by parents and home environments.

c. These programs and curricula rested on the idea that the "spiritual vitality" of parents could rub off onto their children, so that parents were not mere didactic instructors on religious matters but acted as what Bendroth calls "positive agents of grace" in the lives of children, such that parenting mattered from a religious point of view.[34]

Fighting the "Boredom Problem"

At some point, however, the idea that children possess different developmental capacities than do adults began to coincide with changing cultural forms in marketing and entertainment. This combination came to suggest not simply that children could benefit from experience with age-specific religious and educational experiences but also that they would be bored or otherwise possibly harmed by religious involvement that was not specifically directed to their age-related capacities and interests. Just as cartoons came to be seen as a kind of television programming made for children, so, too, was the "children's sermon," or even separate children's church, a development of a specific and age-related kind of religious participation. In the 1940s a parachurch youth ministry organization called Young Life was born, taking as one of its mottoes a statement by founder and Presbyterian minister Jim Rayburn, "It's a sin to bore a kid with the Gospel." Fun and excitement soon became key indicators of good ministry with children and youth. What remains unanalyzed in virtually every historical account of youth ministry and of Young Life in particular is the temporal coincidence between Rayburn's slogan and the explosion of consumerism in which marketers all too readily played on growing parental anxieties about keeping children happy and entertained.

Stearns calls this adult anxiety about childhood boredom "the clearest addition to parental burdens after 1945...Quite simply, boredom increasingly mutated, after the late 1940's, from being an attribute of personality that needed attention to being an inflicted state that demanded correction by others. The importance of boredom increased in this process, along with its growing association with childhood."[35] Stearns contends that the need to keep children entertained through buying commodities became intertwined with the redefinition of parenting as providing fun to children, both to the benefit of the market. The church's ministries with children were hardly immune to such cultural shifts redefining the relationships between children and adults.

Children and Worship

Thus, gradually congregational worship as a multigenerational experience of the whole community came to be replaced increasingly by an hour in which adults participated in worship while children engaged in separate and presumably more entertaining religious education activities.[36] During the 1950s churches, particularly middle-class suburban ones, began to conduct multiple worship services to accommodate the large numbers of people entering their sanctuary doors and education wings. Accordingly, many (especially larger) churches offered multiple sessions of what was then being called "church school" or "Sunday church school," some of which happened concurrent with worship services. As an increasingly hurried pace of living along with intensified patterns of age segregation became more normative elsewhere in the culture (promoted by advertising and further promulgated by the rise of developmental psychological perspectives engaged in educational theory in schools), patterns in congregational activity shifted. Instead of family involvement in a set of activities at the church on Sunday morning, which included both Sunday school and worship, it became more common beginning in the late 1950s for children to attend Sunday school while their parents worshiped. Children and adults operated in separate spheres in the congregation.

In the Children in Congregations Project, only one of the three congregations we studied assumed the regular presence of children for the whole of worship each week, but it did so at the expense of any structured and intentional process of religious education for children. In the other two congregations, parents were among the most vocal opponents to children's participation in the entirety of worship each week. Commonly voiced sentiments of parents mirrored these: "It will turn them off to religion because they will be bored." "It will make every Sunday a battle over coming to church if they have to sit through the sermon and long prayers they can't understand." Others in the congregations expressed concern that the liturgy or preaching would need to be "dumbed down" to accommodate the presence of children in worship.

Children and Congregational Missions

Worship is not the only arena of church life affected by the sequestering of children's education. Our research team observed that in these and other congregations with which we were familiar, efforts appeared especially minimal around the inclusion of children as participants in congregational forms of mission other than those involving putting coins into a special offering basket. The obvious conclusion is that congregations, rather than seeing learning as a constitutive aspect of their various practices, have created learning as a sequestered domain for children that stands separated and abstracted from all practices except those of this separate space of schooling within the church. Instead of seeing classroom learning, such as that which takes place through a Sunday school, as one among multiple sites for learning within a congregational culture, congregations make the unfortunate mistake of construing classroom instruction as *the* place where learning happens. They compound this mistake by making classroom instruction the only legitimate place for children in the congregation. Children's education thus becomes segregated from the rest of what the church does as a separate domain for children and those who care for them.

This separate positioning of children's education simply reiterates the positioning of children in religious discourse on childhood in the United States. Adults in congregations today appear quite ambivalent about children. They seem to pine nostalgically for an age in the church when hallways and classrooms overflowed with children and desire the presence of children in their midst as a sign of vitality today. The level of anxiety about not boring children and of fear that children will not return to church as teens or young adults if they are not adequately entertained plays an extremely influential role in congregations in everything from staffing levels and priorities to mission agendas. At the same time, when children do come to church, they generally are swept off into age-segregated spaces and programs. They may never even participate in a full-length worship service or congregational mission involvement until after their graduation from high school—if at that time they can think of any reason to do so, having little or no previous experience with it!

One observation is interesting and significant. At the very moment in history when marketing moguls seek to capitalize most fully on the specialized segmenting of children and youth into increasingly small market niche groups, congregations also view children and youth and their ministries with them in terms of increasingly age-segmented and segregated experiences. "Success" in children's ministries continues to be symbolized in many congregational contexts by the ability to attract a population of children large enough to create several age-graded classrooms and to draw a good crowd of children forward onto the chancel steps for a children's sermon. The "dysfunctional neurosis" emerging from congregational ambivalence toward children is clearly evident here. In their very anxiety about the absence of children and their desire to include and incorporate their children into the church, congregations develop ways of being with children that effectively create a separate children's church community. These practices insure that children will only be apprenticed in the practices of this separate children's ecclesial culture rather than in the practices commonly held with the "parent" church spawning it.

Children and Adults as Different Cultures?

Perhaps the establishment of parallel organizations within the church, some for children and youth, others for adults, simply reflects what generational theorists increasingly refer to as a clash between different but equally legitimate age-defined "cultures" within the church. Peter W. Rehwaldt[37] has developed an interesting model for conceptualizing different ways adults in congregations may relate to children. Using Malaysian theologian Yap Kim Hao's "five models for cultural interaction,"[38] Rehwaldt suggests that each of these models articulates different ways congregations attempt to mediate the encounter between adults and children in the church.

1. *Ethnocentrism* is a model of interaction in which one's own culture constitutes the norm for all others, which are seen as less developed. This is the model congregations enact when they hold the expectation that "children are to be quiet, little adults in church–sit still, listen, and learn."
2. *Accommodation* refers to a willingness to accommodate to what appear as the good aspects of another culture, while maintaining the "essentials" of one's own culture, refusing to change for the sake of others. Accommodation is the mode congregations engage in when "children are given 'children's sermons'–time is made for children, then children are set aside; [the] goal is slow assimilation to adult culture."
3. *Abandonment* refers to the complete entry into a different culture, giving up one's own culture to such a great extent that the main features of it are set aside, such as in "'family worship' (vs. traditional

worship)–[in which] children's culture (songs, prayers, images, etc.) replaces adults' culture completely."

4. *Relativity* refers to a model in which diverse cultures constitute different meaning systems of value to those who hold them, so that the goal is to peacefully coexist rather than to interact per se. Rehwaldt locates "children's church" under the relativity model as a type of "'liturgical apartheid'…where children meet in one room and adults in the other." This model also expresses the structuring of relationships between children and adults in congregations in which children's education classes meet concurrent with worship.

5. *Openness* offers a way of cultural interaction in which both parties are open to one another's culture and engage in a mutual quest of exploration, exchange, and learning expected to eventuate in enrichment of both cultures. This model is expressed in multigenerational worship and preaching.[39]

Let us accept for a moment the idea that children and adults constitute different "cultures" such that their interactions are comparable to those between the cultures of the type Yap refers in his work on intercultural engagement. Rehwaldt's five-model framework offers a heuristic window into the various strategies congregations may employ to structure the relationships of children and adults within them. In doing so, this model can help congregations give a name to their own ways of organizing generations of people. This framework can help congregations analyze whether some other alternatives might better fit their intentions for how children and adults participate together in the church.

What I wish to note, though, is the particular ecclesiology manifested when children's participation in the church becomes separated from the participation of the rest of the community. This may be justified by the theory that children constitute an inherent (not socially constructed) separate "culture" from that of adults. Such separation may be applied to worship and liturgy, Christian education, advocacy and care, or the congregation's various externally located missional activities of service and care. However applied, the practice of separating out one segment of the church based on its age and creating separate activities and agendas for them that do not intersect with the rest of the church's practice is in effect to create a separate, "parallel" church for children with its own separate practices and identity. In certain times and situations separation into various subgroups (by age, by gender, etc.) may be helpful and desirable, but the potential for these separations to become rigid and permanent features rather than contextual strategies looms large. When that happens and the separations come to be adhered to woodenly, whether or not they are functional and regardless of their larger consequences, then they become problematic. No longer being centered around the purpose of equipping children to participate in the community's practice, this separate and sequestered parallel church comes to educate children into its separate and sequestered practices.

Rationales for Separation

At some point, the rationale for separating children and adults begins to shift from the more benign concern to offer children what they (developmentally speaking) need to that of removing those whose differences, interests, and needs may constitute impediments to perceived adult differences, interests, and needs. Pastors no longer need to cultivate the skills of preaching to a multi-aged group of congregants. Those who plan for the missional activity of the church are excused from the complications and difficulties of thinking through the ways children might contribute in the church's night shelter for housing homeless persons or their local and global peacemaking efforts. Deacons and others responsible for pastoral care, not routinely seeing children or hearing their names included in the pastoral prayers, may come to assume that someone else (perhaps their parents) is providing for their needs for care.

Rhetoric focused on the developmental needs of children masks the less acceptable concern to remove what is messy, complicated, or undesirable in the experience of community shared by adults with children. It becomes a cleverly masked way to remove alterity. Under the guise of more perfectly welcoming the children, many mainline congregations instead simply have set them aside. And the entire congregation misses the opportunities for deeper reflection and transformation of practice that children as relative newcomers to faith can contribute to the communities if they are not effectively denied full participation.

As I have stressed, the "different cultures" model has considerable heuristic value for naming the dynamics at work in various ways congregations structure relations between adults and children, particularly in worship. It also seems useful in helping congregations choose compromise strategies that work toward change amidst complex power arrangements that mediate against children's full participation and welcome in the church. Standing alone, however, as a theory and model of multigenerational engagement in congregations, it is insufficiently critical of the basic assumption that children in congregations necessarily constitute a different "culture" from that of adults. The problem with such a separate-but-equal model that construes children and adults as different "cultures" within the church is its tacit acceptance of the situation created by the separation of Christian education programs for children as the legitimated children's domain within congregational life, separated and abstracted from the full practices of Christian community. That assumption, I contend, has its genesis in consumerist practices that construe human society in terms of age-segmented niches for marketing purposes.

Separating Instruction from Practice in the Education of Children

There remains one important and often overlooked by-product of separating the educational instruction of children from the other practices of faith communities. Bourdieu and others after him perceptively note that education always produces unintended practices.[40] That is, in addition to the outcomes and results intended by teachers and others who design and plan for it, education also brings about unintended and often unanticipated forms of knowledge and practice.

Education's Unintended Results and Practices

In particular, instructional education detached from engagement in social practices, where knowledge is produced and utilized, produces unintended learning and unintended practices that may even undermine the intended education and practices. For instance, the ostensible intended learning and practices of separated Sunday school education for children have as their purpose the education of children into Christian faith and community. These instructional practices with children, therefore, involve such things as developmentally age-appropriate learning about the Christian tradition and the Bible, engagement with peers and adults in relationships that facilitate children's senses of belonging and connection to the community, and the equipping of children in the practices of Christian faith that will eventually allow them to take their places as mature members in the community of faith.

What are the unintended learnings and practices that result from separating instructional learning of children from the rest of the congregation's practice? First, one of the primary things children learn is how to "do" Sunday school. Their "community of practice" becomes reduced to the Sunday school. Instead of being apprenticed into the community of missional, worshiping, serving Christians who are the church, children become apprentices of a set of pedagogical relations (teachers, students, and curricular materials) within the church, but they are not apprenticed in the larger community of practice itself. Lave and Wegner describe this process in other forms of organizations that seek ways to educate newcomers into their practices. When a curriculum is created for instructing newcomers that is separated from the practices of the community, it mediates learning "through an instructor's participation, by an external view of what knowing is about," involving a "prescriptive view of the target practice as subject matter."[41]

Di Pagel, a Christian educator in the San Francisco Bay area, described her appreciation for Godly Play as a method of educating children in the church. She referred to the kinds of teaching methods she used before becoming a Godly Play teacher as "teacher-centered," in which the main learning of children concerned "learning to please the teacher instead of taking pleasure in learning."[42] One of the primary practices taught through schooling concerns how to succeed in school (or not) by test-taking and through other forms of behavior that gain teacher approval. In much the same way, Sunday school's unintended learnings and practices may have more to do with how to successfully navigate the Sunday school environment than with education in the practice of a living and vital faith. Given the understanding of teaching for faith that so many adults bring to Sunday school teaching, children learn that good participation means providing a teacher with certainty in an answer to a question rather than a practice of engagement in curious inquiry of struggle with faith issues. Even very young children learn quickly from the unintended practices of such didactic instruction that sustained inquiry makes many adults uncomfortable and therefore is not "good practice" of doing Sunday school.

Preemptive Instruction

Jerome Bruner, describing the difference between processes of understanding and those of explaining in teaching-learning, asserts that "Understanding, unlike explaining, is not preemptive: one way of constructing the fall of Rome does not preclude other ways."[43] Much didactic instruction in contemporary Christian education with children is preemptive. Children learn that competent participation means responding in the (singularly) accepted manner according to the parameters laid out by the instructor and the culture of schooling in which the classroom experience is situated. It is this phenomenon that accounts for the ironic humor behind jokes about children's Sunday school classes in which a child, asked to say what a certain animal drawing reminds her of, replies, "Well, it looks like a squirrel to me but I know the answer must be Jesus."

Children's "worship readiness" classes, held and advertised in many congregations as a way of equipping children to participate meaningfully in the congregation's worship, provide a helpful example of preemptive instruction. Usually these classes occur apart from children's participation in worship as preparation for their participation at some future time. Separated from children's regular participation in this central practice of the wider community, these classes effectively structure learning through an externally mediated view of what worship is and how to participate in it. In effect this external view becomes the subject matter instead of the practice of worship itself. The main practice is not worship itself but that of learning about worship. These sequestered classroom instructional experiences "school" children in the subject matter of how to be a good worship participant by performing correctly the various components of the practices of worship. Should not such worship readiness classes be sites for learning worship practices and their meanings through intensified reflections on an engaged practice?

Lave and Wenger[44] worked on apprenticeship as "situated learning" through what they call "legitimate peripheral participation" in a community of practice. Through this work they identify several important problematic consequences of sequestered instructional models of learning. First, sequestered learning impacts the source of motivation for learning. Second, it requires learners to take on two separate sets of practices–two separate identities–in order to participate in both segregated age group classrooms and the community at large. Third, the kind of learning taking place in sequestered environments may not be broadly portable to other contexts. I will briefly explore each of these.

In age-segregated models of church education, it is teachers who assume responsibility for motivating newcomers. We see this in congregations in which Sunday school teachers routinely find themselves frustrated by children's complaints of boredom, lack of motivation to be present and to learn, and in the seemingly increasing behavior problems with which teachers must contend in Christian education's Sunday school classrooms. As a self-contained entity that must produce its own motivations in students, the sequestered Sunday school instructional classroom must motivate student desires to participate in the classroom activities. Such motivation must occur in the absence of a larger "culture of participation and membership." The desire for increasing access to such a culture of participation creates an intrinsic motivation for learning that exists beyond the confines of the classroom.

I recall from my own childhood experience, for example, the urgent motivation I felt for learning the words of the Apostle's Creed, Doxology, Gloria Patri, and Lord's Prayer as a fourth-grader who had little previous participation in or exposure to the church. The motivation I felt around learning these various "artifacts" of Christian practice came from my awareness that I could not belong–could not really participate as someone who was a member of my little church community in Richmond, Virginia–if I did not know these creeds, sung responses, and prayers. From there, the interaction between using an artifact of a community's practice and understanding it further motivated me to understand these creeds and songs more deeply. Such interaction constitutes an important part of the learning process and came into play for me with further participation in this faith community.[45] This motivation and learning differed considerably from what I experienced in later years as I participated in Sunday school learning in which the classroom and its teacher had to try to motivate learning intrinsic to the classroom situation. In a community of largely disinterested peers, I learned quickly and early that the appearance of too much interest in and enthusiasm for theology, church, or faith did not fit within the framework of the Sunday school classroom. The Sunday school classroom was, in reality, a community of practice whose purposes as a place of learning and inquiry became subverted by the unintended practices (of resistance to the processes of schooling themselves and of lack of motivation for participating in them) produced therein.

Differences in Learning Practices

Is there any real difference in the experience of, say, an eight-year-old child between learning that comes through engagement in participation in the community's worship practice and that which takes place in classroom instruction on worship? In both, ostensibly, a child can learn "how to worship." In both, it seems, such a child's needs for a sense of competency in practice, so critical to motivation in learning, can be met. So what is the real difference from the perspective of children as learners?

Again, along with Lave and Wenger[46], I assert that learning is only partly about being able to do new activities and accomplish new cognitive understandings. Learning, especially learning in relation to religious faith, fundamentally involves the construction of an identity, a process that is social in nature and takes place through participation in a community of practice in which the identities of persons take shape through sustained participation in that community of practice. There, children learn not just how to talk about what Christians do as a substitute for their participation. They learn through their participation how to talk *as* Christians do. They learn how to engage and tell the stories of scripture in relation to their own lives and that of the world, how to use liturgical language and other forms of "insider speech" that mark them as members of a somewhat odd and idiosyncratic group that is church. An eight-year-old child in a worship readiness class may gain the same technical ability for performing the actions necessary for "competent" participation in worship as will a child who learns those abilities through regular practice of them in the context of the community's worship. The former child's sense of competency comes in the production of external forms that may or may not be "transferable" between settings. The latter child engages in the process of taking on an identity as a participant with increasing abilities to engage in and meaningfully "perform" the various composite practices involved in worship. Through such engagement a child develops ways of negotiating meaning and action as an identity that, as identity, are portable. These learned practices are not confined to the classroom alone, self-contained and not pointing to anything beyond themselves. As elements of an identity, they comprise a way of being in the world.

In short, in a separate "children's church" Christian education apprentices children into the practices of a separate culture held within the Sunday school. When those children step into other-than-Sunday-school arenas of their own lives or of the church's practice, they must in effect move from one set of practices to another separate set of practices. That is, they have to learn two different sets of practices.

The goal, however, is to make learning portable. This can be done if children are apprenticed into identities as Christians who practice a way of life that involves peculiar uses of language, symbol, story, and action. This apprenticeship includes both times of classroom learning and participation in worship. Classroom learning then serves as opportunities for deepened or more focused inquiry into what is already being engaged in the daily and weekly rhythms of practice. In that way children's learning becomes portable. They can move between and among various contexts and setting, within and outside of the church, with their practices forming part of the identity that these children take with them from one place to another.[47]

The Gift of Inexperience

Didactic education sequestered from other aspects of a community of practice engenders yet another important effect upon children in congregations. It significantly curtails their individual and collective "agency" by circumscribing the transformative impact that children have on the congregation as a community of practice. One primary way that such communities maintain their vitality and continually renew their identity is through the reciprocal negotiations of meaning and activity they undergo with all kinds of newcomers, including children. As such, children contribute to congregations! Their inquiries and early efforts at participation involve the mature community of practice in further and perhaps deeper reflection on what it does and says, in ways that help the community stay connected with its own corporate identity and that test that identity through processes of ongoing negotiation and construction. For example, children may ask, "Why do we say 'amen' when we pray?" or, "How does our church really care about poor people when there are none here?" or, "Is God the same as Jesus?" Then members of the community receive opportunities to rethink and rearticulate what their beliefs and actions mean, not only why they do certain things but how they understand them. The members can even renegotiate those meanings in new ways. When children's cries punctuate the sanctuary's silence, the church as a community of practices receives an opportunity to think about what is important about silence. They can reclaim the church's "originary visions" and understandings of how it uses silence, and/or transform those in relation to the new awarenesses brought by the sounds of children.

Often these negotiations involve compromises in meaning and action. Sometimes they involve conflict, especially between "young upstarts" and long-term members of the community. The practices of any community involve an ongoing series of negotiations of meaning and identity by its participants. If children are sequestered away into a parallel, separate experience of church, not only do they lose out by being denied the interactional space to impact community practices, but the congregation also loses the resource of children's inexperience, in effect the gift of their newness to its life as a community of practice. Transformation of practice is critical to the ability of a community to renew and keep vital its life. Obviously, an important aspect of a child's sense of participation in a community relates to their sense that they can shape in some way the various social worlds in which they participate.[48] When children's participation in the church excludes them from contributing to the transformation of its practices, the church stagnates.

Strategies and Tactics for Christian Education with Children in Congregations

By now, it may sound as if I am about to argue for the wholesale abolishing of Sunday school in the education of children in congregations, arguing for its replacement by a socialization model that understands children as learning simply from their imitation of the actions of adults in community. I am not. In fact, I am not denying an appropriate role to the kind of classroom instruction embodied by Sunday school types of education any more than I am moving toward a proposal that socialization into practices alone can be sufficient for educating children in faith (a view that represents, in my thinking, a problematic reification of the "how to" aspects of Christian faith apart from its deep and substantive character as an identity, an aspect requiring study and reflection). What undermines the educational viability of classroom education is not the fact that it is classroom education, but that it is so thoroughly detached from the rest of the wider faith community's practices.

Persons–including children–need to be able to act within and adjust to ever-changing and complex life situations from their identities as people of faith. "Just showing up" or merely socializing persons into the actions and activities of faith without opportunities for sustained reflection, conceptual learning, and dialogue with others is insufficient to permit this kind of flexible "improvisational knowing." Socialization models of Christian education do not provide opportunities for people to encounter new perspectives for understanding scripture, theology, ethics, and Christian life. A question asked by so many seminary students as they first encounter the world-expanding theoretical views of biblical interpretation or theology is, "Why didn't we ever learn about any of this in church?" Their so oft-repeated question speaks to the poverty of education conceived of as socialization alone apart from engagement with the substantive theoretical knowledge resources as part of education in Christian practice.

What tactics and strategies present themselves for educating children into a faith identify that constitutes an alternative identity and practice to that of the dominant consumer-oriented society in which children in the United States live? Recall for a moment my brief reference to a distinction between tactics and strategies, drawn from the writings of Michel de Certeau.[49] With apologies for the military imagery evoked by these terms, I find de Certeau's distinction applicable to the situations educators of children face in congregations. In brief, strategies are longer-term plans, made by those who have the luxury of time for analysis and contemplation of the "big picture." Strategies are used by those who are relatively well-positioned in a conflict or struggle, who have the time to reflect and make the connections between the situation as it stands and the changes and outcomes desired. Tactics, on the other hand, are the activities of people from the underside of a struggle. They have neither the luxury of time nor perhaps the benefit of a thoroughgoing look at the situation as a whole. Nevertheless, they must choose some course of action and attempt to affect the situation, often on the turf and in the discourse of the "other" rather than on their own terms. Tactics are necessarily shorter-term actions, but they can have considerable impact.

In their struggles to educate children in congregations, persons involved in the work of Christian education often engage in tactical forms of action out of positions from the undersides of congregational power and authority, when what are needed in actuality are strategic interventions and plans. At the same time, sometimes tactical maneuvers are necessary to garner momentum or "problematize" the conditions under which children's education in faith takes place in congregations, particularly when those in positions to effect strategy do not grasp the meaning of education or the importance of welcoming and nurturing children.[50] Our goal is to transform Christian educational ministries in churches from pedagogical processes shaped by patterns and practices of consumerism into a ministry that welcomes children into the alternative identity and practices shared by the community of faith. Achieving this goal requires *both* strategies and tactics. In what follows I will paint in broad brush strokes some key strategies for educational ministries that can welcome children and contribute to their flourishing. I will conclude with brief comments on some possible tactics of transformation to use in situations in which resistance is high to reconstructing education as formation in an identity through participation in practices.

An Educational Strategy for Welcoming Children and Contributing to Their Flourishing

The perspective on children's learning in relation to Christian faith that I am proposing here differs from didactic classroom instruction alone or socialization devoid of reflection because it is a view of learning as identity formation in relation to a faith community that understands itself as a community of practice, situated around its central work of enactment of and struggle for the reign of God. As I have said, such learning is not just an accumulation of skills and information. It is a process of becoming that is at heart the formation of identity. Identity formation involves both the ability to participate competently in the here and now practices of a community and also to flexibly improvise in new situations and to imagine alternative futures based upon the ways of making sense or meaning deriving from identity in practice.

What might educational practices that welcome children and contribute to their flourishing look like in the context of a faith community in which children's learning happens in collaboration with seasoned, experienced practitioners of faith?

Hands-on Participation in Missions

A key educational strategy concerns the hands-on participation of children in the missional activities of the congregation. The central purpose of educating children (and other newcomers to the faith) for faith is the formation of identity among learners to enable their full participation in the mission and practices of the faith community. This identity includes their ability, in turn, to impact and transform the practices of that community toward ever-renewed and more adequate instantiations of good news. The paradox at work here is that Christian education, while being about identity, is in an important sense not about the ones being educated at all, but about the world and persons to whom Christian disciples are sent out. The rationale for Christian education with children is not the inculcation of "good values," the development of biblical literacy, or the opportunity to learn "about" God (although these things may be beneficial side effects of such an education in faith). The rationale for Christian education with children is its ability to prepare them to participate in the church's mission and ministry. The integral connection between learning and practice in the very purpose of education is precisely what is missing in many traditional modes of Sunday school learning. In such modes the material to be apprehended by students stands divorced from their practice of faith. Education into an identity contrary to that of "the good consumer" cannot happen through commodified processes of teaching. It can happen only through a community of practice shaping a person into its alternative way of life, centered around ministries of justice, love, and compassion.

What might this look like in congregations? Young children need the help of the scaffolding others provide in a congregation that practices God's hospitality. For example, these young children might engage in conversations with more experienced members. These conversations would lead the children to understand their congregation's practices of advocacy and care among persons without shelter as a ministry of God's welcome. They could at the same time engage in storytelling and learning from scripture in relation to their coparticipation with adults in those hands-on activities of the congregation. In so doing, over time they are formed into people who serve. They learn a set of practices and construct meanings and ways of understanding and relating to poor persons and poverty that have a distinctively Christian perspective.

My son Andrew was four years old when our family moved from the Philippines to San Francisco. He provided our family with an interesting lens of entry into our new home by constantly comparing the poor and homeless people he saw living on sidewalks and under bridges in San Francisco with those he had seen and known in the Philippines. After some months he began to ask important theological questions like, "Why doesn't God make the poor people have what they need?" and, "Why does God let there be more poor people in the Philippines than here?" Through dialogue within our family and in our congregation, Andrew began to develop ways of thinking, commensurate with his cognitive and affective development as a child, about these and other questions in relation to the ways we know and understand God's preferential concern for the poor. In short, Andrew started talking and thinking "like a Christian."

His thinking and discourse, both of which comprise important dimensions of practice, also came together with another aspect of practice, namely actions. Andrew has observed our congregation's practices of hospitality with homeless people through its "Welcome Center" ministries alongside other community practices of interpreting the scriptures in relation to norms of justice and hospitable care for the most marginal persons. Such observations have led Andrew to know himself to be part of a community of Christian people who engage in various forms of ministry and struggle on behalf of persons materially and otherwise deprived of what they need to live well. He did not start out that way, of course. This understanding and identity have emerged through the combination of discourse and actions that constitute faith practice in Andrew's congregational and family life, two overlapping "communities of practice."

For several years now Andrew has been a participant in a faith community that interprets and tries to organize its life around scriptural stories of how Jesus, like the prophets before him, lifted up poor and marginal people and how he calls on us to do the same in our times and contexts. Andrew has spent time in the Welcome Center, greeting its guests and helping them find their ways between areas of the church where they might choose kits of small toiletries and other items, or get a haircut or a shoulder massage. While neither we in his family nor his congregation feel particularly "adequate" in our ability to enact good news among the poor consistently and faithfully, Andrew knows that we continue to work at this and that it is central to our shared understanding of what it means to follow Jesus.

Some congregations, able to "make room for children" in worship and fellowship, nevertheless resist children's participation in mission. Here are some possible tactics of transformation in such situations:

1. Get an adult who is concerned about children's education in faith into a key decision-making position concerning congregational mission.
2. Start with missional activity initiated by children, who then invite adults to participate and collaborate with them.
3. Just show up with children ready to engage in whatever the church is doing–letter writing, construction, making sandwiches, setting tables for a meal, or protesting war.

Linking Sites and Resources for Learning

A second key strategy in educational practices that welcome children involves making links between the various sites and resources for learning that exist within congregations. We may conceive of congregations as possessing multiple sites of pedagogy. The question then becomes how the various learning contexts within a congregation interact with each other to support persons to learn and participate fully in the practices of the community. The congregation needs to create links between various practices, including classroom learning, so that instead of becoming self-contained and self-referential, they become mutually reinforcing.

A good example of these dimensions of links between practices that has importance for children in congregations is hymn singing. Is worship the only location in which children sing hymns? At First Presbyterian Church in San Anselmo, California, pastors can often be heard from the pulpit issuing specific invitations to parents to assist children to follow along in the hymnal as they sing together. In this way the pastors encourage adults to assist children in learning the practice of congregational hymn singing from the hymnal.

Do children sing hymns from a denominational hymnal in the sanctuary, but only "children's songs" in Sunday school and elsewhere? Do the gesturing and movements enjoyed by children in their separate singing find opportunities to destabilize the perhaps too-staid patterns of sanctuary hymn singing? Are there other contexts in which children and adults engage in the practice of hymn singing? Does this happen when the congregation meets to play together or to engage in some act of mission and service? Does language from various hymn texts that children know and sing show up in other forms of discourse, such as classroom instruction about the Trinity, sermons in worship, committee meetings, prayers? Are the kinds of hymns children especially enjoy singing with movement, imaginative imagery, and accessible tunes reflected only in children's separate singing times? Can they be included appropriately in the hymn singing practice of the entire community together? This is but one example of the ways a particular practice across various sites for learning can be linked in the practices of a faith community.

What tactics of transformation might be engaged to overcome the sequestering of children's learning from other sites of learning in congregations so that links may be made between the various resources for learning? A colleague of mine in the Philippines, Dr. Elizabeth Tapia, used to ask students at the end of class to write down one or two of their main learnings or insights from the class. What if we helped people to begin to recognize various activities beyond the classroom in their congregations as educative? We might do this by similarly inviting people to reflect on their learning, whether in a discussion-reflection period or in writing after an activity. Such a small tactical move could go far in increasing awareness of congregations of having multiple sites for learning besides Sunday school.

Increasing Children's Access

A third key strategy involves increasing children's access to the full range of congregational practices and to relationships with particular adults who demonstrate their gifts for mentoring newcomers into those practices. Lave and Wenger refer to the process by which learning through participation takes place as that of "legitimate peripheral participation."[51] This cumbersome expression communicates the way in which newcomers to any community of practice must gain a position of legitimate access to participation in order to learn. By the term *peripheral*, they convey the idea that an apprentice to any practice does not start out participating with the same degree of responsibility, intensity, understanding, or skill that we would expect of an "old timer" in the same community. From their positions of legitimate "peripherality," persons move from this more external status as newcomers to increasingly central positions in relation to the community's practices and identity, coming to be included and to include themselves as stakeholders in its present and future. This description reminds me of church historians' depictions of the catechumenate in the early Christian church and of the practices of many churches today. As learners being both apprenticed and instructed in the practices of the faith community, they occupied a legitimated yet peripheral position of access to those practices. Participating in worship up to the point of the eucharistic meal, full participation–and full responsibility–was reserved for those whose apprenticeship culminating in baptism positioned them no longer at the periphery but in the center of the church's practices.

The question for Christian education with children is what kind of access children have, and whether it is access to the full range of Christian practices in which their communities engage? Lave and Wenger's studies of other kinds of communities of practice into which newcomers seek membership suggest that when newcomers only gain access to menial or inconsequential practices that lack substance and importance for the "core practices" that define that community's identity, they occupy positions of marginality rather than peripherality. Under such conditions, their access to practices remains too limited to form in them an identity. For example, apprentice camp counselors may only get access to the routinized and relatively insignificant work of checking attendance, tying children's shoes, and making sure every child has a lunch. From that position they do not gain enough access to the central and meaningful practices that define camp counselors as a "community of practice," such as planning and engaging in an integrated program of sports activities, arts and crafts, singing and storytelling, camp craft and skill teaching while serving as "parents in absentia." Only by having limited or provisional but legitimate access to these substantive practices of camp counseling can the apprentice counselors-in-training gain an identity within this community of practice. Similarly, for children to gain an identity as members in the community of practice, they must have access not only to its edges but also to its core, in the form of access to its centrally defining practices.

In congregations holding a strong clerical understanding of ministry rather than a theology of shared ministry, even adults may not have legitimate access to substantive and defining practices of Christian community. These are vested in the clergy. That issue notwithstanding, the question of whether children have access, and what kinds of access they have, to participation in practices remains crucial. If children only participate in the less central, less identity-defining practices, then children have little chance of learning–and of being formed and transformed in–an identity through their participation in practices. Less central practices for children may include only singing in a children's choir that "performs" quarterly in congregational worship, with music that differs in theology, substance, and style from the rest of the congregation's practices of singing. The same lack of identity formation occurs when children have limited or no access to a congregation's central practices, such as mission activities, sacraments, ways of interpreting scripture, and patterns of prayer. For children to become genuine apprentices of Christian faith and life, they must have opportunities to participate with others in the "core practices" that define that faith and life.

Two specific tactics come to mind in renegotiating children's access to practices in congregations. The first is straightforward, but undoubtedly too controversial to implement in many settings. Change the schedule so that children's Sunday school does not prevent children and their teachers from access to worship or other core elements of the community of practice.[52] The second tactical suggestion involves a process of continual assessment of children's access. In this, some adults who take particular responsibility for the education of children within the congregation take on the task of continually asking amidst the community's various practices and events: how are children participating? What can we do to better enable the participation of children? What kinds of reflection, instruction, and study in conjunction with this practice would best assist children of different ages and abilities to learn? And, in evaluating practices as sites for learning, what did children's participation teach or contribute to the community's practice and understanding in this particular instance? How are we as a whole changed by the presence and participation of children?

Honoring Children's Thoughts and Initiatives

A fourth strategy for educational practices that welcome children involves the honoring of children's thoughts, ideas, and initiatives in relation to practices of faith. Children not only are shaped by practices in which they participate. They also "act back" on the community of practice, with new insights, ideas, and actions that can contribute to the transformation of those practices and, therefore, of the community. For example, in my son Andrew's emerging understanding of what it means to be Christian in a context in which our family has more than enough while many others struggle for survival, Andrew's interpretations of scripture have transformed some of our family practices. He transforms them by placing before us the sharpness of a child-as-newcomer's concrete and focused attention to our practices with his insights and questions. When we prepare for a drive through the city, Andrew often insists—"because Jesus told us to care about poor people and help them and feed them"—that we carry in our car small bags of food to give to the persons we encounter at stoplights holding signs reading "homeless and hungry: please help." We began to do this when, after hearing the parable of the good Samaritan, Andrew became upset at the idea that we knowingly would drive past someone in need. "We have more than we need so we have to give some to them," he will say by way of explanation.

After conversations in our church and with our family about some of the many issues involved in giving money or other direct assistance to people on the streets, Andrew thought that offering people food might be the best thing he and our family could do in these brief interactions with our homeless neighbors. These conversations included such questions as, Does direct assistance really help others, or mostly help us feel like we've done something? On the other hand, Is that a good enough reason *not* to extend help to someone who needs it? Does giving money invite people to stay in their situation somehow in a way that does not really help them? Does it in some small way fulfill Jesus' saying that whenever we give even a cup of cold water to one in need we do so to him? Is there something we need to be doing to change the "big picture" that creates such poverty in our city? Andrew thinks about these and many other questions.

At age eight, Andrew's participation in a community of practice has not only apprenticed him in performing certain actions, but has also "scaffolded" his thinking and meaning-making in relation to these activities so that he can articulate a rudimentary understanding of how his gesture of compassion is in certain ways limited, a stopgap measure in the face of a large and complex problem that is poverty, even while it is a way of living out a Christian identity as those who care for poor people. Conversely, Andrew's theological inquiries and insights have reshaped our practices in some significant ways, and we continue to learn from the interactive process of thinking with him about such complex questions.

Parents, pastors, and Christian educators often tell me similar stories of the ways their children transform a family or congregational practice with their more concrete and direct sense of awareness. One mother told me that their family was experimenting with being vegetarian after their ten-year-old daughter requested that they not eat meat out of her faith-motivated ethical concern over the mistreatment of animals. "My husband and I were vegetarians in college, but I guess we became 'hardened' to the suffering of animals and just stopped thinking about it. Ana has a very tender empathy for animals and a fierce sense of Christian justice. So we wanted to support that." Similarly, children in one West coast congregation mobilized their congregation to use "fair trade" coffee at the church after studying the situation of coffee producers alongside their reading and reflection on various prophetic texts concerned with justice and land. These are but a few examples of times that adults in Christian communities of practice have changed what they do to honor the insights and wisdom of children.

In our study of congregational practices with children through the Children in Congregations Project, we found (not surprisingly) that congregations vary considerably in their degree of openness to children's agency to transform the church and to the honoring of their initiatives, especially in worship. One tactic of transformation helpful to congregations with such resistance involves identifying a practice in which resistors have less stake and starting there. One congregation frowns on children's participation in worship leadership in its formal service. Children and their adult teachers suggested that since the passing of the peace is one of the "least formal" moments in the service because worshipers get up and move around to greet one another, that might be a good place for children to provide leadership. From that "compromise starting point" of robustly shouting out, "Peace be with you!" children gradually have been welcomed into other roles in the leadership of worship there.

Welcoming Education as a Way to Welcome Children

As a set of strategies (together with a few tactical maneuvers) for educational ministries that welcome children, the above brief list is intended to be suggestive rather than comprehensive. Taken together, these strategies underscore the necessity of embracing an alternative perspective on education in congregations that critiques rather than takes up the consumer-oriented, market-driven educational practices and ideologies operating in so many congregational settings today.

In summary, I envision educational ministries that contribute to the welcome and flourishing of children in the church. To realize that vision, the purpose and function of education with children is that of empowering them to participate in the practices of the community that are formative and constitutive of an alternative identity in the world. That alternative identity is focused around God's redefining of kinship and reordering of power through the call of all persons to be children of God. This is a different purpose than that of providing children with the information they will need to make their own individual decision about religion if and when the Spirit of God concurs with the efforts of Sunday school education and parents at some later date. This purpose does not function to sequester children into a separate space where learning happens, thus serving the tacit function of constituting the church as a kind of "gated community" for adults only, protected from the messiness of children's lives and needs. Rather, this purpose operates to promote children's access to the variety of spaces within the life and practice of the community where learning happens, integrating children in all their messiness into the identity and practices of the faith community.

In addition, the kinds of educational ministries with children that can fund their welcome in the church reframe the role of the various participants in education within the culture of the congregation. In the commonly experienced sequestered classroom learning of many congregations, children take on roles primarily as receivers of knowledge and as passive learners. They are rarely considered "doers" of the Word, active participants in whole of the community's faith practices. Their passive role and position in the congregation in effect deprives them of agency. The kind of education I envision, in contrast, understands children as participants in the practices of the community. From their position as relative newcomers, children offer the gift of their newcomers' insights and knowledge to the larger community. They not only receive knowledge but also produce it and offer it in and through their participation in the community of practice. Children as learners are participants in social processes, practices, and relationships with others, whose collaboration with children not only "scaffolds" the learning of children, but also engenders clarification and renegotiation of meanings and practices within the larger community of practice for its continual renewal and learning.

Teachers are those persons who take on the mentoring/apprenticing responsibilities necessary for the church's thriving and for the formation of children's identities within it, in a particularly intentional way. They actively and intentionally offer scaffolding that allows children to construct meanings and participate in practices beyond that which any could do on their own. Teachers offer this particularly focused and intentional scaffolding of the learning of children, but not out of some contrived or externally authorized role as experts in the knowledge or "data" of Christianity. Teachers offer this scaffolding from their position as longer-term, more seasoned, and more experienced practitioner-mentors, skilled in the practices of Christian faith and life. From that position within the congregation they are able to participate in the education of the young. Accordingly, their educational ministries with children do not remove them from participation in the worship and mission of the congregation, but rather have their basis in teachers' regular participation in the whole life of the church out of which they are able to mentor children. At certain times they may do so from the more distanced perspective-taking of classroom learning, but they also engage in this mentoring across the various locations for learning in the practices of faith that make up congregational life.

All members of the congregation share in the responsibility of educating and nurturing children. In this sense they all embody Karl Barth's theological claim that in the church, parents–but also all adult members–act as presbyters with coresponsibility for children. Pastors, from their roles as spiritual and theological leaders in the community of practice, similarly participate as teachers and presbyters in the education of children. As such they have special responsibilities for supporting the organizing and carrying out of the community's corporate faith practices, offering theological and spiritual resources to the community inclusive of children as it seeks to engage in its practices with faithfulness and integrity. They teach God's hospitality to children through their practices of welcoming children into the church's ministries. As such, they proclaim the good news in sermons and other interpretive activities done with children in mind. They are not "above" involvement with the education of children. In fact, involvement with educating children is central to their pastoral ministry, as the bringing in of newcomers (children) to an identity and practice of Christian faith is the heart of the pastoral tasks of evangelism and mission.

Furthermore, in a liberatory theology of childhood, the contextual situating of children's education in relation to the rest of what the congregation does as a community of practice must undergo a fundamental relocation. From its current positioning as a separate or parallel community of practice, children's education (as well as that of adults, for that matter!) must be repositioned within the liturgical and sacramental, missional, and care-giving ministries of the church. Children's education must become a constitutive aspect of all of these ministries, as children learn through their participation in them, along with periods of intentional reflection upon them. The practices of the community must no longer be divided into those that are learned in the singularly legitimated realm in which children reside within the church (i.e., Sunday school) and those that are central to the church's identity (i.e., worship and sacraments, mission activity, stewardship, etc.). These central community practices must produce and shape persons, including children, into identities as reflective practitioners of this way of life. Such knowledge, while situated in a context, is portable across contexts. Children engaged in learning are learning faith practices and not some other set of practices parallel to them.

Last, this feminist practical theology of childhood critiques the gendered situating of educational ministries in congregations. This critique analyzes how the positioning of education associated with women and children reflects the distribution of power, status, and other forms of symbolic capital in a church that still labors under the sin of sexism and the marginalizing of those deemed lesser or weak, such as children. Obviously, one key reason educational ministries with children remain "sidelined" in so many congregations is that they remain an expression of the uneven power relations between women and men in the church, and between children and adults as well. In larger churches, for example, pastors involved with educational ministries have less status than those whose main portfolio is preaching or administration. In many contexts, those charged with responsibility for Christian education have less education for their jobs (and therefore less credentialing and status) than do persons in other forms of ministry. This situation often reflects the still-gendered distribution of the gifts of ministry that the apostle Paul wrote were given by the Spirit to *each one* for the common good (1 Cor. 11). I imagine the kind of educational ministry with children that is based on their participation in the church as a community of practice. The only relevant status marker is that of being an experienced, skilled, and gifted (i.e., "knowledgeable") reflective practitioner of faith who can apprentice and guide children toward increasingly experienced, skilled, and gifted practice and understanding of practice.

We must reconsider the nature of Christian education with children. We must move it away from its stereotypical rendering as the teaching of morals and right beliefs to children. We must move it toward a reframed perspective as the faith community's apprenticing of children in a "kin-dom identity," a way of life grounded in the Christian community's mission to be about the business of living and proclaiming the reign of God. Then it becomes clear that Christian education of children depends upon adults who actively and intentionally mentor children in practices of faith, and upon the ability of children to have access to and participate in the community's practices. Such a vision of education certainly flies in the face of the increasingly superficial relational bonds between children and adults in far too many settings, including congregations. This view requires adults who do not abdicate their role as mentors in the identity formation of children. These adults must willingly mentor and teach children who may or may not be their "own"; children who may be well-behaved and happy, but also may be sick, dirty, messy, and uncooperative; children whom Jesus calls, blesses, welcomes, and gives over into our care.

Sources Cited

Aronowitz, Stanley, and Henry A. Giroux. *Education Still under Siege.* Westport, Conn.: Bergin and Garvey, 1993.

Barth, Karl. *The Christian Life: Church Dogmatics IV, 4 Lecture Fragments.* Translated by Geoffrey W. Bromiley. Grand Rapids, Mich.: Eerdmans, 1981.

Bendroth, Margaret Lamberts. *Growing Up Protestant: Parents, Children, and Mainline Churches.* New Brunswick, N.J.: Rutgers University Press, 2002.

Blazer, Doris A., ed. *Faith Development in Early Childhood.* Kansas City, Mo.: Sheed and Ward, 1989.

Bourdieu, Pierre. *Outline of a Theory of Practice.* Translated by Richard Nice. Cambridge: Cambridge University Press, 1977.

Bourdieu, Pierre, and Jean-Claude Passeron. *Reproduction in Education, Society and Culture.* Trans. Richard Nice. London: Sage, 1990.

Bruner, Jerome. *The Culture of Education.* Cambridge, Mass.: Harvard University Press, 1996

Christenson, Larry. *The Christian Family.* Minneapolis: Bethany House Publishers, 1970.

de Certeau, Michel. *The Practice of Everyday Life.* Berkeley, Calif.: University of California Press, 1984.

Dobson, James. *Bringing up Boys: Practical Advice and Encouragement for Those Shaping the Next Generation of Men.* Wheaton, Ill.: Tyndale House, 2001.

Epstein, Cynthia Fuchs. *Distinctive Differences: Sex, Gender and the Social Order.* New Haven: Yale University Press, 1985.

Fowler, James W. *Stages of Faith: The Psychology of Human Development and the Quest for Meaning.* San Francisco: Harper and Row, 1981.

Freire, Paulo. *Pedagogy of the Oppressed.* Translated by Myra Bergman Ramos. New York: Continuum, 1987.

Gardner, Howard. *Frames of Mind: The Theory of Multiple Intelligences.* New York: Basic Books, 1993.

Giroux, Henry A. et al., eds. *Counternarratives: Cultural Studies and Critical Pedagogies in Postmodern Spaces.* New York: Routledge, 1996.

Hess, Carol Lakey. *Caretakers of Our Common House: Women's Development in Communities of Faith.* Nashville: Abingdon Press, 1997.

hooks, bell. *Teaching to Transgress: Education as the Practice of Freedom.* New York: Routledge, 1994.

Keely, Barbara Anne, ed. *Faith of Our Foremothers: Women Changing Religious Education.* Louisville: Westminster John Knox Press, 1997.

Kennedy, William Bean. *The Shaping of Protestant Education: An Interpretation of the Sunday School and the Development of Protestant Educational Strategy in the United States, 1789–1860,* Monographs in Christian Education, ed. C. Ellis Nelson. New York: Association Press, 1966.

Lave, Jean, and Etienne Wenger. *Situated Learning: Legitimate Peripheral Participation.* Cambridge: Cambridge University Press, 1991.

Lynn, Robert W., and Elliott Wright. *The Big Little School: 200 Years of the Sunday School.* 2d ed. Birmingham, Ala.: Religious Education Press, 1980.

Marler, Penny Long. "Lost in the Fifties: The Changing Family and the Nostalgic Church." In *Work, Family and Religion in Contemporary Society,* ed. Nancy Tatom Ammerman and Wade Clark Roof, 23–60. New York: Routledge, 1995.

Miller, Vincent J. *Consuming Religion: Christian Faith and Practice in a Consumer Culture.* New York and London: Continuum, 2004.

Russell, Letty M. *Church in the Round: Feminist Interpretations of the Church.* Louisville: Westminster John Knox Press, 1993.

Stearns, Peter N. *Anxious Parents: A History of Modern Childrearing in America.* New York: New York University Press, 2003.

Tanner, Kathryn. *The Politics of God: Christian Theologies and Social Justice.* Minneapolis: Fortress Press, 1992.

Vygotsky, Lev S. *Mind in Society: The Development of Higher Psychological Processes.* Cambridge, Mass.: Harvard University Press, 1978.

Wenger, Etienne. *Communities of Practice: Learning, Meaning, and Identity.* Cambridge: Cambridge University Press, 1998.

Wood, David et al. "The Role of Tutoring in Problem-Solving." *Journal of Child Psychology and Child Psychiatry* 17 (1976): 89–100.

Yap, Kim Hao. *Doing Theology in a Pluralistic World.* Singapore: The Methodist Bookroom, 1990.

Young, Iris Marion. *Justice and the Politics of Difference.* Princeton, N.J.: Princeton University Press, 1990.

CHAPTER SIX

Practicing Liturgy as a Practice of Justice with Children

A few summers ago on a Sunday morning at one of the national conference centers of my denomination, I participated in an outdoors worship service. The beauty of that place was breathtaking, and the liturgy, shaped by a group of adults who had been studying and working together on justice issues in our church's practices of inclusion and exclusion, was inspiring. Throughout that time of worship, several children played quietly around the outside of the seating area, some briefly interrupting their play from time to time to join in singing hymns or to listen to a story. As the celebration of communion approached and the pastors spoke words of invitation to the table, these children approached the front of the worship space with excited, audible whispers: "Is it time for the bread now?" "Mama, I want to share the bread!" "Did they already pour the juice?" The children pushed their way to the location where two adult communion servers, women participating in this conference on justice and inclusion, were just stepping into their places to serve the sacrament.

Then I watched in utter amazement and horror as these servers positioned themselves to stand with *their backs* to the children. They

210

established their serving station between the children and the rest of the congregation, effectively cutting the children off from the (adult) congregation and from participation in the sacrament. The children first looked confused, and then hurt. Obviously no strangers to this moment in the liturgy, they had gone to the location where they believed they could "share the bread," only to find themselves facing the backs of servers. The servers were part of a group speaking words about God's justice and God's abundant welcome of all people to the table, but they did not even acknowledge the children's presence. Apparently justice indeed *is* blind, at least when it comes to children.

Observing this liturgical event caused me to wonder yet again about the connections, and disconnections, between the church's worship practices and the everyday lives of people in the world, particularly children. How did this experience shape the persons participating in it? What did children learn that day about the Lord's supper? What did they learn about their participation and welcome in the body of Christ? What patterns of inclusion and exclusion were modeled for all? In my search for a church that truly welcomes children and actively advocates for their thriving, I especially wonder about the kinds of liturgical practices that can welcome children's participation in worship, form them in Christian identity by teaching them the practices and beliefs of Christians, and contribute to their thriving in the world. In this chapter, I invite readers to wonder with me about how liturgical practices with children in congregations might (or might not) relate to injustices in the lives of children. In what ways might liturgy function as a hopeful resource and strategy for the thriving and welcoming of children, even and especially in a consumerist context such as that occupied by North American mainline congregations? What are "liturgical practices with children"?

The above story of the children seeking to participate in the eucharist reveals three interpretive issues for the present inquiry about how liturgical practices and practices of justice may be related.

Liturgical Practice with Children

The first issue concerns the question of what properly may be considered a liturgical practice with children. The story shows that *a liturgical activity not explicitly oriented toward children nevertheless constitutes part of a community's practices with children by virtue of the implicit and null ways in which it engages and positions children.* The terms *implicit* and *null* draw on the work of educational theorist Elliot Eisner. Eisner writes that three curricula are operating in any given teaching-learning experience.

1. The explicit curriculum refers to that which is planned for, advertised, and intended. In this case, the explicit curriculum was the printed and spoken liturgy of the eucharist with its welcome of all God's children.

2. The implicit curriculum refers to that which is taught not because it is overtly identified and addressed, but by virtue of the process, context, and setting for learning. An example can be seen in asking what a place like a theological seminary teaches by having daily worship, by including racial and ethnic minority persons on its faculty, by engaging in small group pedagogies rather than large lecture classes only, etc. In the case of the communion service, the implicit curriculum concerned its setting at a denominational conference center whose denomination affirms children's participation in communion, its conduct by various adult participants in justice-oriented conferences there, the need to be literate in written English to participate, and the outdoor setting.

3. The null curriculum refers to what is taught by virtue of its absence, exclusion, or erasure. An example of this includes what is taught by having no required courses in Christian education at a seminary—much less any that focus on children—or by the exclusion of texts by persons from other than European American educational and cultural contexts. In the case of this service, the null curriculum concerns such things as the absence of children as worship leaders and the virtual erasure of the children's presence at the point of beginning the communion liturgy.[1]

Eisner's categories can be put to good use in a variety of contexts beyond education, including this one concerning worship life. What then is liturgical practice with children? Nothing about eucharistic practice per se is particularly focused on children. This stands in contrast with the way that a children's sermon, for example, constitutes a practice explicitly organized in relation to children. At the same time, in any given context, eucharistic practices become "liturgical practices with children" by the ways they position children and this sacrament in relation to each other. That is, even in a church whose polity excludes children from the table, their liturgical practices of celebrating the eucharist become practices with children *whether or not children are present or mentioned explicitly.* This is so by virtue of children's required exclusion from participation, enacted whenever the rite is performed. When I talk about "liturgical practices with children," I, therefore, refer not only to those practices in worship directly and intentionally involving children, such as a children's sermon or the baptism of an infant. I also refer to practices that relate to children by virtue of what is not said or done, or by what (or who) is left out. In a society that routinely renders children invisible, liturgical practices with children that require their exclusion exist in a relationship of mutual reinforcement with prevailing social practices that exclude or sequester children.

Complexity of Relationships

Second, the story of the children and the eucharist points *out the complexity of positing a relationship between beliefs and actions, much less between liturgical practices with children enacted in the ritual space of congregational worship and the kinds of social practices with children enacted in the cultural spaces of family relationships, legislative bodies, and educational arenas.* For example, in the eucharist story, in which children were ignored by the servers, many of the worshipers were participating in a seminar addressing the questions of justice in the church's current struggles to define who is included and who is excluded from ordination and membership in the body. During that week's discussions the women participants frequently voiced a concern for advocacy for children in various unconventional family configurations. They showed general interest in the inclusion of children in the church. If liturgical practices functioned as simple enactments of preexisting thoughts, one might logically expect to see the intentional and careful inclusion of children in all aspects of worship to match such an ideology of empowering children's participation.

This did not happen however. Instead, a "disconnect" occurred between the expressed values of a group and their liturgical practice with children. Clearly, no simple one-to-one correspondence can be attributed to the relationship between expressed beliefs about children and liturgical practices with children, just as there is no singular, fixed relationship between beliefs and actions in general. Put differently, liturgical practices with children do not constitute some mere enactment/embodiment of a preexisting belief about children drawn from another "sphere" of life and played out on the liturgical stage. Such a perspective would exemplify an "application" model of the relationship between thought and action, akin to the errant notion that practical theology is the "application" of the thoughts from systematic theology into the realm of human experience, a notion I rejected in chapter 1. This "application" model further makes action separate from and subordinate to thought in a way that I find objectionable.

A similar "disconnect" between expressed values and beliefs about children and liturgical practices with children occurs within congregations throughout North America every Sunday. These congregations claim in various ways that they desire to have children present and involved in their religious life. At the same time, however, they engage in liturgical practices that shun, exclude, or erase children from such an involvement. For example, the pastor or Christian educator of nearly 400 Presbyterian congregations across the U.S. responded to a questionnaire on their various practices with children. Of these, 361 identify themselves as articulating an ideology of welcoming children and wanting to nurture them in Christian faith, only to engage in an action each Sunday of sending the children out of worship after the first ten to twenty minutes! Of the variety of possible and reported patterns for structuring children's participation in worship, this practice was the most prevalent among the congregations surveyed. How might this "disconnect" between ideology that welcomes children and an action that sends them away be accounted for? And, what beliefs does a community create, teach, and enact when, over time, it continues to separate children from the liturgical practices of the community, ostensibly for the purposes of educating them in faith?

Children's Presence in Worship: Full Participation or Brief Appearance?

In these times of declining church membership, mainline congregations put considerable weight on the presence of children as an indicator of congregational vitality. Many a tale of congregational decline begins with words like, "And then we stopped attracting young families with children, and before you knew it we were a dying church." The contrasting tale begins something like, "And then new families with young children began to join our church and we came alive again." Children can bring a sense of life and energy to congregations. That children contribute importantly to congregational vitality is not under dispute here. The issue is whether congregations are as concerned about caring for children and forming them in the faith as they are about having children's presence to enhance congregational vitality.

Children as Symbols of Vitality

For congregations, children symbolize vitality and energy; and, therefore, they come with a kind of spiritual capital that, by all appearances, ought to elevate their status and significance as members of the congregation. What happens instead, all too often, is that under the conditions of consumerism's tutelage, even spiritual capital comes to be commodified for its exchange value. Instead of generating a sense of the value of children themselves as the ones Christ blessed and welcomed, children become spiritual capital in the life of the congregation. They are valued in the more utilitarian mode for being a symbol of vitality, such that it hardly matters what those children do in the congregation or how they participate, but simply that they are present. This may sound rather cynical to some, but the truth of my assertion finds weekly demonstration. This demonstration occurs in the uncritical and casual way many congregations engage children on Sunday mornings. Children's messages are thought up at the last minute *sans* any theological reflection or preparation. Still less thought is given to whether or how a given activity (such as a children's choir) or curriculum helps to form children in beliefs and practices of the faith community. Church leaders give rather more consideration to whether or not these activities keep children coming back. Worshiping the presence of children, instead of including children's presence in worship, becomes the axis around which energies and resources spin under the influence of consumerism.

Of course, many adults of good will are less utilitarian or self-interested in enhancing the appearance of vitality of their congregation than they are in assisting children to be formed in the Christian faith and its worship life. Nevertheless, no small number of adults articulate a belief that children will be bored by the experience of worship and therefore grow to dislike the church. They see this happening if children are "forced" to attend worship when they cannot understand the content of the sermon or the texts or when they will find the hymn singing old-fashioned and anachronistic. They reason that giving children a brief taste of worship, no more than ten or twenty minutes, will allow them to gain some exposure to the liturgy but not so much as to become restless or bored. We can follow two lines of argument within such ideas.

No Boredom Allowed?

The first line of argument concerns children and reflects the view of children fostered by consumerism and postmodern cultural forms. This view contends that children must be in a constant state of arousal and engagement, every moment packed with fun. Boredom becomes the ultimate enemy. As Bauman puts it:

> Boredom is one complaint the consumer world has no room for, and the consumer culture set out to eradicate it. A happy life, as defined by consumer culture, is life insured against boredom, life in which constantly "something happens," something new, exciting, and exciting because new...Nor being bored–ever–is the norm of the consumer's life.[2]

At this point we might do well to question whether the earlier-noted Young Life slogan that "it's a sin to bore a kid with the Gospel" is a theological statement or merely an expression of a religious organization's ideological captivity to the market forces of consumerism, as I have suggested earlier.

The perspective on childhood represented by children's brief participation in worship followed by their departure into separate children's activities further banks on consumer culture's exaggerated divisions of childhood into narrowly segmented age groups. As a marketing technique in the wider culture, we have seen already how this age segmentation assists the market agendas of accelerated consumption, by requiring new products and clothing to fit each distinctive age passage of childhood. When the agenda of accelerated consumption leaks into church worship, it fosters a rationale that age-appropriate opportunities for faith nurture necessarily mean separate and unique modes of worship for each of the identified age groups of children, requiring special curricula, supplies (e.g., separate youth hymnals), and staffing. There is an additional problem with the view of childhood embedded within the practice of giving children brief "exposures" to worship. It posits children's participation in worship as primarily didactic or educational in nature by virtue of their age and in distinction from the participation of adults. Nearly thirty years ago, Christian educators David Ng and Virginia Thomas[3] argued that children, like adults, do not participate in worship to learn about worship. Children, like adults, worship to have an encounter with God: to praise, to confess, to experience forgiveness, and to find renewal in the community of faith. To reduce the experience of children in worship to that which is merely didactic is to engage in a "banking model" of worship participation that mirrors the increasingly consumerist view of participation in the church as a place where one goes to be filled with spiritual goods. Such perspectives miss entirely the transformational, formational, and experiential aspects of regular participation in communally shared practices of liturgy.

Children as Impediments to Adult Worship

The second line of argument concerns adult interests often hidden within the notion that children should be present in worship only briefly and then depart for their age-specific educational activities elsewhere while the adult congregation continues to worship without them. This rationale for children's exclusion from the liturgy reflects the adult argument that children's noise and restlessness impede adult abilities to hear and fully participate in worship. Some adults, recognizing that this line of reasoning puts adult needs and interests over those of children, are understandably uncomfortable explicitly naming this as the reason they structure worship to send children out after a brief time. This agenda, therefore, takes explicit form in terms of the earlier child-focused argument that puts children's developmental needs first and has the appearance of sounding hospitable to children. The prioritizing of adult interests represents adult hostility to children's differences and to their presence. Such hostility actually becomes masked in the rhetoric of doing what is best for the children.

Proclaiming Good News with Children: Children's Sermons and Marginalization

What about the use of children's sermons as a way to welcome children in worship and teach them the faith? In many congregations the desire to offer age-appropriate nurture in Christian faith and to make worship a place that welcomes and affirms the presence of children has evolved into a practice of offering a special children's message or children's sermon. A common pattern is that of gathering the children on the chancel steps for this age-specific message, after which children are dismissed from worship and into other age-specific activities of Christian education or of childcare in the church nursery. Some of these children's messages are highly creative, theologically sound, and no doubt inviting and welcoming of children.

A Strategy to Deal with Conflicting Views

At the same time, though, the separation of preaching into adult sermons and children's sermons, coupled with the exclusion of children from aspects of worship not directly engaging them (as explored above), bespeaks a problematic positioning of children in congregations. The brief presence of children in worship often includes exaggerated attention to them in the form of a "sermon" ostensibly "just for them."[4] Such practice might best be understood as a problematic strategy for holding in tension conflicting views of power relations between children and adults in Christian communities that ideologically affirm children yet are located in a consumerist cultural context that requires their marginalization. This is yet another expression of the wider cultural ambivalence toward children, located this time in liturgical garb.

In such contexts, liturgical practices with children operate as sites for negotiating and performing these power relations. Children's sermons become problematic strategic ways to meet the demands of these two competing realities, as they seem both to affirm children and yet serve also to marginalize them in relationship to adult worship. These practices take shape within the context of consumption-oriented social practices requiring increasing age segmentation and segregation of children into separate spaces.

On the one hand, the brief presence of children in worship for a child-friendly message embodies eschatological and prophetic thoughts that children are welcome by, in a sense, "over-performing" their welcome. On the other hand, the real-time, real-world ideology that sees children as insignificant becomes "performed" in their seemingly necessary exclusion from the major parts of the service. The ritualized practice of their departure has as its ostensible end the opportunity for children to go to an environment more engaging and better suited to them than worship. What is misrecognized in the performance of the practice is the way it actually *produces* both a style of worship only suited to adults and a kind of child who cannot participate in that worship (and therefore "must" go out).

Colluding with Consumerism

I have already described the ways in which the underlying assumption of children's exclusion from worship to allow them to participate in age-segregated activities colludes with consumerist society's intensification of age differences and with engagement of the postmodern cultural form that entails ceaseless quest for novelty and entertainment. The marketing language on the package and in media advertisements for children's breakfast cereal these days transforms a child's breakfast from a simple meal into an exciting adventure with eventlike qualities. In the same way, congregations have taken in the message that the worst possible thing a child can experience is boredom. This message then requires congregations to create more novel and entertaining activities for children than congregational worship seemingly can provide.

Here, I contend that the separation of children from congregational worship (often referred to as "adult worship" in conversations about these matters) produces children who cannot participate in worship, but also adults (lay and ordained) who cannot worship with children.

Unprepared Pastors and Leaders

Worship leaders, often the persons in congregations charged with structuring children's participation in and departure from worship, may also have a stake in children's segregation into age-specific activities and in preaching separately to children and adults. Many pastors feel uncertain about their ability to communicate with children and adults at the same time in the conduct of worship. In the Children in Congregations Project, for example, our interviews and surveys indicate that pastors by and large experienced their seminary educations as preparing them for ministry in congregations populated exclusively by adults. An occasional Christian education course touched upon how to administer a Sunday school for children. Otherwise, pastors told us their formal theological education taught them to preach to an adult-only group, to think of and engage in mission with adults only, to worship with adults only, to provide pastoral care to adults only, and to see themselves as pastor-teachers of adults only. (After all, lay people will teach the children.)

In addition, in our congregational study some preachers expressed fears about "dumbing down" their sermons if they were to preach with the presence of children in mind. Adults in the congregations sometimes expressed a related concern that they would lose the intellectual stimulation and content of sermons if preachers changed their ways of proclaiming the Word to accommodate children. Only rarely did anyone recognize or critique the implicit norm in such perspectives that adult intellectual cognitive appropriation is the norm for preaching and hearing the good news, such that children's arguably different ways of hearing the Word necessarily involve "accommodation."[5] With this kind of adult-focused preparation for ministry, it is little wonder that pastoral leadership also has an often hidden interest in encouraging children's departure from congregational worship after a brief time of participation.

They are not prepared to preach to the whole people of God together in the same room at the same time.

With these comments, I do not mean to imply that there never is an appropriate time for age-specific activities of children in congregations, nor am I suggesting that everything that takes place within worship needs to be equally accessible or interesting to all people at all times. To the contrary! Rather, I contend that in a community of faith that comprises persons of various ages, temperaments, learning styles and abilities, racial-ethnic identities, and other differences, it is not reasonable to expect that everyone will always be equivalently engaged–and that is all right. We are not there to be entertained, nor are our children. We are there to render thanks, praise, and prayers of intercession. We come to worship to proclaim that the kin-dom of God is not the same as the imperial regime of consumer capitalism or any of the other empires that seek our allegiance. At the same time, we are in the business of "making something happen" within our congregations (to paraphrase William Sloane Coffin). If we enter into liturgy expecting and anticipating an encounter with the living God who welcomes us and calls on us to extend that abundant welcome to all, then we need not fear that worship will fail to engage us. The problem of ecclesial captivity to the empire of consumption is that we have unwittingly substituted the market's interest in glitzy, entertaining spectacle for evidence that liturgical practices have power in children's lives and the lives of their adult companions.

Shopping Mall Worship and the Shaping of Worship as Meeting Needs

Practices such as the children's sermon that separate children from congregational worship do not require substantive changes in the overall practices of worship. They may be overtly intended to make the whole worship experience more welcoming of children's participation but do not do so in reality. The children's sermon combined with a sequestered program of Christian education during "adult worship" actually heightens the distinctions between children's ways of participating and those of adults. They operate as a mechanism for creating congregational worship as a private adult space. Certainly, I and most of the adults I know who come to worship on Sunday could use a little space. My weekdays are filled up with noise and conversation, task lists to check off, and nonstop busy-ness. Thus I, as a mother of three children who also works in the paid labor force full time, yearn for that precious bit of contemplative space and stillness that worship affords me.

Adult Perceptions of Children in Worship

Perhaps this thirst for space and stillness is part of the problem when it comes to adult perceptions of children in worship. My colleague Carol

Jacobson[6] points to the absence of other spaces besides Christian worship in adult's lives. For many, worship seems to be the only opportunity to experience stillness and quiet. This results in an over-reliance on worship as "the" one contemplative, quiet space in the week. *This, in turn, leads to the tendency to view children's presence in worship primarily in terms of noise.* With Jacobson, I am suggesting that liturgical practices that exclude children's presence from worship very well may be a way for stressed adults, especially the primarily female caretakers of children, to construct a necessary quiet space in their lives. This desire is not negative in and of itself, but its enactment in liturgical practice has problematic effects upon children. It also falsely construes worship as a clinic for addressing personal needs, such that the needs of adults and those of children are placed into competition with each other.

Such an orientation toward worship reflects, among other things, consumption-oriented social practices. In these practices all of the various activities in which humans participate are rationalized in terms of a need for services or for goods provided by that activity. In church life this results in reshaping ecclesial life around a shopping mall or service station model. Such a model construes worship as primarily being about the personal needs of children and of adults. These needs for services are then pitted against each other. The practice of excluding children from worship so that their parents and other adults can have their own needs for worship met legitimates the church's failure to welcome children.

Insights from Ritual Theory

Many congregations attempt to enhance children's participation in worship by creating separate elements of the service directed toward the children. But efforts to include children in worship by creating children's sermons or messages ostensibly just for them may not be only what they appear to be. Ritual theorist Catherine Bell's notion that liturgical activity is a form of *strategic* ritual practice is instructive here.[7] For Bell, practices are learned forms of activity in which action and thought co-reside. Practices often take on the appearance of being "natural" or "given" forms of social activity because of their somewhat uniform appearance. A practice is a "way of doing things," a way of operating.

To call a practice "strategic," however, is to assert that people do not woodenly follow a script for action but rather make active improvisations to utilize the practice in response to their own contexts, situations, and desires. For example, the official denominational statements may claim that receiving the bread and wine of the eucharist is centrally about our being reconciled to God in Christ. This may not be true, however, for congregational participants. People *may give the appearance of conforming through their participation in the same practice, while, in truth, they engage this practice strategically.* Different individuals may use the eucharist to seek